TOEFL® CBT
practice tests

Bruce Rogers

Australia • Canada • Mexico • Singapore • Spain • United Kingdom • United States

About The Thomson Corporation and Peterson's

With revenues of US$7.8 billion, The Thomson Corporation (www.thomson.com) is a leading global provider of integrated information solutions for business, education, and professional customers. Its Learning businesses and brands (www.thomsonlearning.com) serve the needs of individuals, learning institutions, and corporations with products and services for both traditional and distributed learning.

Peterson's, part of The Thomson Corporation, is one of the nation's most respected providers of lifelong learning online resources, software, reference guides, and books. The Education Supersite^SM at www.petersons.com—the Internet's most heavily traveled education resource—has searchable databases and interactive tools for contacting U.S.-accredited institutions and programs. In addition, Peterson's serves more than 105 million education consumers annually.

I would like to thank the following people for reading and commenting on the manuscript for this text during the development process: Gail Stewart, University of Toronto; Ramon Valenzuela, Boston University; Aise Stromsdorfer, St. Louis University; Sydney Kinneman, University of Oregon; Barbara Sihombing, Economics Institute, Boulder, Colorado; and Jim Price, International English Centre, Bangkok.

"TOEFL" and "TWE" are registered trademarks of Educational Testing Service (ETS). The author and the publisher are in no way affiliated with ETS, nor has ETS endorsed the contents of this text in any way. The test questions and all other testing information are provided in their entirety by the author and Peterson's.

TOEFL Practice Tests is adapted from *Heinle & Heinle's Complete Guide to TOEFL Test: Practice Tests*, second edition, by Bruce Rogers and published by Heinle & Heinle/ITP.

For more information, contact Peterson's, 2000 Lenox Drive, Lawrenceville, NJ 08648; 800-338-3282; or find us on the World Wide Web at www.petersons.com/about.

ISBN 0-7689-1222-9 (text and audiocassettes)
ISBN 0-7689-1221-0 (text with CD)
ISBN 0-7689-1223-7 (text only)

Printed in the United States of America

10 9 8 7 6 5 4 3 2 1   05 04 03

Contents

Preface

If you are preparing for the TOEFL CBT (*Test of English as a Foreign Language Computer Based Test*), you are not alone. More than 780,000 people signed up to take the test in 2002, and the number keeps growing. For almost all nonnative speakers of English who want to study in either undergraduate or graduate programs at universities or colleges in North America, an acceptable score on the exam is a necessity for admission. Many schools are raising the minimal TOEFL scores required for admission, and preparing for this important test can be a difficult, frustrating experience. But we're here to help.

One of the best ways to ensure success on TOEFL exam is to take practice exams. The five tests in this book cover all the types of items that commonly appear on actual exams. All items have been carefully pretested.

This book is designed to supplement Peterson's *TOEFL CBT Success 2004*, which offers an in-depth, point-by-point preparation program for the test. But you can also use this book by itself. This book includes the following features:

- A question-and-answer section tells you about the format of the test, registration for the exam, and how to interpret your scores

- Four tests in a 140-item format (Practice Tests 1, 2, 4, and 5) and one test in a 210-item format (Practice Test 3)

- Highly realistic test items that look and "feel" like items on actual tests

- Ten key strategies that help you do your best on the Writing Section/TWE

- Four Practice Writing Section/TWE tests

- Scoring guides

- Transcripts for all the Listening sections

- Answer keys, including explanatory answers for the Structure and Reading parts

TAKING THE TESTS

- If you purchased the book-only version of *TOEFL CBT Practice Tests*, have a friend read you the transcripts in order to complete the Listening part of these tests.

- If you have the CD or tape version, use the audio to complete the Listening sections.

- Read over the questions and answers about the TOEFL Test before taking the Practice Tests.

- Take each test in its entirety rather than section by section.

- Time yourself carefully during Sections 2 and 3. Do not go ahead to the next section even if you finish early. Do not give yourself extra time even if you haven't finished the section.

- Sit at a desk or table, not in an easy chair or on a sofa, and work away from distractions such as a television or a stereo.

- Mark your answers on the answer sheets rather than in the book.

- After completing the test, mark incorrect answers but do not write in the corrections. Instead, go back and answer these questions a second time.

- If you have time, try to take the entire test over again on another answer sheet. (You may want to make photocopies of the answer sheets in the back of the book before you begin.)

- Use the scoring charts in the back of this book to calculate your scores for each Practice Test.

- Keep track of your scores in the Personal Score Record in the Scoring section of this book.

If you have any comments or questions about this book or the TOEFL Test, I'd like to hear from you. Please contact me in care of the publisher:

Peterson's
2000 Lenox Drive
P.O. Box 67005
Lawrenceville, New Jersey 08648
www.petersons.com/bookstore

Good luck on the TOEFL Test!

WHAT IS THE TOEFL CBT?

In July 1998, Educational Testing Service (ETS) introduced the TOEFL CBT in the United States, Canada, Latin America, Europe, the Middle East, Africa, and selected Asian countries. In 2002, more than 780,000 people took the TOEFL test. According to ETS, in 2005, the new computer-based test will completely replace the paper test. Some parts of the TOEFL CBT are a linear computerized test, which is scored the same way as a paper test. Other parts of the TOEFL are a computer-adaptive test (CAT).

WHAT IS A COMPUTER-ADAPTIVE TEST?

A computer-adaptive test (CAT) is—as the title says—adaptive. That means that each time you answer a question, the computer adjusts to your responses when determining which question to present next. For example, the first question will be of moderate difficulty. If you answer it correctly, the next question will be more difficult. If you answer it incorrectly, the next question will be easier. The computer will continue presenting questions based on your responses, with the goal of determining your ability level.

It is important to understand that questions at the beginning of a section affect your score more than those at the end. That's because the early questions are used to determine your general ability level. Once the computer determines your general ability level, it presents questions to identify your specific ability level. As you progress farther into a section, it will be difficult to raise your score very much, even if you answer most items correctly. That's because the later questions affect your score less, because they are used to pinpoint your exact score once the computer has identified your general ability level. Therefore, take as much time as you can afford to answer the early questions correctly. Your score on each section is based on the number of questions you answer correctly, as well as the difficulty level of those questions.

You need only minimal computer skills to take the computer-based TOEFL. You will have plenty of time at the test center to work through a tutorial that allows you to practice such activities as answering questions, using the mouse, using the word processor (which you will need for your essay responses), and accessing the help function.

The computer-based test is given at designated centers all over the world. The cost of the TOEFL CBT test is US$110.

WHAT KINDS OF QUESTIONS ARE ON THE TOEFL CBT?

Like the paper test, the computer-based TOEFL will have three sections:

1. Listening (40–60 minutes, 30–50 questions, computer adaptive)

2. Structure (15–20 minutes, 20–25 questions, computer adaptive)

3. Reading (70–90 minutes, 44–60 questions, linear)

Some questions will be similar to those on the paper test, whereas others will be very different. The Listening and Reading questions will include question types that are designed specifically for the computer. An essay will also be included that can be handwritten or typed on the computer.

HOW ARE THE TOEFL CBT SCORES CALCULATED?

The computer-based TOEFL reports separate scores for each of the three test sections. The Listening section is scored as a CAT. The Structure section is scored as a CAT and on the basis of the essay. The Reading section is scored as a linear test. The scores for all three sections are factored into a scaled total score, just like on the paper-based test.

2The range of possible scores on each of the three multiple-choice sections is from 0 to 30. The range for the entire test will be from 0 to 300. (The range on the paper version is from 200 to 667.)

TEST-TAKING TIPS FOR THE CAT SECTIONS OF THE TOEFL CBT

The purpose of *TOEFL CBT Practice Tests* is to help you prepare for all forms of the test. You will increase your chances of scoring high on the TOEFL by being completely familiar with the content and format you will encounter on test day. The practice tests provide lots of opportunity to prepare. For the actual exam, keep in mind the following test-taking tips, most of which are unique to the CAT format.

- Understand the directions for each question type. Learn the directions for each type of question. The directions in this book are similar to those on the actual test. Understanding the directions for each question type will save you valuable time on the day of the test.

- Focus on answering the questions at the beginning of Sections 1 and 2 correctly. Remember that questions at the beginning of a section affect your score more than questions at the end. Be especially careful in choosing answers to questions in the first half of both the quantitative and verbal sections. Once the computer determines your general ability level with these initial questions, you will be unable to dramatically improve your score, even if you answer most of the questions toward the end correctly.

- In Sections 1 and 2, be completely sure of each answer before proceeding. With a CAT, you must answer each question as it is presented. You cannot skip a difficult question and return to it later as you can with a paper test. Nor can you review responses to questions that you have already answered. Therefore, you must be confident about your answer before you confirm it and proceed to the next question. If you are completely stumped by a question, eliminate as many answer choices as you can, select the best answer from the remaining choices, and move on.

- Pace yourself. To finish all sections, you will need to work both quickly and accurately to complete each section within the time constraints. You will still receive a score, even if you do not complete all of the questions in a section.

QUESTIONS AND ANSWERS ABOUT THE TOEFL CBT

Q: What is the TOEFL® test?

A: TOEFL stands for *Test of English as a Foreign Language.* The TOEFL® test is designed to measure the English-language ability of people who do not speak English as their first language and who plan to study at colleges and universities in North America. Educational Testing Service (ETS) of Princeton, New Jersey, prepares and administers the TOEFL® test. This organization produces many other standardized tests. Although there are other standardized tests of English, the TOEFL® test is, by far, the most important in North America. ETS has offered this examination since 1965.

Q: What format does the computer-based test follow? How long does it take to complete?

A: The computer-based test is divided into four sections: Listening, Structure, Reading, and Essay Writing, each with its own time limit. The four sections are always given in the same order. Before the actual test, you must take a tutorial that demonstrates the computer skills needed to take the test. This part is ungraded, of course, and untimed. Most test-takers take approximately 40 minutes to complete this section. The first three sections consist mainly of multiple-choice questions, while Essay Writing is a single essay-writing item.

Q: What are the main differences between the paper-based test and the computer-based test?

A: The first three sections of the computer-based test generally have fewer items. For example, on the most recent version of the paper-based test, there are 40 Structure items, whereas on the computer-based version, there are 20 to 25. Another difference is the use of visuals in the Listening section on the CBT. There are also some new "computer-unique" item types in Listening and in Reading.

Computer-Based Format for the TOEFL® Test

Tutorial
Untimed—Average 40 minutes

1. **Listening**
   40–60 minutes
   30–50 questions (computer adaptive)

   Part A: Dialogues 11–17 items
   Part B: Longer Talks
   4–6 Talks/conversations
   3–6 questions per talk

2. **Structure**
   15–20 minutes
   20–25 questions (computer adaptive)

   Sentence Completion and Error Recognition

   Mandatory break—10 minutes

3. **Reading**
   70–90 minutes
   4–5 readings
   44–70 questions (linear)

4. **Essay Writing**
   1 essay prompt—30 minutes

   Total Time: Approximately 4 hours

Q: Are the computer-based test scores simply based on the number of correct answers?

A: No. Test-takers A and B may get the same number of correct answers on one section, but test-taker A may get a higher score because he or she answered more difficult items correctly.

Q: When will I receive my test scores?

A: You will receive unofficial on-screen scores right after you take the test. The scores for Listening and Reading will be final scores, but the score for Structure and your overall score will be reported as a range of scores.

Here is an example of what these on-screen scores look like:

Listening   20
Structure   6–25
Reading   24
Overall   167–230

What your final scores will be depends on the score you receive on the Essay Writing section (which cannot be instantly graded). The Essay Writing score ranges from 0 to 6.

Here are some examples of scores you might receive, depending on your essay score:

Essay Score	Structure Score	Overall Score
0	6–7	167–170
1	9–10	177–180
3	15–16	198–201
5	22–23	220–223
6	24–35	227–230

You and the schools that you designate should receive final scores within two weeks if you word process the essay. If you handwrite the essay, you should receive scores in 4 to 6 weeks.

Q: What is an Institutional TOEFL test?

A: Institutional TOEFL tests are given by English-language schools and other institutions. Sometimes they are used for placement in a school's English program or for testing a student's progress. Institutional tests are composed of items that previously appeared on tests administered by ETS.

Because ETS does not supervise these tests, some universities won't accept the results. However, many other universities will. You should check with the admissions offices of universities to see what their policy is. You must arrange for the institute where you took the examination to send the scores to the university.

Q: Has the format of the Institutional TOEFL® test also changed?

A: No, the Institutional TOEFL® test (a form of the test given by English-language schools and other institutions) is still a paper-based test.

Q: What is TSE?

A: TSE (*Test of Spoken English*) tests your ability to communicate in spoken English. All of your responses are recorded on audiotape so that they can be evaluated later. The test takes approximately 20 minutes to complete and is given twelve times a year at various test centers. On TSE, you must answer questions about pictures or graphs, complete sentences, express your opinions on various topics, give short presentations, and so on. TSE is administered separately from TOEFL and must be paid for separately.

TSE is generally required only for students who are applying for positions as teaching assistants or for special programs or certificates.

Q: How do I register for the computer-based TOEFL® test?

A: There are a several ways to register. You can register for the computer-based test by telephone if you have a credit card (Visa, MasterCard, or American Express). In North America, you can call Prometric TOEFL® Test Registration Center toll-free at 800-GO-TOEFL (800-468-6335) or you may call your local test center. There is a complete list of these in the *TOEFL® Information Bulletin*. Outside North America, call the Regional Registration Center for the country in which you live. These are listed in the *Bulletin*. You will be given a confirmation number and be told when and where to report. You can also register by mail. If you are in North America, you can use the CBT Voucher Test Request Form found in the *Bulletin*. You can pay with a credit card, check, or money order. You will receive a CBT voucher in several weeks. After that, you can call a center to schedule an appointment. If you live outside North America, you need to fill out the International Test Scheduling Form and mail it to your Regional Registration Center. Payment may be in the form of a check, credit card, money order, bank draft, or UNESCO coupons. Outside North America, you may also register by faxing the International Test Scheduling Form to the Regional Registration Center for your country. Fax numbers for these centers are listed in the *Bulletin*. You can register in person by visiting the nearest testing site, and, in the near future, you will probably be able to register on line by going to the TOEFL® Web site.

Q: What computer skills do I need to take the computer-based TOEFL® test?

A: The computer skills required are fairly basic. You only need to know how to point to and click on a choice with a mouse, how to scroll up and down through a document, and how to access help if you need it. If you choose to type your essay on the computer (rather than write it by hand), you will also need basic word-processing skills. Before you take the test at the center, you must complete a tutorial to make sure you have mastered the skills you need.

Q: Where is the computer-based test offered?

A: It is given at designated test centers, universities, binational institutes, and ETS field offices throughout the world. There are two types of test centers, permanent and mobile. Tests are given at mobile centers only during certain months. A complete list of testing centers is given in the *Bulletin*. The computer-based test is not offered at nearly as many centers as the paper-based test was. Depending on where you live, you may have to travel a rather long distance to take the test.

Q: Can I choose whether to take the computer-based test or the paper-based test?

A: No. Once the computer-based test has been phased in, you will no longer have the option of taking the paper-based test.

Q: How much does the computer-based test cost?

A: It will cost US$110. (The paper-based version of the test had cost US$45.) If you need to reschedule the test, you will have to pay a US$40 rescheduling fee.

Q: What should I bring with me to the examination site?

A: You should bring the following:

- Your passport

- Your appointment confirmation number

- Your CBT voucher, if you are using one

- A list of the universities to which you want your scores sent

Don't bring any reference books, such as dictionaries or textbooks, or any electronic devices, such as translators, cellular phones, or calculators. You are not permitted to smoke, eat, or drink in the test center. You do not have to bring pencils or paper.

Q: Is every item on the test scored?

A: No, there is usually at least one unscored item in each part of the test. This is generally the last item in each part. For example, in Section 2, item 15 and item 40 are usually not scored. However, it's not recommended that you skip these items—ETS could always change its system!

Q: What is a passing score on the TOEFL® test?

A: There isn't any. Each university has its own standards for admission, so you should check the catalogs of universities you are interested in or contact their admission offices. Most undergraduate programs require scores between 173 and 213 (between 500 and 550 on the paper-based test), and most graduate programs ask for scores between 195 and 250 (between 525 and 600 on the paper-based test). Recently, there has a been a tendency for universities to raise their minimum requirements for the TOEFL® test.

Q: How are universities informed of my scores?

A: ETS reports your score to three institutions for free. For a charge, ETS will send your scores to additional institutions. There is a form for requesting this service in the *Bulletin*. Some universities will also accept photocopies of the test results that were mailed directly to you.

Q: If I believe I haven't done well on the TOEFL® test, can I cancel my scores?

A: Yes. Right after the test, you may either cancel your scores or view them. You may NOT cancel your scores once you have looked at them. However, if you are not satisfied with your unofficial scores, you can direct ETS to NOT send them on to any universities. Keep in mind that, even if you cancel your scores, you cannot take the test again until the next calendar month. It is generally NOT a good idea to cancel scores.

You may have done better on the test than you thought you did.

Q: Can I get my scores by phone?

A: Yes. Call 888-TOEFL-44 (toll-free) in North America and 609-771-7267 elsewhere fourteen days after the test (four to five weeks after the test if you handwrite the essay). ETS charges a fee for this service.

Q: How many times may I take the computer-based TOEFL® test?

A: There is no limit; you may take it as often as you like. However, you may not take the test more than once in any calendar month.

Q: Will there be other changes to the TOEFL® test in the near future?

A: Yes. In September 2005, ETS will debut a new TOEFL CBT, which willinclude a speaking section, among other changes.

Q: How can I get more information about the TOEFL® test?

A: You can contact ETS via e-mail or get updated information about the test from its home page on the World Wide Web: E-mail: toefl@ets.org; Web site: www.toefl.org.

Q: Is it possible to improve one's score by cheating?

A: It is difficult to have someone else take the examination for you. You must bring an official identification document with your picture on it. You are also required to bring a photo file record with a recent photo of yourself. ETS copies this photo and sends it, with your scores, to universities. If the person in the photo is not the same person who enrolls, that person may not be admitted.

The following are also considered cheating:

- Taking notes during the Listening section

- Talking to or signaling any other test-takers

- Copying any test material

- Working on one section during the time allotted for another section

- Continuing to work on a section after time is called

People who are believed to be cheating will receive a warning for minor acts of cheating. For more serious matters, a person's scores will be canceled.

WHAT IT'S LIKE TO TAKE THE TOEFL® CBT

1. The first step is to call the closest testing center.* You should call at least one month before you need to take the test. There is typically a three-week waiting time, but this may vary by time of year and center. The waiting time for certain days—especially Saturdays—will be longer than for other days. If you have a credit card or have already purchased a CBT voucher, you can make an appointment over the phone to take the test. Otherwise, arrange to stop by the center. If you do make an appointment when you call, you will receive a confirmation number. Write down this number and keep it in a safe place.

2. A week after registering, you will receive directions to the center in the mail (including public transportation routes). Keep this card with your confirmation number. On the day before the test, get this card, your confirmation number, and your passport ready to take with you the following day.

3. Arrive at least a half-hour early for your appointment. At the time you arrive, you will be given a form to complete.

4. At the time of your appointment, or whenever a computer is free, you will be taken into a room near the testing room and given a paragraph to copy and sign. This paragraph says that you really are who you say you are and that you promise not to tell anyone what is on the test. At this time, you will also have to show your passport and you will be photographed. Before you go into the testing room, you will have to sign a register. Center officials will then take you into the testing room and seat you at a computer. There may be several other people in the room taking tests—not only the TOEFL®. Your testing space will resemble a study carrel at a library.

5. Your computer will prompt you to answer some questions about yourself, your plans, and your reason for taking the test. After that, the tutorial will begin. This tutorial teaches you the basic computer skills required to take the test.

6. After you have finished the tutorial (which is not timed), you may begin the Listening section. You will have a chance to adjust the volume, read the directions, and answer a few practice items. Remember, you are NOT allowed to take notes during the Listening section.

7. After the Listening section, you may take a 1-minute break or go directly on to the Structure section.

8. After completing the Structure section, there is a mandatory 10-minute break. You will have to sign out before you leave the testing area.

9. After the break, you will again have to sign in. You will be given six sheets of scrap paper and will be shown back to your computer. The next section of the test is Reading. Remember that this section of the test is NOT computer adaptive and that you can move forward and backward through the readings. You can skip questions (although this is seldom a good idea), and go back and change your answers any time you want.

10. After you finish the Reading section of the test, you may take a one-minute break or proceed with the Essay Writing section. If you choose to word process the essay, you will see a brief tutorial explaining *cut, paste, delete,* and other commands you need to write the essay on the computer. You may use the scrap paper you have been given to write a quick outline for your essay.

11. After you have written your essay, you will receive an unofficial grade report. You will then have a chance to choose from a pull-down menu the universities that will receive your scores. You may then be asked several questions about your experience taking the test. After that, you must hand in your scrap paper. You will then sign out.

12. If you word process your essay, you will receive your final test scores in two weeks.

   If you handwrite your essay, you will receive your final scores in four to five weeks.

---

* *Note:* The testing experience may differ somewhat from center to center.

Practice Test 1

Section 1

LISTENING

This section tests your ability to comprehend spoken English. It is divided into three parts, each with its own directions. During actual exams, you are *not* permitted to turn the page during the reading of the directions or to take notes at any time.

PART A

Directions: Each item in this part consists of a brief conversation involving two speakers. Following each conversation, a third voice will ask a question. You will hear the conversations and questions only once, and they will *not* be written out.

When you have heard each conversation and question, read the four answer choices and select the *one*—(A), (B), (C), or (D)—that best answers the question based on what is directly stated or on what can be inferred. Then fill in the space on your answer sheet that matches the letter of the answer that you have selected.

Here is an example.

You will hear:

M1: Do you think I should lean this chair against the wall or put it somewhere else?

F1: Over by the window, I'd say.

M2: What does the woman think the man should do?

You will read:

(**A**) Open the window.
(**B**) Move the chair.
(**C**) Leave the room.
(**D**) Take a seat.

From the conversation you find out that the woman thinks the man should put the chair over by the window. The best answer to the question, "What does the woman think the man should do?" is (B), "Move the chair." You should fill in (B) on your answer sheet.

Sample Answer

 Ⓐ ● Ⓒ Ⓓ

1. **(A)** This is the first time she's seen the piano.
   (B) The photographs have not been developed.
   (C) The photographs are on the piano.
   (D) The man should photograph the piano.

2. **(A)** Because he was so hungry, he rushed off to eat.
   (B) He found some good buys at the store.
   (C) Everybody was angry at him for leaving.
   (D) He was too mad to say anything when he left.

3. **(A)** She's trying to find a good chair.
   (B) She doesn't know where the chair is now.
   (C) She thinks the chair is actually comfortable.
   (D) She's never sat in that chair before.

4. **(A)** The gardens are on the opposite side of the park.
   (B) The roses in this park are not the best.
   (C) The rose gardens are located on the west side.
   (D) The roses grow outside the park, not inside it.

5. **(A)** He doesn't know where she lives.
   (B) He believes she's going to leave tonight.
   (C) He doesn't know where she's going.
   (D) He didn't hear what she said.

6. **(A)** He has finished cleaning the drain.
   (B) He feels that he has wasted two days.
   (C) He will start his experiment in two days.
   (D) He thinks his experiment was a success.

7. **(A)** She is riding her brother's bicycle now.
   (B) She fixed the bike for her brother.
   (C) Her bicycle can't be repaired.
   (D) Her brother did the repair work.

8. **(A)** A half hour.
   (B) An hour.
   (C) Ninety minutes.
   (D) Two hours.

9. **(A)** She doesn't take her car to campus anymore.
   (B) She doesn't have a long way to drive.
   (C) She doesn't need to go to campus tomorrow.
   (D) She doesn't have a car anymore.

10. **(A)** Swimming is as tiring as dancing.
    (B) She's taking a dancing course.
    (C) Dancing provides good exercise, too.
    (D) She'd rather swim than dance.

11. **(A)** The rain has just begun.
    (B) It's not raining as hard now.
    (C) It only rained a little bit.
    (D) It's raining too hard to go out.

12. **(A)** Robert deserves her thanks for his help.
    (B) Robert didn't help much with the project.
    (C) She finished her project before Robert finished his.
    (D) She and Robert hadn't finished planning their project yet.

13. **(A)** He makes his students work very hard.
    (B) He refused to let the man take his class.
    (C) He stayed home today because he was tired.
    (D) He won't be teaching next semester.

14. **(A)** Send flowers to someone.
    (B) Deliver a package to the hospital.
    (C) Arrange some flowers.
    (D) Talk to a doctor.

15. **(A)** Get a new watch.
    (B) Run around the block.
    (C) Shop for jewelry.
    (D) Have his watch repaired.

16. **(A)** How long he'll be in Montreal.
    (B) How he plans to travel to Montreal.
    (C) What form of transportation he'll use there.
    (D) What other cities he's planning to visit.

17. **(A)** He thinks the woman wants to relax.
 (B) He has plans for the rest of the weekend.
 (C) He believes the woman should be more patient.
 (D) He wants to go to a small, quiet restaurant.

18. **(A)** She doesn't talk very much.
 (B) She'd like to become a better skater.
 (C) She skates a lot these days.
 (D) She doesn't really like skating.

19. **(A)** He can get his money refunded.
 (B) The sweater fits him perfectly.
 (C) The sweater isn't available in a larger size.
 (D) He can't get a refund without a receipt.

20. **(A)** She has never heard of the Fisherman's Grotto.
 (B) She has stopped going to that restaurant.
 (C) She enjoys eating at the Fisherman's Grotto.
 (D) She never goes to the beach anymore.

21. **(A)** Play the guitar while she sings.
 (B) Sing a song with him.
 (C) Write the music for her song.
 (D) Go with her to the guitar concert.

22. **(A)** He should rest before he cleans the kitchen.
 (B) All of his apartment needs to be cleaned.
 (C) Only the kitchen needs to be cleaned up.
 (D) He should wait until this afternoon to begin.

23. **(A)** He doesn't know much about acting.
 (B) The acting seemed professional to him.
 (C) Acting is a very difficult profession.
 (D) He didn't think they were actors.

24. **(A)** Paintbrushes.
 (B) Some soap.
 (C) A can of paint.
 (D) Some milk.

25. **(A)** The bananas have all been eaten.
 (B) He didn't buy any bananas.
 (C) Those are not the right bananas.
 (D) The bananas aren't ready to eat yet.

26. **(A)** Some of the students thought the test was fair.
 (B) There are only a few students in the class.
 (C) Everyone thinks that Professor Murray is unfair.
 (D) Most students thought that the test was too long.

27. **(A)** He wrote a book about great restaurants.
 (B) He always makes reservations for dinner.
 (C) He always finds good places to eat.
 (D) He read a book while he was eating dinner.

28. **(A)** Stay out of the garden.
 (B) Protect himself from the sun.
 (C) Buy another hat.
 (D) Get some new gardening tools.

29. **(A)** No one looked out of the windows.
 (B) Only one window had been locked.
 (C) All the windows were locked.
 (D) Some of the windows were broken.

30. **(A)** He's very friendly.
 (B) He goes out a lot.
 (C) He's out of town now.
 (D) He's quitting his job.

PART B

Directions: This part of the test consists of extended conversations between two speakers. After each of these conversations there are a number of questions. You will hear each conversation and question only once, and the questions are *not* written out.

When you have heard the questions, read the four answer choices and select the one—(A), (B), (C), or (D)—that best answers the question based on what is directly stated or on what can be inferred. Then fill in the space on your answer sheet that matches the letter of the answer that you have selected.

Don't forget: During actual exams, taking notes or writing in your test book is *not* permitted.

31. (A) She didn't know about the painting exhibit.
    (B) She wasn't very familiar with the name "Reynolds Hall."
    (C) She didn't realize the man was speaking to her.
    (D) She wasn't sure where the Art Building was.

32. (A) The main library.
    (B) A painting.
    (C) A service road.
    (D) A metal sculpture.

33. (A) She's a graduate student.
    (B) She works at the library.
    (C) She's waiting for the man.
    (D) She teaches art.

34. (A) Annoyed.
    (B) Apologetic.
    (C) Surprised.
    (D) Cooperative.

35. (A) The possibility of life on other planets.
    (B) Einstein's concept of the speed of light.
    (C) Revolutionary new designs for spaceships.
    (D) The distance from Earth to the closest star.

36. (A) Only a few days.
    (B) Several months.
    (C) Four or five years.
    (D) Hundreds of years.

37. (A) A new means of propelling space-ships.
    (B) A deeper understanding of Einstein's theories.
    (C) Another method for measuring the speed of light.
    (D) A new material from which to build spaceships.

38. (A) As unlikely in the near future.
    (B) As strongly inadvisable.
    (C) As impossible at any time.
    (D) As probably unnecessary.

PART C

Directions: This part of the test consists of several talks, each given by a single speaker. After each of these talks there are a number of questions. You will hear each talk and question only once, and the questions are *not* written out.

When you have heard the question, read the four answer choices and select the *one*—(A), (B), (C), or (D)—that best answers the question based on what is directly stated or on what can be inferred. Then fill in the space on your answer sheet that matches the letter of the answer that you have selected.

Here is an example.

You will hear:

M1: Students, this evening we'll have a chance to observe a phenomenon that we've discussed several times in class. Tonight, there will be a lunar eclipse. As we've said, when an eclipse of the moon occurs, the earth passes between the sun and the moon. Therefore, the shadow of the earth moves across the surface of the moon and obscures it. Because you won't be looking at the sun, it is not necessary to use the special lenses and filters that you need when observing a solar eclipse. You can observe a lunar eclipse with your unaided eye or with a telescope and photograph it with an ordinary camera. So if the weather's not cloudy tonight, go out and take a look at this eclipse of the moon. I'm sure you'll find it interesting.

Now here is a sample question.

You will hear:

M2: In what course is this lecture probably being given?

You will read:

(A) Philosophy.
(B) Meteorology.
(C) Astronomy.
(D) Photography.

The lecture concerns a lunar eclipse, a topic that would typically be discussed in an astronomy class. The choice that best answers the question "In what course is this lecture probably being given?" is (C), "Astronomy." You should fill in (C) on your answer sheet.

Sample Answer

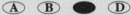

Here is another sample question.

You will hear:

M2: According to the speaker, which of the following occurs during a lunar eclipse?

You will read:

(A) The earth's shadow moves across the moon.
(B) Clouds block the view of the moon.
(C) The moon moves between the earth and the sun.
(D) The sun can be observed without special equipment.

From the lecture, you learn that a lunar eclipse occurs when the earth moves between the sun and the moon and the shadow of the earth passes across the moon. The choice that best answers the question "According to the speaker, which of the following occurs during a lunar eclipse?" is (A), "The earth's shadow moves across the moon." Don't forget: During actual exams, taking notes or writing in your test book is *not* permitted.

Sample Answer

39. (A) Journalism students.
    (B) Reporters.
    (C) Editorial writers.
    (D) Teachers.

40. (A) The International Desk.
    (B) The Circulation Department.
    (C) The Production Department.
    (D) The City Desk.

41. (A) Distributing the newspaper through-out the city.
    (B) Reporting local news.
    (C) Printing the newspaper.
    (D) Gathering news from international sources.

42. (A) The background of the professors.
    (B) Costs.
    (C) Social events.
    (D) The academic program.

43. (A) Archaeology.
    (B) History.
    (C) Architecture.
    (D) Language.

44. (A) The Eastern Mediterranean program.
    (B) The Southeast Asian program.
    (C) The North American program.
    (D) The Western Mediterranean program.

45. (A) They are exactly like classes at Hunt University.
    (B) They take up all of the participants' time.
    (C) They can earn students credit at their universities.
    (D) They are completely optional.

46. (A) Instructors in the program.
    (B) Students from the professor's class at Hunt University.
    (C) Representatives of "Semester Afloat."
    (D) Former participants in the program.

47. (A) Better types of skates.
    (B) Improved conditions on ice tracks.
    (C) Changes in skating techniques.
    (D) New world records.

48. (A) They all had equal opportunities of winning.
    (B) They couldn't compete in the Winter Olympics.
    (C) They all wore the same kinds of skates.
    (D) They had to skate on outdoor tracks.

49. (A) It chips easily.
    (B) It becomes covered with frost.
    (C) It becomes too soft.
    (D) It provides too much resistance.

50. (A) Speed skating will become more popular.
    (B) Speed skaters will skate faster than ever before.
    (C) Speed skating events will return to outside tracks.
    (D) New rules for speed skating will be needed.

THIS IS THE END OF SECTION 1: LISTENING.

STOP WORK ON SECTION 1.

Section 2

This section tests your ability to recognize grammar and usage suitable for standard written English. It is divided into two parts, each with its own directions.

SENTENCE COMPLETION

Directions: Items in this part are incomplete sentences. Following each of these sentences, there are four words or phrases. You should select the *one* word or phrase—(A), (B), (C), or (D)—that best completes the sentence. Then fill in the space on your answer sheet that matches the letter of the answer that you have selected.

Example I

Pepsin _____ an enzyme used in digestion.

(A) that
(B) is
(C) of
(D) being

This sentence should properly read "Pepsin is an enzyme used in digestion." You should fill in choice (B) on your answer sheet.

Sample Answer

(A) ● (C) (D)

Example II

_____ large natural lakes are found in the state of South Carolina.

(A) There are no
(B) Not the
(C) It is not
(D) No

This sentence should properly read "No large natural lakes are found in the state of South Carolina." You should fill in choice (D) on your answer sheet. As soon as you understand the directions, begin work on this part.

Sample Answer

(A) (B) (C) ●

1. _____ dancer Isadora Duncan played a major role in the revolution in dance that took place in the early twentieth century.

   (A) Because the
   (B) The
   (C) She was a
   (D) Being a

2. Water pressure _____ cracks open small rocks but also breaks great slabs of stone from the faces of cliffs.

   (A) either
   (B) not only
   (C) and so
   (D) moreover

3. _____ types of guitars: acoustic and electric.

   (A) Basically, there are two
   (B) Two of the basic
   (C) Basically, two
   (D) They are two basic

4. Both longitude and latitude _____ in degrees, minutes, and seconds.

   (A) measuring
   (B) measured
   (C) are measured
   (D) being measured

5. New words are constantly being invented _____ new objects and concepts.

   (A) to describe
   (B) a description of
   (C) they describe
   (D) describe

6. Modern saw blades are coated with a special _____ plastic.

   (A) reduction of friction
   (B) reduced-friction
   (C) friction is reduced
   (D) friction-reducing

7. Bricks baked in a kiln are much harder _____ that are dried in the sun.

   (A) those
   (B) than do those
   (C) than those
   (D) ones

8. Exactly _____ humans domesticated animals is not known.

   (A) how
   (B) by means of
   (C) if
   (D) by which

9. Jerome Kern's most famous work is *Showboat*, _____, most enduring musical comedies.

   (A) it is one of the finest
   (B) of the finest one
   (C) the finest one
   (D) one of the finest

10. _____ snowfield on a mountain slope reaches a depth of about 100 feet, it begins to move slowly forward under its own weight.

    (A) Whenever a
    (B) A
    (C) That a
    (D) Should a

11. Most comets have two kinds of tails, one made up of dust, _____ made up of electrically charged particles called plasma.

    (A) one another
    (B) the other
    (C) other ones
    (D) each other

12. By 1820, there were over sixty steamboats on the Mississippi River, _____ were quite luxurious.

    (A) many of them
    (B) which many
    (C) many of which
    (D) many that

13. _____ in 1772, Maryland's state capitol is still in use and is one of the most attractive public buildings in the United States.

    (A) It was built
    (B) Built
    (C) To build it
    (D) Building

14. Four miles off the southeastern coast of Massachusetts _____, a popular summer resort.

   (A) lies the island of Martha's Vineyard

   (B) the island of Martha's Vineyard lies there

   (C) does lie the island of Martha's Vineyard

   (D) where the island of Martha's Vineyard lies

15. Copperplate, a highly ornate form of handwriting, is _____ longer in common use.

   (A) not

   (B) none

   (C) never

   (D) no

ERROR IDENTIFICATION

Directions: The items in this part have four underlined words or phrases. You must identify the *one* underlined expression—(A), (B), (C), or (D)—that must be changed for the sentence to be correct. Then fill in the space on your answer sheet that matches the letter of the answer that you have selected.

Example I

Lenses may to have either concave or convex shapes.
      A   **B** **C**   **D**

This sentence should read "Lenses may have either concave or convex shapes." You should therefore select choice (A).

Sample Answer

● Ⓑ Ⓒ Ⓓ

Example II

When painting a fresco, an artist is applied paint directly to the damp plaster of a wall.
  A   **B**   **C**   **D**

This sentence should read "When painting a fresco, an artist applies paint directly to the wet plaster of a wall." You should therefore select choice (B). As soon as you understand the directions, begin work on this part.

Sample Answer

Ⓐ ● Ⓒ Ⓓ

16. In an essay writing in 1779, Judith Sargeant
          A   B
Murray promoted the cause of
                C
women's education.
      D

17. A metallic object that is in contact with a
            A   B
magnet becomes a magnet themselves.
         C   D

18. The change from summer to winter occurs
          A   B
very abrupt in the tundra regions of North
     C   D
America.

19. In outer space, spacecraft can be maneu-
   A   B
vered by means small steering rockets.
      C   D

20. Echoes occur when sound waves strike a
         A   B
smooth surface and bounces backward.
   C   D

21. A good carpentry must possess a wide
     A   B
variety of skills.
  C   D

22. Grover Cleveland was the only American
              A
president which served two nonconsecu-
     B   C
tive terms.
  D

23. The American soprano Mary Gardner,

who had one of the greatest operatic voices
    A   B
of her era, retired at the height of the
              C   D
career.

24. On nights when is the sky clear and the air
          A
calm, the earth's surface rapidly radiates
  B   C
heat into the atmosphere.
  D

25. Dreams are commonly made up of both
        A   B
visual or verbal images.
  C   D

26. The trap-door spider makes a hole in the
         A
ground, lines it with silk, and closing it
         B   C
with a hinged door.
    D

27. Sleepiness is one symptom of hypothermia,
   A   B
the extreme lost of body heat.
   C   D

28. The flute is the only woodwind instrument
   A   B
that is not done of wood.
   C   D

29. F. Scott Fitzgerald's novel *The Great Gatsby*

is about the pursuit of wealthy, status, and
    A   B   C
love in the 1920s.
  D

30. Whenever there are red, orange, or brown
     A   B
coloring in sandstone, iron ore is probably
                 C
present.
  D

31. Feathers keep birds warm and dry also
         A   B
enable them to fly.
  C D

32. Some species of penicillin mold are used to
   A   B
ripe cheeses.
  C D

33. In about 1920, experimental psychologists
 A   B
have devoted more research to learning
              C
than to any other topic.
  D

34. Natural asphalt lakes are find in many parts
        A   B   C
of the world.
  D

35. All living creatures pass on inherited traits
   A   B
from one generation to other.
 C   D

36. Many of the events that led up to the
        A   B
American Revolution took placed in
         C D
Massachusetts.

37. Mass production is the manufacture of
                                    A
machineries and other articles in standard
        B   C
sizes and large numbers.
                  D

38. Not much people realize that apples
        A   B
have been cultivated for over 3,000 years.
              C   D

39. The destructive force of running water
                            A   B
depends entirely almost on the velocity
                        C
of its flow.
        D

40. The eastern bluebird is considered the
                                        A
most attractive bird native of North America
              B   C
by many bird-watchers.
            D

THIS IS THE END OF SECTION 2.

IF YOU FINISH BEFORE THE TIME LIMIT, CHECK YOUR WORK
ON SECTION 2 ONLY.

DO NOT READ OR WORK ON ANY OTHER SECTION OF THE TEST.

Section 3

READING
TIME—55 MINUTES

This section of the test measures your ability to comprehend written materials.

Directions: This section contains several passages, each followed by a number of questions. Read the passages and, for each question, choose the *one* best answer—(A), (B), (C), or (D)—based on what is stated in the passage or on what can be inferred from the passage. Then fill in the space on your answer sheet that matches the letter of the answer that you have selected.

Read the Following Passage

Line Like mammals, birds claim their own territories. A bird's territory may be small or large. Some birds claim only their nest and the area right around it, while others claim far larger territories that include their feeding areas. Gulls, penguins, and other waterfowl nest in huge colonies, but even in the biggest colonies, each male and his mate have small territories of their own
5 immediately around their nests.
 Male birds defend their territory chiefly against other males of the same species. In some cases, a warning call or threatening pose may be all the defense needed, but in other cases, intruders may refuse to leave peacefully.

Example I

What is the main topic of this passage?

(A) Birds that live in colonies
(B) Birds' mating habits
(C) The behavior of birds
(D) Territoriality in birds

The passage mainly concerns the territories of birds. You should fill in choice (D) on your answer sheet.

Sample Answer

Example II

According to the passage, male birds defend their territory primarily against which of the following?

(A) Female birds
(B) Birds of other species
(C) Males of their own species
(D) Mammals

The passage states that "Male birds defend their territory chiefly against other males of the same species." You should fill in choice (C) on your answer sheet. As soon as you understand the directions, begin work on this section.

Sample Answer

QUESTIONS 1–10

Line Just as optical fibers have transformed communication, they are also revolutionizing medicine. These ultra-thin, flexible fibers have opened a window into the living tissues of the body. By inserting optical fibers through natural openings or small incisions and threading them along the body's established pathways, physicians can look into the lungs, intestines, heart, and other areas that were
5   formerly inaccessible to them.

      The basic fiber-optics system is called a fiberscope, which consists of two bundles of fibers. One, the illuminating bundle, carries light to the tissues. It is coupled to a high-intensity light source. Light enters the cores of the high-purity silicon glass and travels along the fibers. A lens at the end of the bundle collects the light and focuses it into the other bundle, the imaging bundle. Each fiber in
10   the bundle transmits only a tiny fraction of the total image. The reconstructed image can be viewed through an eyepiece or displayed on a television screen. During the last five years, improved methods of fabricating optical fibers have led to a reduction in fiberscope diameter and an increase in the number of fibers, which in turn has increased resolution.

      Optical fibers can also be used to deliver laser light. By use of laser beams, physicians can
15   perform surgery inside the body, sometimes eliminating the need for invasive procedures in which healthy tissue must be cut through to reach the site of disease. Many of these procedures do not require anesthesia and can be performed in a physician's office. These techniques have reduced the risk and the cost of medical care.

1. What is the main subject of the passage?

    (A) A revolution in communication
    (B) The invention of optical fibers
    (C) New surgical techniques
    (D) The role of optical fibers in medicine

2. In line 2, the author uses the expression *have opened a window* to indicate that the use of optical fibers

    (A) has enabled scientists to make amazing discoveries.
    (B) sometimes requires a surgical incision.
    (C) allows doctors to see inside the body without major surgery.
    (D) has been unknown to the general public until quite recently.

3. Which of the following is closest in meaning to the word *formerly* in line 5?

    (A) Previously
    (B) Completely
    (C) Usually
    (D) Theoretically

4. The word *them* in line 5 refers to

    (A) optical fibers.
    (B) pathways.
    (C) other areas of the body.
    (D) physicians.

5. According to the passage, what is the purpose of the illuminating bundle in a fiberscope?

    (A) To carry light into the body
    (B) To collect and focus light
    (C) To reconstruct images
    (D) To perform surgery inside the body

6. Which of the following is closest in meaning to the word *cores* in line 8?

    (A) Tips
    (B) Centers
    (C) Clusters
    (D) Lines

7. According to the passage, how do the fiberscopes used today differ from those used five years ago?

    (A) They use brighter lights.
    (B) They are longer.
    (C) They contain more fibers.
    (D) They are larger in diameter.

8. The word *resolution* in line 13 is closest in meaning to which of the following?

    (A) Strength
    (B) Sharpness
    (C) Inconvenience
    (D) Efficiency

9. Which of the following is NOT mentioned by the author as one of the advantages of laser surgery techniques?

   (A) They can be performed in a physician's office.
   (B) They are safer than conventional surgery.
   (C) They can often be performed without anesthesia.
   (D) They are relatively easy to teach to physicians.

10. Where in the passage does the author provide a basic description of a fiberscope?

    (A) Lines 1–2
    (B) Line 6
    (C) Lines 10–11
    (D) Line 14

QUESTIONS 11–18

Line Alice Walker has written books of poetry and short stories, a biography, and several novels. She is
probably best known for her novel *The Color Purple*, published in 1982. The book vividly narrates
the richness and complexity of black people—especially black women—in Georgia in the 1920s and
1930s. Although the novel came under bitter attack by certain critics and readers, it was applauded
5   by others and won both the American Book Award and the Pulitzer Prize for fiction. It became a
bestseller, selling over 4 million copies, and it was made into a successful film by noted director
Steven Spielberg. The novel reveals the horror, drudgery, and joy of black life in rural Georgia. It gets
much of its special flavor from its use of the words, rhythm, and grammar of black English and from
its epistolary style. Telling a story through letters was a narrative structure commonly used by
10   eighteenth-century novelists, but it is not often used in contemporary fiction. Unlike most epistolary
novels, which have the effect of distancing the reader from the events described by the letter writer,
The Color Purple uses the letter form to draw the reader into absolute intimacy with the poor,
uneducated, but wonderfully observant Celie, the main character of the novel. So the reader applauds
when Celie, like William Faulkner's character Dilsey, does not simply survive, but prevails.

11. What is the passage mainly about?
    - **(A)** A film by Steven Spielberg
    - **(B)** The life of Alice Walker
    - **(C)** Characters in the novels of William Faulkner
    - **(D)** A book by Alice Walker and reactions to it

12. According to the passage, *The Color Purple* is a book of
    - **(A)** poetry.
    - **(B)** criticism.
    - **(C)** fiction.
    - **(D)** biography.

13. The word *vividly* in line 2 is closest in meaning to
    - **(A)** intellectually.
    - **(B)** graphically.
    - **(C)** surprisingly.
    - **(D)** temporarily.

14. Which of the following is closest in meaning to the word *drudgery* in line 7?
    - **(A)** Hard work
    - **(B)** Culture
    - **(C)** Uniqueness
    - **(D)** Long history

15. The author mentions eighteenth-century novelists (line 10) because
    - **(A)** their books, like *The Color Purple*, made use of the epistolary style.
    - **(B)** *The Color Purple* is based on episodes in their books.
    - **(C)** their novels have a sense of absolute intimacy.
    - **(D)** their books, like those of Alice Walker, were attacked by critics but enjoyed by readers.

16. Why does the author mention Dilsey in line 14?
    - **(A)** He is a main character in *The Color Purple*.
    - **(B)** He is similar to Celie in one way.
    - **(C)** He is the person on whom Celie was based.
    - **(D)** He wrote a book somewhat similar to *The Color Purple*.

17. The word *prevails* in line 14 is closest in meaning to
    - **(A)** changes.
    - **(B)** resists.
    - **(C)** triumphs.
    - **(D)** impresses.

18. The attitude of the author toward *The Color Purple* is best described as one of
    - **(A)** admiration.
    - **(B)** alarm.
    - **(C)** indifference.
    - **(D)** anger.

QUESTIONS 19–30

Line   Many flowering plants woo insect pollinators and gently direct them to their most fertile blossoms by
changing the color of individual flowers from day to day. Through color cues, the plant signals to the
insect that it would be better off visiting one flower on its bush than another. The particular hue tells
the pollinator that the flower is full of far more pollen than are neighboring blooms. That nectar-rich
5   flower also happens to be fertile and ready to disperse its pollen or to receive pollen the insect has
picked up from another flower. Plants do not have to spend precious resources maintaining reser-
voirs of nectar in all their flowers. Thus, the color-coded communication system benefits both plant
and insect.

For example, on the lantana plant, a flower starts out on the first day as yellow, when it is rich
10   with pollen and nectar. Influenced by an as-yet-unidentified environmental signal, the flower changes
color by triggering the production of the pigment anthromyacin. It turns orange on the second day
and red on the third. By the third day, it has no pollen to offer insects and is no longer fertile. On
any given lantana bush, only 10 to 15 percent of the blossoms are likely to be yellow and fertile. But
in tests measuring the responsiveness of butterflies, it was discovered that the insects visited the
15   yellow flowers at least 100 times more than would be expected from haphazard visitation. Experiments with paper flowers and painted flowers demonstrated that the butterflies were responding to
color cues rather than, say, the scent of the nectar.

In other types of plants, blossoms change from white to red, others from yellow to red, and so
on. These color changes have been observed in some 74 families of plants.

19. The first paragraph of the passage implies that insects benefit from the color-coded communication system because

   (A) the colors hide them from predators.
   (B) they can gather pollen efficiently.
   (C) the bright colors attract fertile females.
   (D) other insect species cannot understand the code.

20. The word *woo* in line 1 is closest in meaning to

   (A) frighten.
   (B) trap.
   (C) deceive.
   (D) attract.

21. The word *it* in line 3 refers to a(n)

   (A) plant.
   (B) insect.
   (C) signal.
   (D) blossom.

22. The word *hue* in line 3 is closest in meaning to

   (A) smell.
   (B) texture.
   (C) color.
   (D) shape.

23. The word *Thus* in line 7 is closest in meaning to which of the following?

   (A) However
   (B) Therefore
   (C) Probably
   (D) Generally

24. Which of the following describes the sequence of color changes that lantana blossoms undergo?

   (A) Red to yellow to white
   (B) White to red
   (C) Yellow to orange to red
   (D) Red to purple

25. The word *triggering* in line 11 is closest in meaning to

   (A) maintaining.
   (B) renewing.
   (C) limiting.
   (D) activating.

26. The passage implies that insects would be most attracted to lantana blossoms

   (A) on the first day that they bloom.
   (B) when they turn orange.
   (C) on the third day that they bloom.
   (D) after they produce anthromyacin.

27. According to the passage, what is the purpose of the experiments involving paper flowers and painted flowers?

   (A) To strengthen the idea that butterflies are attracted by the smell of flowers

   (B) To prove that flowers do not always need pollen to reproduce

   (C) To demonstrate how insects change color depending on the type of flowers they visit

   (D) To support the idea that insects respond to the changing color of flowers

28. The word *haphazard* in line 15 is closest in meaning to which of the following?

   (A) Dangerous

   (B) Random

   (C) Fortunate

   (D) Expected

29. What is known from the passage about the *other types of plants* mentioned in line 18?

   (A) They follow various sequences of color changes.

   (B) They use scent and other methods of attracting pollinators.

   (C) They have not been studied as thoroughly as the lantana.

   (D) They have exactly the same pigments as the lantana.

30. According to the passage, in approximately how many families of plants has the color-changing phenomenon described in the passage been observed?

   (A) 10

   (B) 15

   (C) 74

   (D) 100

Questions 31–39

Line The 1960s, however, saw a rising dissatisfaction with the Modernist movement, especially in North America where its failings were exposed in two influential books, Jane Jacobs' *The Death and Life of Great American Cities* in 1961 and Robert Venturi's *Complexity and Contradiction in Architecture* in 1966. Jacobs highlighted the destruction of the richness of American cities by massive, impersonal
5 buildings. Venturi implied that Modernist structures were without meaning because they lacked the complexity and intimacy of historical buildings.

    This dissatisfaction was translated into action in 1972 with the demolition of several fourteen-story Modernist apartment blocks that only twenty years before had won architectural prizes. Similar housing developments were destroyed elsewhere in North America in the following decades, but it
10 was in St. Louis that the post-Modernist era began.

    Post-Modernist architects have little in common in terms of style or theory. They are united mainly in their opposition to the Modernist style. Robert Venturi's designs show wit, humanity, and historical reference. These tendencies can be seen in his bold design for the Tucker House (1975) in Katonah, New York, and the Brant-Johnson House (1975) in Vail, Colorado, which owes something
15 to the Italian Renaissance. Similar characteristics are apparent in the work of Venturi's disciple Michael Graves. Graves' Portland Public Service Building (1982) in Portland, Oregon, and his Humana Tower (1986) in Louisville, Kentucky, have the bulk of skyscrapers but incorporate historical souvenirs such as colonnades, belvederes, keystones, and decorative sculpture.

    Other post-Modernists rejected the playfulness of Venturi and his group. They chose a more
20 historically faithful classical style, as in Greenberg and Blateau's reception rooms at the U.S. Department of State in Washington, D.C. (1984–86). The most complete instance of historical accuracy is the J. Paul Getty Museum in Malibu, California (1970–75), designed by Langdon and Wilson. They relied on archaeological advice to achieve the authentic quality of a Roman villa.

31. With which of the following topics did the paragraph preceding the passage probably deal?

(A) The Modernist movement
(B) Architecture outside North America
(C) A history of post-Modernism
(D) Books of the 1950s

32. Which of the following is closest in meaning to the word *highlighted* in line 4?

(A) Celebrated
(B) Denied
(C) Emphasized
(D) Exaggerated

33. The word *they* in line 5 refers to

(A) historical buildings.
(B) Venturi and Jacobs.
(C) North American cities.
(D) Modernist structures.

34. According to the passage, what do the two books mentioned in the first paragraph have in common?

(A) They were both written by the same author.
(B) They both lack complexity.
(C) They are both critical of Modernism.
(D) They both outline post-Modernist theory.

35. According to the author, which event signalled the beginning of post-Modernism?

(A) The publication of a book
(B) The building of a housing development
(C) The awarding of a prize
(D) The destruction of some buildings

36. The author mentions that a house designed by Robert Venturi in a style influenced by the Italian Renaissance was built in

(A) Katonah, New York
(B) Vail, Colorado
(C) Portland, Oregon
(D) Louisville, Kentucky

37. Which of the following is closest in meaning to *disciple* in line 15?

    (A) Adviser

    (B) Follower

    (C) Critic

    (D) Partner

38. What does the author imply about the Portland Public Service Building and the Humana Building?

    (A) They are popular places for tourists to visit and to buy souvenirs.

    (B) They have great historical significance.

    (C) They feature elements not generally seen in modern buildings.

    (D) They are much smaller than most skyscrapers.

39. The J. Paul Getty Museum is given as an example of

    (A) a massive, impersonal Modernist building.

    (B) a faithful reproduction of classical architecture.

    (C) a typical Malibu structure.

    (D) playful architecture.

Questions 40–50

Line While many nineteenth-century reformers hoped to bring about reform through education or by eliminating specific social evils, some thinkers wanted to start over and remake society by founding ideal, cooperative communities. The United States seemed to them a spacious and unencumbered country where models of a perfect society could succeed. These communitarian thinkers hoped their
5 success would lead to imitation, until communities free of crime, poverty, and other social ills would cover the land. A number of religious groups, notably the Shakers, practiced communal living, but the main impetus to found model communities came from nonreligious, rationalistic thinkers.

Among the communitarian philosophers, three of the most influential were Robert Owen, Charles Fourier, and John Humphrey Noyes. Owen, famous for his humanitarian policies as owner of
10 several thriving textile mills in Scotland, believed that faulty environment was to blame for human problems and that these problems could be eliminated in a rationally planned society. In 1825, he put his principles into practice at New Harmony, Indiana. The community failed economically after a few years but not before achieving a number of social successes. Fourier, a commercial employee in France, never visited the United States. However, his theories of cooperative living influenced many
15 Americans through the writings of Albert Brisbane, whose *Social Destiny of Man* explained Fourierism and its self-sufficient associations or "phalanxes." One or more of these phalanxes was organized in every Northern state. The most famous were Red Bank, New Jersey, and Brook Farm, Massachusetts. An early member of the latter was the author Nathaniel Hawthorne. Noyes founded the most enduring and probably the oddest of the utopian communities, the Oneida Community of upstate
20 New York. Needless to say, none of these experiments had any lasting effects on the patterns of American society.

40. The main topic of the passage is
- **(A)** nineteenth-century schools.
- **(B)** American reformers.
- **(C)** the philosophy of Fourierism.
- **(D)** model communities in the nineteenth century.

41. Which of the following is NOT given in the passage as one of the general goals of communitarian philosophers?
- **(A)** To remake society
- **(B)** To spread their ideas throughout the United States
- **(C)** To establish ideal communities
- **(D)** To create opportunities through education

42. The Shakers are mentioned in line 6 as an example of
- **(A)** a communal religious group.
- **(B)** radical reformers.
- **(C)** rationalistic thinkers.
- **(D)** an influential group of writers.

43. Which of the following is closest in meaning to the word *impetus* in line 7?
- **(A)** Stimulus
- **(B)** Commitment
- **(C)** Drawback
- **(D)** Foundation

44. Which of the following is closest in meaning to the word *thriving* in line 10?
- **(A)** Prosperous
- **(B)** Famous
- **(C)** Failing
- **(D)** Pioneering

45. The "phalanxes" described in the second paragraph were an idea originally conceived by
- **(A)** Albert Brisbane.
- **(B)** Robert Owen.
- **(C)** Charles Fourier.
- **(D)** John Humphrey Noyes.

46. Why does the author mention Nathaniel Hawthorne in line 18?
- **(A)** He founded Brook Farm in Massachusetts.
- **(B)** He was a critic of Charles Fourier.
- **(C)** He wrote a book that led to the establishment of model communities.
- **(D)** He was at one time a member of the Brook Farm community.

47. Which of the following communities lasted longest?
- **(A)** New Harmony
- **(B)** The Oneida Community
- **(C)** Red Bank
- **(D)** Brook Farm

48. The word *oddest* in line 19 is closest in meaning to which of the following?

(A) Earliest
(B) Most independent
(C) Largest
(D) Most unusual

49. The author implies that, for readers, the conclusion of the passage is

(A) obvious.
(B) surprising.
(C) absurd.
(D) practical.

50. Why did the author probably divide the passage into two paragraphs?

(A) To compare nineteenth-century reforms with twentieth-century reforms
(B) To present an overview of a concept in the first paragraph and specific examples in the second
(C) To contrast the work of utopian thinkers with that of practical reformers
(D) To give the causes for a phenomenon in the first paragraph and its consequences in the second

THIS IS THE END OF SECTION 3.

IF YOU FINISH BEFORE THE TIME LIMIT, CHECK YOUR WORK
ON SECTION 3 ONLY.

DO NOT READ OR WORK ON ANY OTHER SECTION OF THE TEST.

Practice Test 2

Section 1

LISTENING

This section tests your ability to comprehend spoken English. It is divided into three parts, each with its own directions. During actual exams, you are *not* permitted to turn the page during the reading of the directions or to take notes at any time.

PART A

Directions: Each item in this part consists of a brief conversation involving two speakers. Following each conversation, a third voice will ask a question. You will hear the conversations and questions only once, and they will *not* be written out.

When you have heard each conversation and question, read the four answer choices and select the one—(A), (B), (C), or (D)—that best answers the question based on what is directly stated or on what can be inferred. Then fill in the space on your answer sheet that matches the letter of the answer that you have selected.

Here is an example.

You will hear:

M1: Do you think I should lean this chair against the wall or put it somewhere else?

F1: Over by the window, I'd say.

M2: What does the woman think the man should do?

You will read:

(A) Open the window.
(B) Move the chair.
(C) Leave the room.
(D) Take a seat.

From the conversation, you find out that the woman thinks the man should put the chair over by the window. The best answer to the question "What does the woman think the man should do?" is (B), "Move the chair." You should fill in (B) on your answer sheet.

Sample Answer

 Ⓐ ● Ⓒ Ⓓ

1. (A) He closed the suitcase.
   (B) He just left on a trip.
   (C) He put the suitcase away.
   (D) He packed his clothes.

2. (A) He came too late to have lunch.
   (B) He is going to eat dinner early.
   (C) He's not very hungry.
   (D) He's not going to eat anything.

3. (A) She adjusted to college life easily.
   (B) It was hard for her to get into college.
   (C) She no longer attends college.
   (D) It doesn't take her long to get to campus.

4. (A) Encouraged.
   (B) Indifferent.
   (C) Insulted.
   (D) Responsible.

5. (A) Her mistakes weren't serious.
   (B) She made mistakes because she rushed.
   (C) She must hurry to the laboratory.
   (D) Her work in the laboratory isn't finished.

6. (A) The post office.
   (B) Monroe Street.
   (C) The courthouse.
   (D) Fourth Avenue.

7. (A) He knew Lynn was majoring in economics.
   (B) He doesn't think they have anything in common.
   (C) He knows Mitch better than he knows Lynn.
   (D) He's planning to study economics himself.

8. (A) How he's going to contact Tony.
   (B) Why he needs to speak to Tony.
   (C) Where he will meet Tony.
   (D) When he's going to call Tony.

9. (A) Prepared a meal.
   (B) Went to a wedding.
   (C) Shopped for groceries.
   (D) Worked in a garden.

10. (A) He's expecting guests.
    (B) He can give the introduction.
    (C) He's very well known.
    (D) He'll be the main speaker.

11. (A) Tea, not coffee.
    (B) Either milk or sugar in her coffee.
    (C) Nothing to drink right now.
    (D) Black coffee without sugar.

12. (A) It was indeed exciting.
    (B) It was too frightening.
    (C) It was mildly interesting.
    (D) It was extremely long.

13. (A) He doesn't mind moving.
    (B) He won't move for two weeks.
    (C) He'd rather not be moving.
    (D) He's decided not to move.

14. (A) She may telephone Arthur.
    (B) Perhaps rehearsal should be canceled.
    (C) She can't practice any other evening.
    (D) Rehearsal has already been postponed.

15. (A) Drink some more lemonade.
    (B) Put on his glasses.
    (C) Make a glass of lemonade.
    (D) Buy some more fruit.

16. (A) It's near the entrance.
    (B) He doesn't know where it is.
    (C) It's not in this building.
    (D) The directory doesn't list it.

17. (A) They're always expensive.
    (B) They haven't been cleaned.
    (C) They're inexpensive now.
    (D) There aren't any available.

18. (A) Have lunch with the man.
    (B) Join a club.
    (C) Skip the meeting.
    (D) Walk with the man.

19. (A) It may take more than half an hour.
    (B) The stadium is the best place to go now.
    (C) The stadium will probably be only half full.
    (D) It's not a good idea to hurry right now.

20. (A) Joan is really an easygoing person.
    (B) No one believes Joan.
    (C) He's more easygoing than Joan.
    (D) No one knows Joan as well as he does.

21. (A) Its lyrics are hard to understand.
    (B) It needs a stronger melody.
    (C) It has become very popular.
    (D) Its melody is hard to forget.

22. (A) She has a stamp exactly like his.
(B) She knows a lot about stamps.
(C) She thinks the stamp is worthless.
(D) She's never seen this type of stamp.

23. (A) They must go to an orientation session.
(B) They are not new students.
(C) They won't be allowed to register.
(D) They were given the wrong schedule.

24. (A) He lives a long way from a good library.
(B) Up to now, he hasn't had any problems.
(C) He's not happy with the quality of the research.
(D) When he's finished the project, he'll be happy.

25. (A) They're both working on a ship.
(B) They're taking summer vacations together.
(C) They own the same type of boat.
(D) They both have summer jobs.

26. (A) She thinks Professor Fuller's class is boring.
(B) She doesn't know Professor Fuller.
(C) She agrees with the man's remark.
(D) She doesn't understand the man's comment.

27. (A) She doesn't want to be photographed.
(B) The man can have the picture she took.
(C) Not all the pictures are good.
(D) The man may take her photograph.

28. (A) She loves all kinds of books.
(B) She doesn't read poetry anymore.
(C) She doesn't like all poetry.
(D) She writes many types of poems.

29. (A) In a few days.
(B) Before they eat.
(C) During lunch.
(D) When lunch is over.

30. (A) That the man had not bought the motorcycle.
(B) That the weather wouldn't be good today.
(C) That the man would ride to work today.
(D) That the man did not have to work today.

PART B

Directions: This part of the test consists of extended conversations between two speakers. After each of these conversations there are a number of questions. You will hear each conversation and question only once, and the questions are *not* written out.

When you have heard the questions, read the four answer choices and select the *one*—(A), (B), (C), or (D)—that best answers the question based on what is directly stated or on what can be inferred. Then fill in the space on your answer sheet that matches the letter of the answer that you have selected.

Don't forget: During actual exams, taking notes or writing in your test book is *not* permitted.

31. (A) He'd lost his driver's license.
    (B) His identification wasn't acceptable.
    (C) He didn't have his checkbook.
    (D) The ticket office was closed.

32. (A) On campus.
    (B) In the Midvale Shopping Mall.
    (C) On Southland Parkway.
    (D) Downtown.

33. (A) A passport.
    (B) A check.
    (C) A driver's license.
    (D) A ticket.

34. (A) Drive him to the concert.
    (B) Cash his check.
    (C) Sell him her tickets.
    (D) Lend him some money.

35. (A) Doctor and nurse.
    (B) Librarian and library patron.
    (C) Forest ranger and hiker.
    (D) Nurse and patient.

36. (A) Saturday.
    (B) Sunday.
    (C) Monday.
    (D) Tuesday.

37. (A) An allergy to animals.
    (B) A reaction to toxic chemicals.
    (C) An allergy to food.
    (D) Contact with a noxious plant.

38. (A) Look at photographs in the library.
    (B) Take a drug that prevents rashes.
    (C) Avoid certain foods.
    (D) Stay out of the woods.

PART C

Directions: This part of the test consists of several talks, each given by a single speaker. After each of these talks there are a number of questions. You will hear each talk and question only once, and the questions are *not* written out.

When you have heard the question, read the four answer choices and select the one—(A), (B), (C), or (D)—that best answers the question based on what is directly stated or on what can be inferred. Then fill in the space on your answer sheet that matches the letter of the answer that you have selected.

Here is an example.

You will hear:

M1: Students, this evening we'll have a chance to observe a phenomenon that we've discussed several times in class. Tonight, there will be a lunar eclipse. As we've said, when an eclipse of the moon occurs, the earth passes between the sun and the moon. Therefore, the shadow of the earth moves across the surface of the moon and obscures it. Because you won't be looking at the sun, it is not necessary to use the special lenses and filters that you need when observing a solar eclipse. You can observe a lunar eclipse with your unaided eye or with a telescope and photograph it with an ordinary camera. So if the weather's not cloudy tonight, go out and take a look at this eclipse of the moon. I'm sure you'll find it interesting.

Now here is a sample question.

You will hear:

M2: In what course is this lecture probably being given?

You will read:

(A) Philosophy.
(B) Meteorology.
(C) Astronomy.
(D) Photography.

The lecture concerns a lunar eclipse, a topic that would typically be discussed in an astronomy class. The choice that best answers the question "In what course is this lecture probably being given?" is (C), "Astronomy." You should fill in (C) on your answer sheet.

Sample Answer

Here is another sample question.

You will hear:

M2: According to the speaker, which of the following occurs during a lunar eclipse?

You will read:

(A) The earth's shadow moves across the moon.
(B) Clouds block the view of the moon.
(C) The moon moves between the earth and the sun.
(D) The sun can be observed without special equipment.

From the lecture, you learn that a lunar eclipse occurs when the earth moves between the sun and the moon and the shadow of the earth passes across the moon. The choice that best answers the question "According to the speaker, which of the following occurs during a lunar eclipse?" is (A), "The earth's shadow moves across the moon." Don't forget: During actual exams, taking notes or writing in your test book is *not* permitted.

Sample Answer

39. (A) On a bus.
(B) At Crater Lake National Park.
(C) In a hotel.
(D) In Portland, Oregon.

40. (A) Its mineral content.
(B) The reflection of blue sky in the water.
(C) The depth and clarity of the lake.
(D) Its low temperature.

41. (A) It rises rapidly when the snow melts.
(B) It stays more or less the same all year.
(C) It varies greatly from year to year.
(D) It drops quickly because of evaporation and seepage.

42. (A) Communications
(B) Mining
(C) Transportation
(D) Journalism.

43. (A) Nebraska
(B) California
(C) Utah
(D) Missouri

44. (A) 5
(B) 10
(C) 50
(D) 200

45. (A) Useless
(B) Dangerous
(C) Boring
(D) High-paying

46. (A) The invention of the telephone.
(B) The beginning of the Civil War.
(C) The expansion of the railroad system.
(D) The completion of the transcontinental telegraph.

47. (A) To urge the audience to attend a play.
(B) To introduce a speaker.
(C) To welcome some new members to a club.
(D) To describe opportunities in acting.

48. (A) At a meeting.
(B) During a drama class.
(C) At a rehearsal.
(D) During auditions for a play.

49. (A) Performing in a television series.
(B) Directing a television commercial.
(C) Acting in a New York play.
(D) Appearing in a movie.

50. (A) Became president of the Drama Club.
(B) Studied in the Drama Department.
(C) Acted in campus plays.
(D) Directed a number of performances.

THIS IS THE END OF SECTION 1: LISTENING.

STOP WORK ON SECTION 1.

Section 2

This section tests your ability to recognize grammar and usage suitable for standard written English. It is divided into two parts, each with its own directions.

SENTENCE COMPLETION

Directions: Items in this part are incomplete sentences. Following each of these sentences, there are four words or phrases. You should select the *one* word or phrase—(A), (B), (C), or (D)—that best completes the sentence. Then fill in the space on your answer sheet that matches the letter of the answer that you have selected.

Example I

Pepsin _____ an enzyme used in digestion.

(A) that
(B) is
(C) of
(D) being

This sentence should properly read "Pepsin is an enzyme used in digestion." You should fill in choice (B) on your answer sheet.

Sample Answer

Ⓐ ● Ⓒ Ⓓ

Example II

_____ large natural lakes are found in the state of South Carolina.

(A) There are no
(B) Not the
(C) It is not
(D) No

This sentence should properly read "No large natural lakes are found in the state of South Carolina." You should fill in choice (D) on your answer sheet. As soon as you understand the directions, begin work on this part.

Sample Answer

Ⓐ Ⓑ Ⓒ ●

1. In 1793, Charles Newbold designed a cast iron plow that _____ than the wooden plows then in use.

   (A) was more efficient
   (B) was of more efficiency
   (C) had more efficiency
   (D) it was more efficient

2. _____ think of metallurgy as a modern field of science, but it is actually one of the oldest.

   (A) Although many people
   (B) Many people
   (C) Many people who
   (D) In spite of many people

3. Part of Jane Colden's work involved collecting plant specimens, cataloging plants, and _____ with other botanists.

   (A) exchanging correspondence
   (B) her exchange of correspondence
   (C) correspondence exchanging
   (D) correspondence was exchanged

4. The walls of arteries _____ into three layers.

   (A) they divide
   (B) dividing
   (C) to be divided
   (D) are divided

5. The art of storytelling is _____ humanity.

   (A) as old
   (B) old as
   (C) as old as
   (D) old

6. A cloud is a dense mass of _____ water vapor or ice particles.

   (A) or
   (B) whether
   (C) both
   (D) either

7. Centuries of erosion have exposed _____ rock surfaces in the Painted Desert of northern Arizona.

   (A) rainbow-colored
   (B) colored like a rainbow
   (C) in colors of the rainbow
   (D) a rainbow's coloring

8. Nellie Ross of Wyoming was the first woman _____ governor in the United States.

   (A) who elected
   (B) to be elected
   (C) was elected
   (D) her election as

9. Dry farming is a type of agriculture used in areas _____ less than 20 inches of rainfall.

   (A) there are
   (B) in which is
   (C) where there is
   (D) which has

10. Once known as the "Golden State" because of its gold mines, _____.

    (A) North Carolina today mines few metallic minerals
    (B) few metallic minerals are mined in North Carolina today
    (C) there are few metallic minerals mined in North Carolina today
    (D) today in North Carolina few metallic minerals are mined

11. Indoor heating systems have made _____ for people to live and work comfortably in temperate climates.

    (A) possible that
    (B) it possible
    (C) possible
    (D) it is possible

12. _____ of liquids through pipes.

    (A) The flow controlled by valves
    (B) For valves to control the flow
    (C) Valves control the flow
    (D) Controlled by valves, the flow

13. Honey is the only form of naturally occurring sugar that _____ to be refined before it can be eaten.

    (A) has not
    (B) does not have
    (C) not having
    (D) does not

14. _____ species of wild goats, only one, the Rocky Mountain goat, is native to North America.

    (A) The ten
    (B) Ten of the
    (C) Of the ten
    (D) There are ten

15. Snare drums produce a sharp, rattling sound _____.

    (A) as striking
    (B) when are struck
    (C) struck
    (D) when struck

42

ERROR IDENTIFICATION

Directions: The items in this part have four underlined words or phrases. You must identify the *one* underlined expression—(A), (B), (C), or (D)—that must be changed for the sentence to be correct. Then fill in the space on your answer sheet that matches the letter of the answer that you have selected.

Example I

Lenses may to have either concave or convex shapes.
       A   **B** **C**   **D**

This sentence should read "Lenses may have either concave or convex shapes." You should therefore select choice (A).

Sample Answer

● Ⓑ Ⓒ Ⓓ

Example II

When painting a fresco, an artist is applied paint directly to the damp plaster of a wall.
A   **B**   **C**   **D**

This sentence should read "When painting a fresco, an artist applies paint directly to the wet plaster of a wall." You should therefore select (B). As soon as you understand the directions, begin work on this part.

Sample Answer

Ⓐ ● Ⓒ Ⓓ

16. Much superstitions and symbols are
    $\overline{\text{A}}$ $\overline{\text{B}}$ $\overline{\text{C}}$
    connected with Halloween.
    $\overline{\text{D}}$

17. Luray Caverns in northern Virginia contain
    $\overline{\text{A}}$
    acres of colorful rock formations
    $\overline{\text{B}}$ $\overline{\text{C}}$
    illumination by electric lights.
    $\overline{\text{D}}$

18. Furniture makers use glue

    to hold joints together and sometimes to
    $\overline{\text{A}}$ $\overline{\text{B}}$ $\overline{\text{C}}$
    reinforce it.
    $\overline{\text{D}}$

19. Anthracite contains a higher percent of
    $\overline{\text{A}}$ $\overline{\text{B}}$ $\overline{\text{C}}$
    carbon than bituminous coal.
    $\overline{\text{D}}$

20. Sheep have been domesticated for over
    $\overline{\text{A}}$ $\overline{\text{B}}$ $\overline{\text{C}}$
    5,000 years ago.
    $\overline{\text{D}}$

21. The hard, out surface of the tooth is called
    $\overline{\text{A}}$ $\overline{\text{B}}$ $\overline{\text{C}}$ $\overline{\text{D}}$
    enamel.

22. Aneroid barometers are smaller than
    $\overline{\text{A}}$ $\overline{\text{B}}$
    mercury barometers and are more easy
    $\overline{\text{C}}$
    to carry.
    $\overline{\text{D}}$

23. Liquids take the shape of any container
    $\overline{\text{A}}$
    which in they are placed.
    $\overline{\text{B}}$ $\overline{\text{C}}$ $\overline{\text{D}}$

24. The earliest form of artificial lighting was
    $\overline{\text{A}}$ $\overline{\text{B}}$
    fire, which also provided warm and
    $\overline{\text{C}}$ $\overline{\text{D}}$
    protection.

25. Publishers of modern encyclopedias employ
    $\overline{\text{A}}$
    hundreds of specialists and large editorials
    $\overline{\text{B}}$ $\overline{\text{C}}$ $\overline{\text{D}}$
    staffs.

26. Automobiles begun to be equipped with
    $\overline{\text{A}}$ $\overline{\text{B}}$
    built-in radios around 1930.
    $\overline{\text{C}}$ $\overline{\text{D}}$

27. The thread used in knitting may be woolen
    $\overline{\text{A}}$ $\overline{\text{B}}$
    yarn, cotton, or synthetic fabric threads
    $\overline{\text{C}}$
    such rayon.
    $\overline{\text{D}}$

28. All mammals have hair, but not always
    $\overline{\text{A}}$ $\overline{\text{B}}$ $\overline{\text{C}}$ $\overline{\text{D}}$
    evident.

29. Asparagus grows well in soil that is
    $\overline{\text{A}}$ $\overline{\text{B}}$
    too much salty for most crops to grow.
    $\overline{\text{C}}$ $\overline{\text{D}}$

30. A professor of economic and history at
    $\overline{\text{A}}$ $\overline{\text{B}}$
    Atlanta University, W. E. B. Du Bois

    promoted full racial equality.
    $\overline{\text{C}}$ $\overline{\text{D}}$

31. Bubbles of air in ice cream make it soft and
    $\overline{\text{A}}$ $\overline{\text{B}}$
    enough smooth to eat.
    $\overline{\text{C}}$ $\overline{\text{D}}$

32. However type of raw materials are used
    $\overline{\text{A}}$ $\overline{\text{B}}$
    in making paper, the process is essentially
    $\overline{\text{C}}$
    the same.
    $\overline{\text{D}}$

33. Ducks are less susceptible to infection than
    $\overline{\text{A}}$ $\overline{\text{B}}$
    another types of poultry.
    $\overline{\text{C}}$ $\overline{\text{D}}$

34. Lake Tahoe's great deep of 1,600 feet
    $\overline{\text{A}}$ $\overline{\text{B}}$
    prevents it from freezing in the winter.
    $\overline{\text{C}}$ $\overline{\text{D}}$

35. By 1675, Boston was the home port for
    $\overline{\text{A}}$ $\overline{\text{B}}$
    almost 750 ships, ranging in size between
    $\overline{\text{C}}$ $\overline{\text{D}}$
    30 to 250 tons.

36. The silk thread that spiders spin is much
    $\overline{\text{A}}$ $\overline{\text{B}}$
    finer than the silk that it comes from
    $\overline{\text{C}}$ $\overline{\text{D}}$
    silkworms.

37. Needles are simple looking tools, but they
    $\overline{\text{A}}$ $\overline{\text{B}}$
    are very relatively difficult to make.
    $\overline{\text{C}}$ $\overline{\text{D}}$

38. Winslow Homer, who had no formally
                           A   B
training in art, became famous for his
                              C
paintings of the sea and seacoast.
    D

39. The reflection of sunshines off snow can be
                         A   B
so intense that it causes a condition known
      C   D
as "snow blindness."

40. The first rugs were made by the hand, and
                           A   B
the finest ones are still handmade.
         C   D

THIS IS THE END OF SECTION 2.

IF YOU FINISH BEFORE THE TIME LIMIT, CHECK YOUR WORK
ON SECTION 2 ONLY.

DO NOT READ OR WORK ON ANY OTHER SECTION OF THE TEST.

Section 3

READING
TIME—55 MINUTES

This section of the test measures your ability to comprehend written materials.

Directions: This section contains several passages, each followed by a number of questions. Read the passages and, for each question, choose the *one* best answer—(A), (B), (C), or (D)—based on what is stated in the passage or on what can be inferred from the passage. Then fill in the space on your answer sheet that matches the letter of the answer that you have selected.

Read the Following Passage

Line   Like mammals, birds claim their own territories. A bird's territory may be small or large. Some birds claim only their nest and the area right around it, while others claim far larger territories that include their feeding areas. Gulls, penguins, and other waterfowl nest in huge colonies, but even in the biggest colonies, each male and his mate have small territories of their own
5   immediately around their nests.
    Male birds defend their territory chiefly against other males of the same species. In some cases, a warning call or threatening pose may be all the defense needed, but in other cases, intruders may refuse to leave peacefully.

Example I

What is the main topic of this passage?

(A) Birds that live in colonies
(B) Birds' mating habits
(C) The behavior of birds
(D) Territoriality in birds

The passage mainly concerns the territories of birds. You should fill in choice (D) on your answer sheet.

Sample Answer

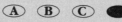

Example II

According to the passage, male birds defend their territory primarily against which of the following?

(A) Female birds
(B) Birds of other species
(C) Males of their own species
(D) Mammals

The passage states that "Male birds defend their territory chiefly against other males of the same species." You should fill in choice (C) on your answer sheet. As soon as you understand the directions, begin work on this section.

Sample Answer

46

QUESTIONS 1–12

Line Clipper ships were the swiftest sailing ships that were ever put to sea and the most beautiful. These
ships had their days of glory in the 1840s and 1850s. The first were built in Baltimore, but most were
constructed in the shipyards of New England. It was Chinese tea that brought them into existence.
Tea loses its flavor quickly when stored in the hold of a vessel, and merchants were willing to pay
5   top prices for fast delivery. American shipbuilders designed clippers to fill this need. Then came the
California Gold Rush of 1849, when Clippers took gold seekers from the East Coast to the West by
way of Cape Horn.

   Clippers were built for speed, and considerations of large carrying capacity and economical
operation were sacrificed for this purpose. They had long, slender hulls with sharp bows. Their three
10   slanted masts carried a huge cloud of canvas sail, including topgallants and royal sails, and sometimes
skysails and moonrakers, to capture the power of the winds. They required a hard-driving captain and
a large, experienced crew.

   Many records were set by clippers. *Sovereign of the Seas* made it from San Francisco to New
York in eighty-two days. *Flying Cloud* did 374 miles in one day. *Lightning* traveled from New York
15   to Liverpool in thirteen days, and *Ino* made it from New York to Singapore in eighty-six days.

   Some 500 clippers were built in American shipyards. British yards turned out some twenty-
seven tea clippers, as the British ships were called. Unlike the wooden American ships, British
clippers were "composite" with iron frames and wooden planking. The most famous tea clipper was
the *Cutty Sark.*
20   By 1860, the age of the clippers was fading. Gold diggings in California were nearly exhausted.
American investors found railroad building more profitable than clippers. Most importantly, there was
a technological innovation that doomed the clipper, and in fact, the entire age of sail: the development of the steamship.

1. What is the author's main purpose in writing?
   (A) To describe the tea trade in the 1840s
   (B) To contrast clipper ships and steamships
   (C) To discuss nineteenth-century shipbuilding techniques
   (D) To provide a brief history of clipper ships

2. Which of the following is closest in meaning to the word *swiftest* in line 1?
   (A) Fastest
   (B) Best armed
   (C) Largest
   (D) Most expensive

3. According to the passage, where were the majority of clipper ships built?
   (A) California
   (B) Baltimore
   (C) New England
   (D) Great Britain

4. In line 4, the word *vessel* could best be replaced by which of the following?
   (A) Container
   (B) Ship
   (C) Cargo
   (D) Merchant

5. According to the passage, how did the California Gold Rush affect clipper ships?
   (A) It encouraged the development of railroads, which competed directly with clipper ships.
   (B) The newly discovered gold was used to finance the construction of new ships.
   (C) It stimulated the demand for tea on the West Coast.
   (D) People who wanted to participate in the Gold Rush became passengers on clipper ships.

6. According to the passage, which of the following considerations was of the most importance to the owners of clipper ships?
   (A) Maximum speed
   (B) Reduced operating costs
   (C) Increased cargo capacity
   (D) Small crews

7. Which of the following is closest in meaning to the word *slanted* in line 10?

    (A) Tilted
    (B) Slender
    (C) Strengthened
    (D) Towering

8. What can be inferred from the passage about skysails and moonrakers?

    (A) Skysails were the highest sails on the mast, and moonrakers were the lowest.
    (B) They were not always used on clipper ships.
    (C) They were much larger than royal sails and topgallants.
    (D) They were never used on clipper ships.

9. According to the passage, the record for the fastest trip between New York and Liverpool was set by

    (A) *Sovereign of the Sea*.
    (B) *Flying Cloud*.
    (C) *Lightning*.
    (D) *Ino*.

10. It can be inferred from the passage that the tea clipper *Cutty Sark*

    (A) was faster than most American clippers.
    (B) had more than three masts.
    (C) could be powered by steam as well as by sails.
    (D) had a metal frame and wooden planking.

11. All of the following are given in the passage as reasons for the decline of clipper ships EXCEPT

    (A) the end of the California Gold Rush.
    (B) competition with British tea clippers.
    (C) the development of steamships.
    (D) investment in railroads.

12. In the next paragraph, the author will most likely discuss

    (A) the beginnings of the age of steam.
    (B) railroad travel in the United States.
    (C) further developments in sailing ships.
    (D) the relationship between speed and ship design.

Questions 13–22

Line Ralph Earl was born into a Connecticut farm family in 1751. He chose early to become a painter and
looked for what training was available in his home state and in Boston. Earl was one of the first
American artists to paint landscapes. Among his first paintings were scenes from the Revolutionary
War battles of Lexington and Concord. In 1778, Earl went to London to study with Benjamin West
5   for four years.

When Earl returned to the United States, he was jailed for fourteen months for outstanding
debts. While still a prisoner, he painted portraits of some of New York City's most elegant society
women and their husbands. After his release, he took up the trade of itinerant portrait painter,
working his way through southern New England and New York. Earl didn't flatter his subjects, but
10 his portraits show a deep understanding of them, perhaps because he had sprung from the same
roots.

Among Earl's most famous paintings is his portrait of Justice Oliver Ellsworth and his wife,
Abigail. To provide counterpoint to the severity of the couple, he accurately details the relative
luxury of the Ellsworth's interior furnishings. The view through the window behind them shows
15 sunlit fields, well-kept fences, and a bend of the Connecticut River. One of Earl's paintings is something of an anomaly. *Reclining Hunter*, which for many years was attributed to Thomas Gainsborough, shows a well-dressed gentleman resting beneath a tree. In the foreground, he displays a pile of
birds, the result of a day's hunt. The viewer can also see a farmer's donkey lying in the background,
another of the hunter's victims. This outrageously funny portrait couldn't have been commis-
20 sioned—no one would have wanted to be portrayed in such an absurd way. However, this painting
uncharacteristically shows Earl's wit as well as his uncommon technical skills.

13. What is the author's main purpose?

   (A) To discuss the life and work of an
American painter

   (B) To compare the art of Ralph Earl and
Thomas Gainsborough

   (C) To trace Ralph Earl's artistic influences

   (D) To describe the art scene in New
York in the late eighteenth century

14. Which of the following is NOT given in the
passage as a subject of one of Earl's
paintings?

   (A) People

   (B) Landscapes

   (C) Battle scenes

   (D) Fruit and flowers

15. According to the passage, Benjamin West
was Ralph Earl's

   (A) subject.

   (B) teacher.

   (C) student.

   (D) rival.

16. Which of the following could be substituted
for *outstanding* (line 6) without changing
the meaning of the sentence?

   (A) Excellent

   (B) Shocking

   (C) Unpaid

   (D) Illegal

17. The word *itinerant* in line 8 is closest in
meaning to which of the following?

   (A) Traveling

   (B) Successful

   (C) Talented

   (D) Innovative

18. The author uses the phrase *sprung from
the same roots* (lines 10–11) to indicate
that Ralph Earl and his subjects

   (A) lived in the same town.

   (B) were about the same age.

   (C) were equally successful.

   (D) had the same background.

19. According to the passage, one of the
distinguishing features of the portrait of
Oliver and Abigail Ellsworth is the contrast
between the

   (A) plainness of the figures and the luxury
of the furnishings.

   (B) two styles used to paint the two
figures.

   (C) sunlit fields and the dark interior.

   (D) straight fences and the curving
Connecticut River.

20. Why does the author refer to *Reclining Hunter* as "something of an anomaly" in line 16?

    (A) It is so severe.

    (B) It is quite humorous.

    (C) It shows Earl's talent.

    (D) It was commissioned.

21. The word *he* in line 17 refers to

    (A) Ralph Earl.

    (B) the farmer.

    (C) the hunter.

    (D) Thomas Gainsborough.

22. The author's attitude toward Ralph Earl is

    (A) admiring.

    (B) antagonistic.

    (C) neutral.

    (D) unflattering.

Questions 23–30

Line For centuries, sky watchers have reported seeing mysterious flashes of light on the surface of the moon. Modern astronomers have observed the same phenomenon, but no one has been able to satisfactorily explain how or why the moon sporadically sparks. However, researchers now believe they have found the cause.

5   Researchers have examined the chemical content of Moon rocks retrieved by astronauts during the Apollo missions and have found that they contain volatile gases such as helium, hydrogen, and argon. The researchers suggest that stray electrons, freed when the rock cracks, may ignite these gases. Indeed, lunar rock samples, when fractured in the lab, throw off sparks.

     What causes these rocks to crack on the lunar surface? The flashes are most often seen at the
10   borders between sunlight and shade on the moon, where the surface is being either intensely heated or cooled. A sudden change in temperature may cause thermal cracking. Another possibility is that meteors may strike the rocks and cause them to crack. Finally, lunar rocks may be fractured by seismic events—in other words, by tiny moonquakes.

23. Which of the following statements describes the organization of the passage?

(A) A popular notion is refuted.
(B) A generalization is made, and examples of it are given.
(C) The significance of an experiment is explained.
(D) A phenomenon is described, and a possible explanation is proposed.

24. According to the passage, how long have people been aware of the mysterious lights on the moon?

(A) For the last ten years
(B) Since the Apollo moon missions
(C) For hundreds of years
(D) For thousands of years

25. The word *sporadically* (line 3) is closest in meaning to which of the following?

(A) Reputedly
(B) Occasionally
(C) Mysteriously
(D) Constantly

26. According to the passage, the theory that Moon rocks give off sparks when they crack is supported by

(A) a telescopic study of the moon.
(B) experiments conducted by astronauts.
(C) observations made centuries ago.
(D) an analysis of rocks from the moon.

27. In line 6, the word *they* refers to

(A) helium, hydrogen, and argon.
(B) researchers.
(C) Apollo spacecraft.
(D) lunar rocks.

28. The word *stray* in line 7 is closest in meaning to which of the following?

(A) Loose
(B) Speeding
(C) Fiery
(D) Spinning

29. Which of the following situations is an example of "thermal cracking" as described in the passage?

(A) A dam breaks when water rises behind it.
(B) A stone cracks open because of the pressure of tree roots.
(C) A cool glass breaks when it is filled with boiling water.
(D) An ice cube melts in the heat of the sun.

30. All of the following are given as reasons for Moon rocks cracking EXCEPT

(A) seismic actions.
(B) sudden temperature changes.
(C) the action of meteors.
(D) the pressure of gases.

QUESTIONS 31–41

Line In addition to the great ridges and volcanic chains, the oceans conceal another form of undersea mountains: the strange guyot, or flat-topped seamount. No marine geologist even suspected the existence of these isolated mountains until they were discovered by geologist Harry H. Hess in 1946. He was serving at the time as a naval officer on a ship equipped with a fathometer. Hess named
5   these truncated peaks for the nineteenth-century Swiss-born geologist Arnold Guyot, who had served on the faculty of Princeton University for thirty years. Since then, hundreds of guyots have been discovered in every ocean but the Arctic. Like offshore canyons, guyots present a challenge to oceanographic theory. They are believed to be extinct volcanoes. Their flat tops indicate that they once stood above or just below the surface, where the action of waves leveled off their peaks. Yet
10   today, by definition, their summits are at least 600 feet below the surface, and some are as deep as 8,200 feet. Most lie between 3,200 feet and 6,500 feet. Their tops are not really flat but slope upward to a low pinnacle at the center. Dredging from the tops of guyots has recovered basalt and coral rubble, and that would be expected from the eroded tops of what were once islands. Some of this material is over 80 million years old. Geologists think the drowning of the guyots involved two
15   processes: The great weight of the volcanic mountains depressed the sea floor beneath them, and the level of the sea rose a number of times, especially when the last Ice Age ended, some 8,000 to 11,000 years ago.

31. What is the author's main purpose in writing this passage?

    (A) To trace the career of Arnold Guyot
    (B) To describe one feature of the undersea world
    (C) To present the results of recent geologic research
    (D) To discuss underwater ridges and volcano chains

32. The word *conceal* in line 1 is closest in meaning to which of the following?

    (A) Contain
    (B) Erode
    (C) Hide
    (D) Create

33. The passage implies that guyots were first detected by means of

    (A) a fathometer.
    (B) computer analysis.
    (C) a deep-sea diving expedition.
    (D) research submarines.

34. The author indicates that Arnold Guyot

    (A) was Harry Hess's instructor.
    (B) invented the fathometer.
    (C) named the guyot after himself.
    (D) taught at Princeton University.

35. What does the passage say about the Arctic Ocean?

    (A) The first guyot was discovered there.
    (B) No guyots have ever been found there.
    (C) There are more guyots there than in any other ocean.
    (D) It is impossible that guyots were ever formed there.

36. The author states that offshore canyons and guyots have which of the following characteristics in common?

    (A) Both are found on the ocean floor near continental shelves.
    (B) Both present oceanographers with a mystery.
    (C) Both were formed by volcanic activity.
    (D) Both were, at one time, above the surface of the sea.

37. According to the passage, most guyots are found at a depth of

    (A) less than 600 feet.
    (B) between 600 and 3,200 feet.
    (C) between 3,200 and 6,500 feet.
    (D) more than 8,200 feet.

38. Which of the following is closest in meaning to the word *rubble* in line 13?

    (A) Fragments
    (B) Mixture
    (C) Columns
    (D) Core

39. Which of the following is the best depiction of the top of a guyot?

(A)

(B)

(C)

(D)

40. According to the passage, which of the following two processes were involved in the submersion of guyots?

(A) Erosion and volcanic activity
(B) The sinking of the sea floor and the rising of sea level
(C) Mountain building and the action of ocean currents
(D) High tides and earthquakes

41. According to the passage, when did sea level significantly rise?

(A) In 1946
(B) In the nineteenth century
(C) From 8,000 to 11,000 years ago
(D) 80 million years ago

QUESTIONS 42–50

Line The demand for the vote by American women was first formulated in earnest at the Seneca Falls
      Convention in upstate New York in 1848. After the Civil War, agitation for women's suffrage in-
      creased. Suffragists Susan B. Anthony and Julia Ward Harris founded the National Women's Suffrage
      Association to work on the federal level. Lucy Stone created the American Women's Suffrage Associa-
5   tion, which worked to secure the ballot through state legislation. In 1890, the two groups united to
      form the National American Women's Suffrage Association (NAWSA). While still a territory, Wyoming
      enfranchised women in 1869. The first state to enfranchise women was Utah in 1870; the second
      was Colorado in 1893. By 1920, women were voting in all the Western states except New Mexico.
         As the pioneer suffragists withdrew from the movement, younger women assumed leadership.
10   One of the most astute was Carrie Chapmann Catt, who was named president of NAWSA in 1915.
      Another prominent suffragist was Alice Paul. Forced to resign from NAWSA because of her insistence
      on direct-action techniques, she organized the National Women's Party, which used such tactics as
      mass marches and hunger strikes.
         Economics and the role played by women in World War I also contributed to the success of the
15   drive. Women were surging into the workforce. In 1900, there were 3 million working women. By
      1915, there were 8 million. During the war, women moved into jobs that had once been the
      province of men.
         In 1918, the House of Representatives passed the Nineteenth Amendment, which removed
      voting discrimination on the basis of gender. The Senate voted for it the following year. In August
20   1920, the amendment became law. The 1920 presidential election was thus the first in which women
      voted. Like men, they voted overwhelmingly for Warren G. Harding.

42. What is the main topic of the passage?

   (A) The importance of the Seneca Falls Convention

   (B) The role of women in World War I

   (C) The effects of the Nineteenth Amendment

   (D) The campaign by American women to secure the vote

43. The phrase *in earnest* in line 1 is closest in meaning to

   (A) seriously.

   (B) originally.

   (C) theoretically.

   (D) primarily.

44. According to the passage, how did the National Women's Suffrage Association differ from the American Women's Suffrage Association?

   (A) It advocated direct-action techniques rather than indirect tactics.

   (B) It tried to achieve change at the national level rather than at the state level.

   (C) It had more members and more power.

   (D) Its members were generally older women rather than younger women.

45. Women first won the right to vote in

   (A) Utah.

   (B) Colorado.

   (C) the Wyoming territory.

   (D) New Mexico.

46. Which of the following is closest in meaning to the phrase *most astute* in line 10?

   (A) Most independent

   (B) Youngest

   (C) Cleverest

   (D) Most experienced

47. According to the passage, which of the following women formed the National Women's Party?

   (A) Susan B. Anthony and Julia Ward Harris

   (B) Lucy Stone

   (C) Carrie Chapmann Catt

   (D) Alice Paul

48. The author uses the word *province* (line 17) to refer to a

   (A) region of the country.

   (B) group of people with similar backgrounds.

   (C) sphere of activity reserved for a certain group.

   (D) specific era of history.

49. What does the passage imply about Warren G. Harding?

    (A) He was elected president in 1920.
    (B) He first entered politics in the 1920 election.
    (C) He strongly supported women's voting rights.
    (D) He was favored by women voters but not by men.

50. Where in the passage does the author specifically mention the growth of women in the work force?

    (A) Lines 3–4
    (B) Line 9
    (C) Line 15
    (D) Lines 18–19

THIS IS THE END OF SECTION 3.

IF YOU FINISH BEFORE THE TIME LIMIT, CHECK YOUR WORK ON SECTION 3 ONLY.

DO NOT READ OR WORK ON ANY OTHER SECTION OF THE TEST.

Practice Test 3
(Long Form)

Section 1

LISTENING

This section tests your ability to comprehend spoken English. It is divided into three parts, each with its own directions. During actual exams, you are *not* permitted to turn the page during the reading of the directions or to take notes at any time.

PART A

Directions: Each item in this part consists of a brief conversation involving two speakers. Following each conversation, a third voice will ask a question. You will hear the conversations and questions only once, and they will *not* be written out.

When you have heard each conversation and question, read the four answer choices and select the one—(A), (B), (C), or (D)—that best answers the question based on what is directly stated or on what can be inferred. Then fill in the space on your answer sheet that matches the letter of the answer that you have selected.

Here is an example.

You will hear:

M1: Do you think I should lean this chair against the wall or put it somewhere else?

 F1: Over by the window, I'd say.

M2: What does the man think the man should do?

You will read:

 (A) Open the window.
 (B) Move the chair.
 (C) Leave the room.
 (D) Take a seat.

From the conversation you find out that the woman thinks the man should put the chair over by the window. The best answer to the question "What does the woman think the man should do?" is (B), "Move the chair." You should fill in (B) on your answer sheet.

Sample Answer

 Ⓐ ● Ⓒ Ⓓ

1. (A) They had to move her truck.
   (B) There was only one thing wrong with her truck.
   (C) The engine had to be taken out of her truck.
   (D) She had to hire an engineer.

2. (A) He intends to relax for a few weeks.
   (B) The final exams he took were easy.
   (C) It's too early for him to make plans.
   (D) He still has a couple of tests to take.

3. (A) He can teach her that program too.
   (B) He owns several computers himself.
   (C) He's busier than Greg right now.
   (D) He taught himself that program.

4. (A) Every two days, a bus goes there.
   (B) It's faster to take the bus than to run there.
   (C) Two times a day, a bus goes to Springsdale.
   (D) There's no longer bus service to Springsdale.

5. (A) This is the first paper the professor has assigned.
   (B) The man doesn't like the choice of topics.
   (C) The professor will assign the class specific topics.
   (D) The students must have the topic of their papers approved.

6. (A) The man has many photos of the old dormitory.
   (B) The appearance of the dormitory has changed over the years.
   (C) In the photograph, the dormitory looks quite old.
   (D) These are photographs of many different dormitories.

7. (A) How he got to class.
   (B) What he set up.
   (C) Why he looked angry.
   (D) Where he went.

8. (A) She won't be allowed to attend the party.
   (B) She thinks it will be a noisy party.
   (C) She would hate to miss this party.
   (D) She always has the best parties.

9. (A) New York.
   (B) Denver.
   (C) Phoenix.
   (D) Chicago.

10. (A) She'd watched the movie a long time ago.
    (B) She left before the movie was half over.
    (C) She saw only half the movie before.
    (D) She realized the film was 4 years old.

11. (A) He stopped Professor Beasley to ask him a question.
    (B) He doesn't ask Professor Beasley questions anymore.
    (C) He's finally gotten used to Professor Beasley's questions.
    (D) He no longer attends Professor Beasley's class.

12. (A) He's been looking everywhere for the puzzle.
    (B) He hardly looked at the puzzle.
    (C) His comment puzzled the woman.
    (D) He thought the puzzle would be easier to solve.

13. (A) She fell ill on her trip.
    (B) She won't travel until the fall.
    (C) She had to cancel her trip.
    (D) She has just returned from her trip.

14. (A) He's gone to bed.
    (B) He's not cold anymore.
    (C) He's frightened.
    (D) He isn't feeling better.

15. (A) She just got a job at a florist's shop.
    (B) She needs to go shopping before dinner.
    (C) She has to clean up the dining room.
    (D) She got a lot of flowers for the party.

16. (A) Professor Mitchie gave him the schedule by mistake.
    (B) The schedule contains several errors.
    (C) Professor Mitchie has a very busy schedule.
    (D) The woman's mistakes were pointed out by Professor Mitchie.

17. (A) Making hotel reservations.
    (B) Writing postcards.
    (C) Washing the windows.
    (D) Looking at photographs.

18. (A) Steve's directions are not clear.
    (B) It will be impossible for them to go camping.
    (C) She's been to the campground many times.
    (D) Steve has no idea how to get to the campground.

19. (A) He's going to wear the blue jacket tonight.
    (B) He doesn't know what they are going to do.
    (C) He doesn't know which jacket he will wear.
    (D) He's going to go somewhere else tonight.

20. (A) She enjoyed hearing Walter's story.
    (B) She doesn't believe Walter had a flat tire.
    (C) Walter's story was a lot like hers.
    (D) She thinks Walter should fix his flat tire right away.

21. (A) They should go to the coffee shop now.
    (B) They need to change the time of their meeting.
    (C) She wants to buy some more coffee.
    (D) They'll have to change the location of their meeting.

22. (A) The damage done to the woman's car.
    (B) The purchases that the woman made yesterday.
    (C) The repairs that the woman did at home.
    (D) The parking problem at the shopping mall.

23. (A) He likes it the best of all his classes.
    (B) He wasn't able to sign up for it.
    (C) He thinks it may be too difficult for him.
    (D) He's worried that it will be canceled.

24. (A) That the woman had caught the fish herself.
    (B) That he wouldn't be invited to dinner.
    (C) That the woman would not serve fish.
    (D) That the woman did not have her own garden.

25. (A) He needs to find a new job.
    (B) He can't get to his keys.
    (C) His car needs to be repaired.
    (D) He doesn't know where his keys are.

26. (A) Try it on.
    (B) Paint a picture of it.
    (C) Throw it away.
    (D) Hammer a nail with it.

27. (A) Both articles are equally useful.
    (B) She's not familiar with the articles.
    (C) These are the wrong articles.
    (D) He should read the longer article.

28. (A) The woman would enjoy the mountain scenery.
    (B) The weather has been hot this month.
    (C) The weather in the mountains is unusual.
    (D) The woman probably doesn't like cool weather.

29. (A) The change machine was still out of order.
    (B) Change would not be required.
    (C) The change machine had already been repaired.
    (D) Someone had replaced the change machine.

30. (A) It has exceptionally good service.
    (B) It has excellent food.
    (C) The service there is disappointing.
    (D) Everything there is wonderful.

31. (A) As funny.
    (B) As dishonest.
    (C) As foolish.
    (D) As polite.

32. (A) Jump off the diving board.
    (B) Give up on the project.
    (C) Add some illustrations.
    (D) Plan the paper over again.

33. (A) If she'd helped make it.
    (B) If she wants more.
    (C) If she likes it.
    (D) If she wants something else.

34. (A) He thought other science courses would be harder.
    (B) It's a required class for all students.
    (C) He's studied geology before.
    (D) It was the only science course open to him.

35. (A) He's never played professional basketball.
(B) He seldom watches television.
(C) He's never seen a professional basketball game in person.
(D) He plans to attend a professional basketball game soon.

36. (A) When she will answer the questions.
(B) Where she drove.
(C) What kind of car she has.
(D) Why she asked so many questions.

37. (A) Shopping for gifts.
(B) Buying a target for Jennifer.
(C) Practicing archery.
(D) Trying to find Allen.

38. (A) He thinks it will be better than the old one.
(B) He's anxious for it to be completed.
(C) He's worried that it's not long enough.
(D) He feels that it shouldn't have been built.

39. (A) He should have left after 2 hours.
(B) His roommate should have seen the doctor too.
(C) He's exaggerating the length of the wait.
(D) His roommate can't always be believed.

40. (A) He's studying to be a pilot.
(B) He broke the handle.
(C) He's running a high fever.
(D) He gets angry easily.

41. (A) She gave it two weeks ago.
(B) She is going to give it right now.
(C) She plans to give it next week.
(D) She will give it in two weeks.

42. (A) Lend him some money.
(B) Pick up some laundry for him.
(C) Bring back some detergent.
(D) Deposit some money for him.

43. (A) He wore a tie when he met her.
(B) He had trouble talking to her.
(C) He couldn't understand a word she said.
(D) He told her the truth.

44. (A) Its size.
(B) Its low mileage.
(C) Its color.
(D) Its appearance.

45. (A) He should try another type of film.
(B) He needs to learn how to take pictures.
(C) She thinks he should buy a better camera.
(D) She wants him to teach her about photography.

46. (A) He seldom has trouble with translations.
(B) He worked on a simpler passage.
(C) Even he was late for the train this time.
(D) He was the only person to have a problem.

47. (A) He doesn't enjoy jazz very much.
(B) He hasn't heard any music for a long time.
(C) He'd prefer silence for a while.
(D) He'd like to hear some jazz.

48. (A) From the party.
(B) Through her best friend.
(C) From high school.
(D) Through her roommate.

49. (A) It surprised her.
(B) She hasn't seen it.
(C) It has been misplaced.
(D) She found it believable.

50. (A) There are already enough members of the group.
(B) She forgot to remind the man of the last group meeting.
(C) She doesn't care if a few others join their group.
(D) The man should have spoken to her before he asked anyone to join.

PART B

Directions: This part of the test consists of extended conversations between two speakers. After each of these conversations there are a number of questions. You will hear each conversation and question only once, and the questions are *not* written out.

When you have heard the questions, read the four answer choices and select the *one*—(A), (B), (C), or (D)—that best answers the question based on what is directly stated or on what can be inferred. Then fill in the space on your answer sheet that matches the letter of the answer that you have selected.

Don't forget: During actual exams, taking notes or writing in your test book is *not* permitted.

51. (A) A letter that she received.
(B) A performance that she attended.
(C) A conversation with a friend.
(D) A poster that she saw.

52. (A) He was fired by the bandleader.
(B) He didn't have enough time.
(C) He had an offer to join a better band.
(D) He felt he wasn't talented enough.

53. (A) He played the trumpet.
(B) He led the band.
(C) He was the drummer.
(D) He played the saxophone.

54. (A) Visit him at home.
(B) Telephone him.
(C) See him perform.
(D) Wait for a call from him.

55. (A) At a newspaper.
(B) At an advertising agency.
(C) At a furniture store.
(D) At a real estate office.

56. (A) A two-bedroom apartment.
(B) A sofa.
(C) A chair.
(D) A roommate.

57. (A) Her phone number.
(B) The location of the apartment.
(C) The best time to call her.
(D) Her first name.

58. (A) $5.
(B) $15.
(C) $30.
(D) $250.

59. (A) A vacation the woman took.
(B) French influence in New Orleans.
(C) New Orleans's Mardi Gras festival.
(D) A business trip.

60. (A) By bus.
(B) By car.
(C) By plane.
(D) By train.

61. (A) The weather.
(B) The food.
(C) The architecture.
(D) The music.

62. (A) The Spanish.
(B) The French.
(C) The British.
(D) The Americans.

63. (A) He was president when the city was purchased.
(B) He led the American forces in a nearby battle.
(C) He designed Jackson Square in the French Quarter.
(D) He helped found New Orleans.

PART C

Directions: This part of the test consists of several talks, each given by a single speaker. After each of these talks there are a number of questions. You will hear each talk and question only once, and the questions are *not* written out.

When you have heard the question, read the four answer choices and select the *one*—(A), (B), (C), or (D)—that best answers the question based on what is directly stated or on what can be inferred. Then fill in the space on your answer sheet that matches the letter of the answer that you have selected.

Here is an example.

You will hear:

M1: Students, this evening we'll have a chance to observe a phenomenon that we've discussed several times in class. Tonight, there will be a lunar eclipse. As we've said, when an eclipse of the moon occurs, the earth passes between the sun and the moon. Therefore, the shadow of the earth moves across the surface of the moon and obscures it. Because you won't be looking at the sun, it is not necessary to use the special lenses and filters that you need when observing a solar eclipse. You can observe a lunar eclipse with your unaided eye or with a telescope and photograph it with an ordinary camera. So if the weather's not cloudy tonight, go out and take a look at this eclipse of the moon. I'm sure you'll find it interesting.

Now here is a sample question.

You will hear:

M2: In what course is this lecture probably being given?

You will read:

  (A) Philosophy.
  (B) Meteorology.
  (C) Astronomy.
  (D) Photography.

The lecture concerns a lunar eclipse, a topic that would typically be discussed in an astronomy class. The choice that best answers the question "In what course is this lecture probably being given?" is (C), "Astronomy." You should fill in (C) on your answer sheet.

Sample Answer

Here is another sample question.

You will hear:

M2: According to the speaker, which of the following occurs during a lunar eclipse?

You will read:

  (A) The earth's shadow moves across the moon.
  (B) Clouds block the view of the moon.
  (C) The moon moves between the earth and the sun.
  (D) The sun can be observed without special equipment.

From the lecture, you learn that a lunar eclipse occurs when the earth moves between the sun and the moon and the shadow of the earth passes across the moon. The choice that best answers the question "According to the speaker, which of the following occurs during a lunar eclipse?" is (A), "The earth's shadow moves across the moon." Don't forget: During actual exams, taking notes or writing in your test book is *not* permitted.

Sample Answer

64. (A) Books about science.
    (B) Western movies.
    (C) The stories of H. G. Wells.
    (D) Science fiction films.

65. (A) *Things to Come.*
    (B) *The Day the Earth Stood Still.*
    (C) *Duel in the Sun.*
    (D) *Star Wars.*

66. (A) They are all unintentionally funny.
    (B) They are all unforgettable classics.
    (C) They were all made during the 1950s.
    (D) They all involve spectacular special effects.

67. (A) Write a paper.
    (B) Discuss their reactions.
    (C) Take a test.
    (D) Watch several films.

68. (A) Discouraged.
    (B) Critical.
    (C) Alarmed.
    (D) Optimistic.

69. (A) Rotary engines.
    (B) Piston-driven engines.
    (C) Electric engines.
    (D) Hydrogen-powered engines.

70. (A) Oxygen.
    (B) Toxic gases.
    (C) Water vapor.
    (D) Carbon dioxide.

71. (A) The time required to recharge engines with hydrogen.
    (B) The danger of explosions.
    (C) Engine backfiring.
    (D) The lack of large hydrogen-producing facilities.

72. (A) To explain why parrots are such popular pets.
    (B) To clear up some incorrect ideas the audience may have about parrots.
    (C) To show the audience how to teach parrots to talk.
    (D) To describe the colorful plumage of parrots.

73. (A) High mountains.
    (B) Warm, humid forests.
    (C) Dry deserts.
    (D) Areas near glaciers.

74. (A) It has the best singing voice.
    (B) It has the brightest plumage.
    (C) It has the largest vocabulary.
    (D) It has the best sense of rhythm.

75. (A) They can sing exactly on key.
    (B) They can make up songs of their own.
    (C) They can remember several hundred words.
    (D) They understand the meaning of songs.

76. (A) Stone.
    (B) Skins.
    (C) Wood.
    (D) Snow.

77. (A) In Labrador.
    (B) In northern Alaska.
    (C) In Greenland.
    (D) In north-central Canada.

78. (A) Only a house made of snow.
    (B) Any summer house.
    (C) Only an all-season house.
    (D) Any type of house.

79. (A) They were made in the shape of a dome.
    (B) Their entrance tunnels were lower than their floors.
    (C) They had an unsupported dome.
    (D) They could be built in a short time.

80. (A) To cover the hole in the top.
    (B) To line the inside of the house.
    (C) To serve as a bed.
    (D) To cover the entrance tunnel.

THIS IS THE END OF SECTION 1, LISTENING.

STOP WORK ON SECTION 1.

Section 2

This section tests your ability to recognize grammar and usage suitable for standard written English. It is divided into two parts, each with its own directions.

SENTENCE COMPLETION

Directions: Items in this part are incomplete sentences. Following each of these sentences, there are four words or phrases. You should select the *one* word or phrase—(A), (B), (C), or (D)—that best completes the sentence. Then fill in the space on your answer sheet that matches the letter of the answer that you have selected.

Example I

Pepsin _____ an enzyme used in digestion.

(A) that
(B) is
(C) of
(D) being

This sentence should properly read "Pepsin is an enzyme used in digestion." You should fill in choice (B) on your answer sheet.

Sample Answer

Ⓐ ● Ⓒ Ⓓ

Example II

_____ large natural lakes are found in the state of South Carolina.

(A) There are no
(B) Not the
(C) It is not
(D) No

This sentence should properly read "No large natural lakes are found in the state of South Carolina." You should fill in choice (D) on your answer sheet. As soon as you understand the directions, begin work on this part.

Sample Answer

Ⓐ Ⓑ Ⓒ ●

1. Extensive forests, _____, abundant wildlife, and beautiful waterfalls are among the attractions of Glacier National Park.

   (A) it has spectacular mountain scenery
   (B) the mountain scenery is spectacular
   (C) spectacular mountain scenery
   (D) and the spectacular scenery of the mountains

2. A network of railroads to unite the continent and encourage Western settlement _____ before the Civil War by Asa Whitney.

   (A) when proposed
   (B) a proposal
   (C) was proposed
   (D) to propose

3. The chief advantage of using satellites to predict weather _____ can survey vast regions of the earth at one time.

   (A) they
   (B) is that they
   (C) is that
   (D) that they

4. The small, _____ farms of New England were not appropriate for the Midwest.

   (A) self-support
   (B) they supported themselves
   (C) self-supporting
   (D) supporting themselves

5. _____ art appreciation is an individual matter, no work of art is ever perceived by two people in exactly the same way.

   (A) Since
   (B) According to
   (C) Because of
   (D) Perhaps

6. _____ a black singer and actor, first came to the public's attention for his role in Eugene O'Neill's play *The Emperor Jones*.

   (A) Paul Robeson was
   (B) Because Paul Robeson
   (C) It was Paul Robeson, as
   (D) Paul Robeson,

7. Dragonflies remain stationary in the air while _____ their prey to come near.

   (A) waited for
   (B) they wait
   (C) waiting for
   (D) to wait

8. Fiction writer Zona Gale wrote about the small Wisconsin town _____ she grew up, showing both its positive and negative qualities.

   (A) in which
   (B) which in
   (C) which
   (D) in where

9. A collectible coin _____ in mint condition when it looks as it did when it was made.

   (A) to be is said
   (B) said is to be
   (C) is to be said
   (D) is said to be

10. Dust storms most often occur in areas where the ground has little vegetation to protect _____ of the wind.

    (A) from the effects
    (B) it the effects
    (C) it from the effects
    (D) the effects from it

11. _____ of their size and weight, grizzly bears are remarkably nimble animals.

    (A) Animals
    (B) For animals
    (C) As animals
    (D) To be animals

12. _____ most fruits, cherries must ripen on the vine.

    (A) Unlikely
    (B) Different
    (C) Dislike
    (D) Unlike

13. _____ who made Thanksgiving an official holiday in the United States.

    (A) Abraham Lincoln
    (B) He was Abraham Lincoln
    (C) Abraham Lincoln was
    (D) It was Abraham Lincoln

14. The higher _____ octane number of gasoline, the less knocking occurs in the engine as the fuel is burned.

    (A) some
    (B) the
    (C) is
    (D) than

15. Historian Barbara Tuchman was the first woman _____ president of the Academy of Arts and Sciences.

    (A) whose election as
    (B) to elect
    (C) was elected
    (D) to be elected

16. Although drama is a form of literature, _____ from the other types in the way it is presented.

    (A) it differs
    (B) is different
    (C) despite the difference
    (D) but it is different

17. Not only _____ the most populous city in the United States in 1890, but it also had become the most congested.

    (A) was New York City
    (B) that New York City was
    (C) New York City was
    (D) has New York City

18. In 1989, President George Bush appointed Carla A. Hills _____ a special trade representative.

    (A) to
    (B) as
    (C) like
    (D) be

19. Iguanas are different from most other lizards _____ they are not carnivores.

    (A) in spite of
    (B) even
    (C) so that
    (D) in that

20. _____ are considered humorous is mainly due to his characters' use of slang.

    (A) Damon Runyan's stories
    (B) Damon Runyan's stories, which
    (C) That Damon Runyan's stories
    (D) Because Damon Runyan's stories

21. The spores of ferns are almost microscopic and are far simpler than _____ in structure.

    (A) that of seeds
    (B) so are seeds
    (C) seeds do
    (D) seeds

22. Good pencil erasers are soft enough not _____ paper but hard enough so that they crumble gradually when used.

    (A) by damaging
    (B) so that they damage
    (C) to damage
    (D) damaging

23. _____ the outer rings of a gyroscope are turned or twisted, the gyroscope itself continues to spin in exactly the same position.

    (A) However
    (B) Somehow
    (C) Otherwise
    (D) No matter

ERROR IDENTIFICATION

Directions: The items in this part have four underlined words or phrases. You must identify the *one* underlined expression—(A), (B), (C), or (D)—that must be changed for the sentence to be correct. Then fill in the space on your answer sheet that matches the letter of the answer that you have selected.

Example I

Lenses may to have either concave or convex shapes.
　　　　　　A　　　　　**B**　**C**　　　　**D**

This sentence should read "Lenses may have either concave or convex shapes." You should therefore select choice (A).

Sample Answer

● Ⓑ Ⓒ Ⓓ

Example II

When painting a fresco, an artist is applied paint directly to the damp plaster of a wall.
　A　　　　　　　　　　　**B**　　　　　**C**　　　　　　　　　**D**

This sentence should read "When painting a fresco, an artist applies paint directly to the wet plaster of a wall." You should therefore select choice (B). As soon as you understand the directions, begin work on this part.

Sample Answer

Ⓐ ● Ⓒ Ⓓ

24. Alike the United States, Canada conducts a
     A   B
complete census of its population every ten
    C   D
years.

25. Natural resources provide the raw material
    A
are needed to produce finished goods.
  B   C   D

26. Because they are so secretive, blind snakes
      A
are seldom seen, and its habits are not
    B   C
well known.
    D

27. The main rotor and tail rotor of a helicopter
                             A
make the same job as the wings, propellers,
 B   C   D
and rudder of an airplane.

28. X rays are too powerful that they can
        A
penetrate most solids as easily as light
      B   C
passes through glass.
    D

29. Machines that use hydraulic pressure
        A
including elevators, dentist chairs, and
    B   C
automobile brakes.
    D

30. The Franklin stove, which became common
            A   B
in the 1780s, burned wood more efficiency
                      C
than an open fireplace.
   D

31. The coastline of Maine is marked by
       A   B
thousand of islands and inlets.
  C   D

32. Metals can be beaten into thin sheets,
         A   B
melted and poured into molds, or drawing
           C   D
into fine wire.

33. Stone Mountain, a huge dome of granite
               A
near the city of Atlanta, is 1,686 feet height
 B   C
and measures 7 miles around at its base.
                  D

34. Since ancient times, some people wore
          A   B
amulets, objects that are supposed to give
                 C
the wearer magical powers.
       D

35. Dance notation is a means of recording the
            A   B
movements of dances by using of special
       C   D
symbols.

36. Approximately the third of Alaska's
            A
land area lies north of the Arctic Circle.
  B   C   D

37. No cactus has flowers most beautiful or
 A   B
fragrant than those of the night-blooming
       C   D
cereus.

38. The poet Amy Lowell sometimes wrote
    A   B
literary criticism and biographical.
  C   D

39. Each of the chemical elements have its own
     A   B   C
D standard symbol.

40. A balloon rises because of the hot air or gas
              A   B
inside the balloon is lighter than the air
                 C
outside.
  D

41. Just three years afterwards Martha Graham's
                      A
first dance lesson, she starred in the ballet
     B   C   D
Xochitl.

42. The delicate color of rose quartz is due the
                 A   B
presence of manganese in the mineral.
   C   D

43. Most large corporations have personnel
        A
departments responsible to hiring and firing
                         B   C
workers and for keeping employee records.
                              D

44. Costume jewelry is made of plastic, wood,
                          A
or inexpensive metal, and they may
     B   C
be set with semiprecious or imitation
   D
stones.

45. The medicine of prehistoric people
              A
probably consisted of a mixture of
              B
scientific practices, superstitions, and
              C
religious believes.
              D

46. The sculptors of Louise Nevelson typically
             A   B
consisted of complex arrangements of
                              C
large black wooden boxes.
              D

47. Engineering is a profession who puts
              A   B
scientific knowledge to practical use.
     C   D

48. Fire blight, a common disease of apples and
                    A   B
pear trees, can sometimes be controlled
                              C
with an antibiotic spray.
   D

49. Radio stations at which broadcast
                      A
only news first appeared in the 1970s.
     B   C   D

50. Newspaper editor James G. Bennett
                      A
believed that the journalist's task was

not merely to inform readers but to startle
     B   C
them as well as.
              D

51. In the tundra regions of North America,
        A
the change from summer to winter occurs
        B   C
very sudden.
     D

52. Natural bridges of stone are formed the
                           A   B
action of water or wind-driven sand.
                 C   D

53. In *Babbitt* and other novels, Sinclair Lewis
                 A
presented critical portraits of middle-class
              B
Americans who thought of them as model
                 C   D
citizens.

54. Quite logically, nearly all early roads
        A   B
followed course of river valleys.
        C   D

55. The plants of the desert are so

spaced widely because of a scarcity of
     A   B
water that there is little or no competition
                        C
for water among them.
              D

56. Drowsiness is one symptom of hypother-
                        A
mia, the extreme lost of body heat.
     B   C   D

57. A globe presents a picture of the earth with
            A   B
practically not distortions.
     C   D

58. It is about 125 years for the cedar tree to
$\overline{A}$ $\overline{B}$
reach its full height.
$\overline{C}$ $\overline{D}$

59. Compared to those of animals, the fossil
$\overline{A}$ $\overline{B}$
record for plants is quite sketchy.
$\overline{C}$ $\overline{D}$

60. Life that we know it is based on the
$\overline{A}$ $\overline{B}$ $\overline{C}$
element carbon.
$\overline{D}$

THIS IS THE END OF SECTION 2.

IF YOU FINISH BEFORE THE TIME LIMIT, CHECK YOUR WORK ON SECTION 2 ONLY.

DO NOT READ OR WORK ON ANY OTHER SECTION OF THE TEST.

Section 3

This section of the test measures your ability to comprehend written materials.

Directions: This section contains several passages, each followed by a number of questions. Read the passages and, for each question, choose the *one* best answer—(A), (B), (C), or (D)—based on what is stated in the passage or on what can be inferred from the passage. Then fill in the space on your answer sheet that matches the letter of the answer that you have selected.

Read the Following Passage

Line   Like mammals, birds claim their own territories. A bird's territory may be small or large. Some birds claim only their nest and the area right around it, while others claim far larger territories that include their feeding areas. Gulls, penguins, and other waterfowl nest in huge colonies, but even in the biggest colonies, each male and his mate have small territories of their own
5   immediately around their nests.
       Male birds defend their territory chiefly against other males of the same species. In some cases, a warning call or threatening pose may be all the defense needed, but in other cases, intruders may refuse to leave peacefully.

Example I

What is the main topic of this passage?

(A) Birds that live in colonies
(B) Birds' mating habits
(C) The behavior of birds
(D) Territoriality in birds

The passage mainly concerns the territories of birds. You should fill in choice (D) on your answer sheet.

Sample Answer

Example II

According to the passage, male birds defend their territory primarily against which of the following?

(A) Female birds
(B) Birds of other species
(C) Males of their own species
(D) Mammals

The passage states that "Male birds defend their territory chiefly against other males of the same species." You should fill in choice (C) on your answer sheet. As soon as you understand the directions, begin work on this section.

Sample Answer

QUESTIONS 1–11

Line Lighthouses are towers with strong lights that help mariners plot their position, inform them that
land is near, and warn them of dangerous rocks and reefs. They are placed at prominent points on
the coast and on islands, reefs, and sandbars.

  Every lighthouse has a distinctive pattern of light, known as its characteristic. There are five
5 basic characteristics: fixed, flashing, occulting, group flashing, and group occulting. A fixed signal is a
steady beam. A flashing signal has periods of darkness longer than periods of light, while an occulting
signal's periods of light are longer. A group-flashing light gives off two or more flashes at regular
intervals, and a group-occulting signal consists of a fixed light with two or more periods of darkness
at regular intervals. Some lighthouses use lights of different colors as well, and today, most light-
10 houses are also equipped with radio beacons. The three types of apparatus used to produce the
signals are the catoptric, in which metal is used to reflect the light; the dioptric, in which glass is
used; and the catadioptric, in which both glass and metal are used.

  In the daytime, lighthouses can usually be identified by their structure alone. The most typical
structure is a tower tapering at the top, but some, such as the Bastion Lighthouse on the Saint
15 Lawrence River, are shaped like pyramids, and others, such as the Race Rock Light, look like wooden
houses sitting on high platforms. Still others, such as the American Shoal Lighthouse off the Florida
Coast, are skeletal towers of steel. Where lighthouses might be confused in daylight, they can be
distinguished by day-marker patterns—designs of checks and stripes painted in vivid colors on
lighthouse walls.
20 In the past, the job of lighthouse keeper was lonely and difficult, if somewhat romantic.
Lighthouse keepers put in hours of tedious work maintaining the lights. Today, lighthouses are almost
entirely automated with humans supplying only occasional maintenance. Because of improvements in
navigational technology, the importance of lighthouses has diminished. There are only about 340
functioning lighthouses in existence in the United States today, compared to about 1,500 in 1900,
25 and there are only about 1,400 functioning lighthouses outside the United States. Some decommis-
sioned lighthouses have been preserved as historical monuments.

1. Which of the following is NOT mentioned in the passage as one of the functions of lighthouses?

 (A) To help sailors determine their location
 (B) To warn of danger from rocks and reefs
 (C) To notify sailors that bad weather is approaching
 (D) To indicate that land is near

2. The word *their* in line 1 refers to

 (A) mariners'.
 (B) lighthouses'.
 (C) dangers'.
 (D) lights'.

3. The word *prominent* in line 2 is closest in meaning to

 (A) dangerous.
 (B) conspicuous.
 (C) picturesque.
 (D) famous.

4. In the context of this passage, the author uses the term *characteristic* (line 4) to refer to a

 (A) period of darkness.
 (B) person who operates a lighthouse.
 (C) pattern painted on a lighthouse.
 (D) distinctive light signal.

5. According to the passage, what kind of signal has long periods of light that are regularly broken by two or more periods of darkness?

 (A) Group occulting
 (B) Flashing
 (C) Occulting
 (D) Group flashing

6. According to the passage, a catoptric apparatus is one that uses

 (A) lights of various colors.
 (B) metal.
 (C) glass.
 (D) a radio beacon.

7. For which of the following does the author NOT provide a specific example in the third paragraph?

    (A) A lighthouse shaped like a pyramid
    (B) A lighthouse made of steel
    (C) A lighthouse with day-marker patterns
    (D) A lighthouse that resembles a house on a platform

8. The word *tapering* in line 14 is closest in meaning to which of the following?

    (A) Narrowing
    (B) Soaring
    (C) Opening
    (D) Rotating

9. It can be concluded from the passage that lighthouses with day-marker patterns would most likely be found in areas where

    (A) the weather is frequently bad.
    (B) the structures themselves cannot be easily seen by passing mariners.
    (C) there are not many lighthouses.
    (D) there are a number of lighthouses with similar structures.

10. The author implies that, compared to those of the past, contemporary lighthouses

    (A) employ more powerful lights.
    (B) require less maintenance.
    (C) are more difficult to operate.
    (D) are more romantic.

11. There is information in the fourth paragraph to support which of these statements?

    (A) There are more lighthouses in the United States now than there were in 1900.
    (B) There are more lighthouses in the United States today than in any other single country.
    (C) There are more functioning lighthouses in the United States today than there are lighthouses preserved as historical monuments.
    (D) There were more lighthouses in the United States in 1900 than there are elsewhere in the world today.

QUESTIONS 12–23

Line   Although both Luther Burbank and George Washington Carver drastically changed American agriculture and were close friends besides, their methods of working could hardly have been more dissimi-
lar. Burbank's formal education ended with high school, but he was inspired by the works of Charles
Darwin. In 1872, on his farm near Lunenberg, Massachusetts, he produced his first "plant cre-
5   ation"—a superior potato developed from the Early Rose variety. It still bears his name. After moving
to Santa Rosa, California, in 1875, Burbank created a stream of creations, earning the nickname "the
plant wizard." He developed new varieties of fruits, vegetables, flowers, and other plants, many of
which are still economically important. He began his work some thirty years before the rediscovery
of Gregor Mendel's work on heredity, and while he did not participate in the developing science of
10   plant genetics, his work opened the country's eyes to the productive possibilities of plant breeding.
However, the value of his contributions was diminished by his methods. He relied on his keen
memory and powers of observation and kept records only for his own use. He thus thwarted
attempts by other scientists to study his achievements.

      Carver, on the other hand, was a careful researcher who took thorough notes. Born a slave, he
15   attended high school in Kansas, Simpson College in Iowa, and Iowa State College, which awarded
him a master's degree. When the eminent black educator Booker T. Washington offered him a
position at Tuskegee Institute in Alabama, he accepted. While Burbank concentrated on developing
new plants, Carver found new uses for existing ones. He produced hundreds of synthetic products
made from the soybean, the sweet potato, and especially the peanut, helping to free Southern
agriculture from the tyranny of cotton.

12. What is the author's main purpose in
writing the passage?

   (A) To compare the products created by
two agricultural scientists

   (B) To demonstrate how Carver and
Burbank influenced American agriculture

   (C) To contrast the careers and methods
of two scientists

   (D) To explain how Charles Darwin
inspired both Carver and Burbank

13. The word *drastically* in line 1 is closest in
meaning to

   (A) dramatically.

   (B) initially.

   (C) unintentionally.

   (D) potentially.

14. According to the passage, which of the
following best describes the relationship
between Burbank and Carver?

   (A) They were competitors.

   (B) Carver was one of Burbank's teachers.

   (C) Burbank invited Carver to work with
him.

   (D) They were personal friends.

15. It can be inferred that Burbank's first "plant
creation" is known as the

   (A) Early Rose potato.

   (B) Burbank potato.

   (C) Lunenberg potato.

   (D) Wizard potato.

16. The word *his* in line 10 refers to

   (A) George Washington Carver's.

   (B) Gregor Mendel's.

   (C) Luther Burbank's.

   (D) Charles Darwin's.

17. Which of the following is closest in
meaning to the word *thwarted* in line 12?

   (A) Restored

   (B) Predated

   (C) Nurtured

   (D) Defeated

18. The word *thorough* in line 14 is closest in
meaning to

   (A) complete.

   (B) general.

   (C) puzzling.

   (D) precise.

19. The author implies that a significant difference between the techniques of Burbank and those of Carver is that

    (A) while Carver kept careful research records, Burbank did not.
    (B) Carver popularized his achievements, but those of Burbank were relatively unknown.
    (C) unlike Burbank, Carver concentrated mainly on developing new varieties of plants.
    (D) Burbank bred both plants and animals, but Carver worked only with plants.

20. According to the passage, what school awarded Carver a master's degree?

    (A) Simpson College
    (B) Iowa State College
    (C) Tuskegee Institute
    (D) The University of Alabama

21. Carver developed new uses for all of the following crops EXCEPT

    (A) cotton.
    (B) soybeans.
    (C) peanuts.
    (D) sweet potatoes.

22. The word *tyranny* in line 20 is closest in meaning to

    (A) history.
    (B) dependence.
    (C) control.
    (D) unreliability.

23. At what point in the passage does the author focus on Burbank's weaknesses as a researcher?

    (A) Lines 3–4
    (B) Lines 5–7
    (C) Line 11
    (D) Lines 16–17

QUESTIONS 24–36

Line Visitors to Prince Edward Island, Canada, delight in the "unspoiled" scenery—the well-kept farms and peaceful hamlets of the island's central core and the rougher terrain of the east and west. In reality, the Island ecosystems are almost entirely artificial.

5   Islanders have been tampering with the natural environment since the eighteenth century and long ago broke down the Island's natural forest cover to exploit its timber and clear land for agriculture. By 1900, 80 percent of the forest had been cut down and much of what remained had been destroyed by disease. Since then, however, some farmland has been abandoned and has returned to forest through the invasion of opportunist species, notably spruce. Few examples of the original climax forest, which consisted mostly of broadleaved trees such as maple, birch, and oak, survive

10 today.

    Apart from a few stands of native forest, the only authentic habitats on Prince Edward Island are its sand dunes and salt marshes. The dunes are formed from sand washed ashore by waves and then dried and blown by the wind to the land beyond the beach. The sand is prevented from spreading farther by marram grass, a tall, long-rooted species that grows with the dunes and keeps them

15 remarkably stable. Marram grass acts as a windbreak and allows other plants such as beach pea and bayberry to take hold. On dunes where marram grass is broken down—for instance, where it is trampled—the dunes may spread inland and inundate agricultural lands or silt up fishing harbors. The white dunes of the north coast are the most impressive. There are also white dunes on the east and west coasts. Only in the south are there red dunes, created when the soft sandstone cliffs crumble

20 into the sea and subsequently wash ashore as red sand. The dunes were once used as cattle pasture but were abandoned as the early settlers moved inland.

    Salt marshes are the second remaining authentic habitat. These bogs are the result of the flooding of low coastal areas during unusually high tides. In the intervals between tides, a marsh area remains and plants take root, notably cord grass, the "marsh hay" used by the early settlers as winter

25 forage for their livestock. Like the dunes, though, the marshes were soon dismissed as wasteland and escaped development.

---

24. On what aspect of Prince Edward Island does the author focus?

  (A) Its tourist industry
  (B) Its beaches
  (C) Its natural habitats
  (D) Its agriculture

25. Why does the author use quotation marks around the word *unspoiled* in line 1?

  (A) He is quoting from another author.
  (B) The scenery is not as attractive as it once was.
  (C) The scenery looks unspoiled but is not.
  (D) He disagrees with the ideas in this paragraph.

26. The word *hamlets* in line 2 is closest in meaning to

  (A) villages.
  (B) forests.
  (C) rivers.
  (D) pastures.

27. The phrase *tampering with* in line 4 is closest in meaning to

  (A) preserving.
  (B) interfering with.
  (C) remembering.
  (D) dealing with.

28. What can be inferred about Prince Edward Island's forests?

  (A) Only a few small stands of trees still exist.
  (B) They are more extensive than they were in 1900.
  (C) They are virtually the same as they were in the eighteenth century.
  (D) About 80 percent of the island is covered by them.

29. Which of the following types of trees is most common in the forests of Prince Edward Island today?

  (A) Oak
  (B) Birch
  (C) Spruce
  (D) Maple

30. What does the author say about beach pea and bayberry?

(A) They have become commercially important plants.

(B) They grow on dunes after marram grass is established.

(C) They were once an important food crop for early settlers.

(D) They are spreading across the Island, destroying important crops.

31. According to the passage, what effect does the destruction of marram grass have?

(A) It permits the sand dunes to cover farmland.

(B) It creates better conditions for fishing.

(C) It allows seawater to flood agricultural land.

(D) It lets the sand wash into the sea.

32. The word *trampled* in line 17 is closest in meaning to

(A) ripped up.

(B) flooded.

(C) stepped on.

(D) burned.

33. Which of the following words in paragraph 4 is given as a synonym for the word *marshes* (line 22)?

(A) Tides

(B) Plants

(C) Bogs

(D) Settlers

34. According to the passage, in which part of Prince Edward Island are red sand dunes found?

(A) The north

(B) The east

(C) The south

(D) The west

35. What conclusion can be drawn from the passage about both the sand dunes and salt marshes of Prince Edward Island?

(A) They have never been used.

(B) They were once used but have long since been abandoned.

(C) They have been used continuously since the island was first settled.

(D) They were long unused but have recently been exploited.

36. In which of these paragraphs does the author discuss the destruction of an ecosystem?

(A) The first

(B) The second

(C) The third

(D) The fourth

QUESTIONS 37–44

Line   Lichens may grow on the bark of a tree in a steaming tropical rain forest, on the bricks of big-city
buildings, on rocks in hot springs, on wind-swept mountain tops, and in the driest desserts. In the
Arctic, they provide the principal food for caribou, and they are one of the few plants that grow in
Antarctica. They are pioneers, appearing in barren rocky areas and starting the formation of soil in
5   which mosses, then ferns, and then other plants can take root.

Lichens are a partnership of two plants—fungi and algae. The lichen body is made up of a
network of fungal strands. In the upper layers of these grow groups of algae. The two organisms live
together to the benefit of both, a relationship known as symbiosis. The fungi provide support, absorb
water, and shelter the tender algae from direct sunlight. The algae carry on photosynthesis and
10   provide the fungi with food. The algae can live independently and are recognizable as a species that
grows alone. The fungi, on the other hand, cannot live apart from their partners. They can be placed
in known classes of fungi but are unlike any species that live independently.

So definite are the form, color, and characteristics of these double organisms that for hundreds
of years, they were classified as one. More than 15,000 "species" were named. If these organisms are
15   classified as separate species, it is difficult to fit them into the existing system of classification. But if
they are classified separately, these species of fungi seem rather strange. Lichens are a splendid
example of the difficulties faced by taxonomists in classifying species.

37. What does the author imply about lichens
in the first paragraph?

  (A) They require a lot of moisture to live.
  (B) They primarily live in cold places.
  (C) They can live anywhere except
around people.
  (D) They have adapted to a wide variety
of environments.

38. Why does the author call lichens *pioneers*
(line 4)?

  (A) Because they developed so early in
the history of the planet
  (B) Because of their primitive structure
  (C) Because they prepare soil for other
plants
  (D) Because they were the first plants to
live in Antarctica

39. The word *barren* in line 4 is closest in
meaning to

  (A) lifeless.
  (B) frigid.
  (C) jagged.
  (D) uncovered.

40. Which of the following is an example of
symbiosis as it is described in the second
paragraph?

  (A) Certain types of tall grass conceal
tigers because of the tigers' striped
markings.
  (B) Fish called remoras attach themselves
to sharks and eat the scraps of the
sharks' meals.
  (C) Mistletoe, a type of shrub, grows on
trees and harms them by extracting
water and nutrients.
  (D) Protozoa in the intestines of termites
digest the cellulose that the termites
eat, and their waste products nourish
the termites.

41. Which of the following can be inferred
about the effect of direct sunlight on
lichens?

  (A) It damages the algae.
  (B) It helps the fungi absorb water.
  (C) It is required for the algae to carry on
photosynthesis.
  (D) It destroys the fungi.

42. Why does the author say that "these species
of fungi seem rather strange" (line 16)?

  (A) They are larger than typical fungi.
  (B) Unlike other fungi, they can produce
their own food.
  (C) They exist only as partners of algae.
  (D) They do not fit into any known class
of fungi.

43. Which of the following best expresses the main idea of the second paragraph?

(A) Because of their characteristics as double organisms, it is difficult to classify lichens.

(B) Over 15,000 varieties of lichens have been identified.

(C) Double organisms should always be classified as separate species.

(D) Taxonomists always find it difficult to classify new species of plants.

44. The word *splendid* in line 16 is closest in meaning to

(A) unique.

(B) improbable.

(C) excellent.

(D) famous.

QUESTIONS 45–53

Line Fifty-five delegates representing all thirteen states except Rhode Island attended the Constitutional
      Convention in Philadelphia from May to September 1787. The delegates had been instructed by the
      Continental Congress to revise the old Articles of Confederation, but most believed that a stronger
      central government was needed. There were differences, however, about what structure the govern-
5   ment should take and how much influence large states should have.

      Virginia was by far the most populous state, with twice as many people as New York, four
      times as many as New Jersey, and ten times as many as Delaware. The leader of the Virginia delega-
      tion, James Madison, had already drawn up a plan for government, which became known as the
      Large State Plan. Its essence was that congressional representation would be based on population. It
10   provided for two or more national executives. The smaller states feared that under this plan, a few
      large states would lord over the rest. New Jersey countered with the Small State Plan. It provided for
      equal representation for all states in a national legislature and for a single national executive. Angry
      debate, heightened by a stifling heat wave, led to deadlock.

      A cooling of tempers seemed to come with lower temperatures. The delegates hammered out
15   an agreement known as the Great Compromise—actually a bundle of shrewd compromises. They
      decided that Congress would consist of two houses. The larger states were granted representation
      based on population in the lower house, the House of Representatives. The smaller states were given
      equal representation in the upper house, the Senate, in which each state would have two senators
      regardless of population. It was also agreed that there would be a single executive, the president.
20   This critical compromise broke the logjam, and from then on, success seemed within reach.

45. What is the main topic of this passage?

(A) James Madison's plan to create a stable structure for the government of the United States

(B) A disagreement at the Constitutional Convention and a subsequent compromise

(C) The differences in population and relative power between the original states

(D) The most important points of the Small State Plan

46. According to the passage, how many states were represented at the Constitutional Convention?

(A) Twelve
(B) Thirteen
(C) Fourteen
(D) Fifty-five

47. It can be inferred from the passage that the Articles of Confederation

(A) were supported by a majority of the delegates at the Convention.

(B) were revised and presented as the Large State Plan.

(C) allowed small states to dominate large ones.

(D) provided for only a weak central government.

48. According to the passage, in 1787 which of the following states had the FEWEST people?

(A) Virginia
(B) Delaware
(C) New York
(D) New Jersey

49. In line 10, the phrase *this plan* refers to

(A) the Small State Plan.
(B) a plan suggested by the national legislature.
(C) the Large State Plan.
(D) a compromise plan.

50. According to the passage, the weather had what effect on the Constitutional Convention?

(A) Hot weather intensified the debate while cooler weather brought compromise.

(B) Bad weather prevented some of the delegates from reaching Philadelphia.

(C) Delegates hurried to achieve an agreement before winter arrived.

(D) Cold temperatures made Independence Hall an uncomfortable place to work.

51. The word *shrewd* in line 15 is closest in meaning to

(A) practical.

(B) unfair.

(C) important.

(D) clever.

52. Which of the following is NOT given in the passage as one of the provisions of the Great Compromise?

(A) There would be only one national executive.

(B) The president would be elected by popular vote.

(C) Each state would have two senators.

(D) Congress would be divided into two bodies.

53. The author uses the phrase *broke the logjam* (line 20) to indicate that

(A) the government was nearly bankrupt.

(B) some major problems had been solved.

(C) the Convention came to a sudden end.

(D) the situation had become desperate.

Questions 54–60

Line   Wood has long been a popular building material in North America because it has generally been
plentiful and cheap. Swedish settlers in Delaware built log cabins as early as the 1630s. In New
England, British colonists built wooden "saltbox houses." Most of the wooden homes of Colonial
times could be built with simple tools and minimal skills.

5   In the early nineteenth century, the standard wooden house was built with beams set into
heavy posts and held together with wooden pegs. This method of construction was time consuming
and required highly skilled workers with special tools. The balloon-frame house, invented in 1833 in
Chicago by a carpenter from Hartford, Connecticut, used a framework of lightweight lumber, mostly
2 × 4 and 2 × 6 inches. This type of house could be assembled by any careful worker who could saw

10   in a straight line and drive a nail.
     This revolution in building was made possible by improved sawmills that could quickly cut
boards to standard sizes and the lower cost of lumber that resulted. There were also new machines
that could produce huge quantities of inexpensive nails. Skeptics predicted that a strong wind would
send such houses flying through the air like balloons and, at first "balloon frame" was a term of

15   derision. But the light frames proved practical, and wooden houses have been basically built this way
ever since.

54. What is the main purpose of this passage?

  (A) To trace the influence of Swedish and British settlers on American styles of building

  (B) To stress the importance of wood as a building material

  (C) To compare methods of constructing wooden houses in various parts of the country

  (D) To describe a revolutionary technique for constructing wooden houses

55. According to the passage, where did the inventor of the balloon-frame house originally come from?

  (A) Connecticut
  (B) Chicago
  (C) Sweden
  (D) Delaware

56. Which of the following questions about the balloon-frame house is NOT answered in the passage?

  (A) Where was it invented?
  (B) What was its inventor's name?
  (C) What size was most of the lumber used in its framework?
  (D) In what year was it invented?

57. The author implies that which of the following types of houses required the most skill to produce?

  (A) The log cabins built by Swedish settlers
  (B) Saltbox houses
  (C) Standard wooden houses of the early nineteenth century
  (D) Balloon-frame houses

58. All of the following are factors in the development of the balloon-frame house EXCEPT

  (A) the invention of sophisticated tools.
  (B) the production of cheap nails.
  (C) improvements in sawmills.
  (D) the falling price of lumber.

59. According to the passage, why was the term *balloon frame* (line 7) applied to certain houses?

  (A) They could be moved from place to place.
  (B) They could be easily expanded.
  (C) They had rounded frames that slightly resembled balloons.
  (D) They were made of lightweight materials.

60. The word *derision* in line 15 is closest in meaning to

  (A) affection.
  (B) ignorance.
  (C) ridicule.
  (D) regret.

QUESTIONS 61–70

Line Rachel Carson was born in 1907 in Springsdale, Pennsylvania. She studied biology in college and
zoology at Johns Hopkins University, where she received her master's degree in 1933. In 1936, she
was hired by the U.S. Fish and Wildlife Service, where she worked most of her life.

        Carson's first book, *Under the Sea Wind,* was published in 1941. It received excellent reviews,
5   but sales were poor until it was reissued in 1952. In that year, she published *The Sea Around Us,*
which provided a fascinating look beneath the ocean's surface, emphasizing human history as well as
geology and marine biology. Her imagery and language had a poetic quality. Carson consulted no less
than 1,000 printed sources. She had voluminous correspondence and frequent discussions with
experts in the field. However, she always realized the limitations of her nontechnical readers.

10   In 1962, Carson published *Silent Spring,* a book that sparked considerable controversy. It
proved how much harm was done by the uncontrolled, reckless use of insecticides. She detailed how
they poison the food supply of animals, kill birds and fish, and contaminate human food. At the time,
spokesmen for the chemical industry mounted personal attacks against Carson and issued propaganda
to indicate that her findings were flawed. However, her work was vindicated by a 1963 report of the
15   President's Science Advisory Committee.

61. The passage mainly discusses Rachel Carson's work

    (A) as a researcher.
    (B) at college.
    (C) at the U.S. Fish and Wildlife Service.
    (D) as a writer.

62. According to the passage, what did Carson primarily study at Johns Hopkins University?

    (A) Oceanography
    (B) History
    (C) Literature
    (D) Zoology

63. When she published her first book, Carson was closest to the age of

    (A) 26.
    (B) 29.
    (C) 34.
    (D) 45.

64. It can be inferred from the passage that in 1952, Carson's book *Under the Sea Wind*

    (A) was outdated.
    (B) became more popular than her other books.
    (C) was praised by critics.
    (D) sold many copies.

65. Which of the following was NOT mentioned in the passage as a source of information for *The Sea Around Us*?

    (A) Printed matter
    (B) Talks with experts
    (C) A research expedition
    (D) Letters from scientists

66. Which of the following words or phrases is LEAST accurate in describing *The Sea Around Us*?

    (A) Highly technical
    (B) Poetic
    (C) Fascinating
    (D) Well researched

67. The word *reckless* in line 11 is closest in meaning to

    (A) unnecessary.
    (B) limited.
    (C) continuous.
    (D) irresponsible.

68. According to the passage, *Silent Spring* is primarily a(n)

    (A) attack on the use of chemical preservatives in food.
    (B) discussion of the hazards insects pose to the food supply.
    (C) warning about the dangers of misusing insecticides.
    (D) illustration of the benefits of the chemical industry.

69. Which of the following is closest in meaning to the word *flawed* in line 14?

(A) Faulty
(B) Deceptive
(C) Logical
(D) Offensive

70. Why does the author of the passage mention the report of the President's Science Advisory Committee (line 15)?

(A) To provide an example of government propaganda
(B) To support Carson's ideas
(C) To indicate a growing government concern with the environment
(D) To validate the chemical industry's claims

THIS IS THE END OF SECTION 3.

IF YOU FINISH BEFORE THE TIME LIMIT, CHECK YOUR WORK ON SECTION 3 ONLY.

DO NOT READ OR WORK ON ANY OTHER SECTION OF THE TEST.

Practice Test 4

Section 1

LISTENING

This section tests your ability to comprehend spoken English. It is divided into three parts, each with its own directions. During actual exams, you are not permitted to turn the page during the reading of the directions or to take notes at any time.

PART A

Directions: Each item in this part consists of a brief conversation involving two speakers. Following each conversation, a third voice will ask a question. You will hear the conversations and questions only once, and they will *not* be written out.

When you have heard each conversation and question, read the four answer choices and select the *one*—(A), (B), (C), or (D)—that best answers the question based on what is directly stated or on what can be inferred. Then fill in the space on your answer sheet that matches the letter of the answer that you have selected.

Here is an example.

You will hear:

M1: Do you think I should lean this chair against the wall or put it somewhere else?

F1: Over by the window, I'd say.

M2: What does the woman think the man should do?

You will read:

(A) Open the window.
(B) Move the chair.
(C) Leave the room.
(D) Take a seat.

From the conversation you find out that the woman thinks the man should put the chair over by the window. The best answer to the question "What does the woman think the man should do?" is (B), "Move the chair." You should fill in (B) on your answer sheet.

Sample Answer

 Ⓐ ● Ⓒ Ⓓ

1. (A) He wants to know how Donna feels.
   (B) Maybe Donna can organize the slide show.
   (C) He wants to know what present Donna got.
   (D) Donna has already seen the show.

2. (A) Make some tea.
   (B) Wash out a cup.
   (C) Get the key.
   (D) Clean the spoon.

3. (A) He hasn't been alone lately.
   (B) He hasn't been here recently.
   (C) He has been acting strangely.
   (D) He has to be reminded several times.

4. (A) She will do anything but play golf.
   (B) She seldom wants to do anything.
   (C) She never plays, but she'd like to.
   (D) She is an enthusiastic golfer.

5. (A) It's too hot to eat.
   (B) There's not enough of it.
   (C) He doesn't like the way it tastes.
   (D) He thinks it's too cool.

6. (A) The merchandise is in storage.
   (B) That store sells fine housewares.
   (C) No one knows where the store is.
   (D) The goods are upstairs somewhere.

7. (A) She finds reading poetry rewarding.
   (B) She made some beautiful pottery.
   (C) She wrote some award-winning poems.
   (D) She is now writing for a newspaper.

8. (A) They were free.
   (B) He's going to give them away.
   (C) They were inexpensive.
   (D) He has to return them soon.

9. (A) He repaired her guitar.
   (B) He sold her a new guitar.
   (C) He has a better guitar now.
   (D) He's a good guitarist.

10. (A) He isn't going out today.
    (B) The wind is dying down.
    (C) He thinks today is Wednesday.
    (D) The wind is strong today.

11. (A) His picture appears on the book.
    (B) His photographs are in the box.
    (C) He autographed the new book.
    (D) His new book is very interesting.

12. (A) He didn't understand the manual.
    (B) The electricity has gone off.
    (C) He couldn't find the manual.
    (D) The printer is out of order.

13. (A) She's not home now.
    (B) He's not sure if she's there.
    (C) She's talking on another phone.
    (D) He can see her.

14. (A) Forget about the concert.
    (B) Spend some time practicing.
    (C) Find a new place to live.
    (D) Go to another concert.

15. (A) He didn't like mathematics.
    (B) He'll be a great mathematician someday.
    (C) He's no longer studying mathematics.
    (D) He was failing mathematics.

16. (A) Anger.
    (B) Surprise.
    (C) Confusion.
    (D) Happiness.

17. (A) She couldn't get dinner reservations.
    (B) She didn't need reservations for dinner.
    (C) She was the last person to arrive at the restaurant.
    (D) She had made reservations for dinner a long time ago.

18. (A) Go to a lecture.
    (B) Call her sister.
    (C) Attend a planning meeting.
    (D) Go bowling.

19. (A) Where he went to buy the camcorder.
    (B) How much a good used camcorder costs.
    (C) What condition the camcorder is in.
    (D) How many days he's had his camcorder.

20. (A) She should wear her old glasses.
    (B) Her headaches will soon disappear.
    (C) She ought to take off her glasses.
    (D) Her glasses look a little like his.

21. (A) He paid it today for the first time.
    (B) He pays it after it's due.
    (C) He pays it on the last day of the month.
    (D) He's planning to pay it tomorrow.

22. (A) She'll be home on time.
(B) She was late for work.
(C) She's working overtime.
(D) She missed work again.

23. (A) The man must wait before taking it.
(B) The second half is even more difficult.
(C) The man should take only the first half.
(D) It's not as hard as the man thinks.

24. (A) She only read it two times.
(B) She doesn't understand it.
(C) She likes it very much.
(D) She has dozens of copies.

25. (A) Make an important discovery.
(B) Perform an experiment with penicillin.
(C) Study something other than biology.
(D) Discover a substitute for penicillin.

26. (A) A lot of people attended.
(B) The debate involved only a few issues.
(C) Many people changed their plans.
(D) The debate lasted a long time.

27. (A) Order a meal.
(B) Write a check.
(C) Look for the waiter.
(D) Get the waiter's atttention.

28. (A) She will probably win.
(B) She hasn't improved her game recently.
(C) No one ever sees her on the court.
(D) She doesn't think she can win.

29. (A) They couldn't finish cleaning in time.
(B) They helped her clean the apartment.
(C) They didn't have much cleaning to do.
(D) They had to work and couldn't clean.

30. (A) After class today.
(B) After today's meeting.
(C) Before class on Friday.
(D) After class on Friday.

PART B

Directions: This part of the test consists of extended conversations between two speakers. After each of these conversations there are a number of questions. You will hear each conversation and question only once, and the questions are *not* written out.

When you have heard each questions, read the four answer choices and select the *one*—(A), (B), (C), or (D)—that best answers the question based on what is directly stated or on what can be inferred. Then fill in the space on your answer sheet that matches the letter of the answer that you have selected.

Don't forget: During actual exams, taking notes or writing in your test book is *not* permitted.

31. (A) A multiple-choice exam.
    (B) A chemistry exam.
    (C) An essay exam.
    (D) A geology exam.

32. (A) Its relative hardness.
    (B) Its true color.
    (C) Its chemical composition.
    (D) Its relative purity.

33. (A) They are never effective.
    (B) They are simple to perform.
    (C) They are not always conclusive.
    (D) They are usually undependable.

34. (A) Flight attendant.
    (B) Rental-car agent.
    (C) Hotel manager.
    (D) Travel agent.

35. (A) Miami.
    (B) Minneapolis.
    (C) Key West.
    (D) Chicago.

36. (A) A hotel room.
    (B) A flight to Chicago.
    (C) A rental car.
    (D) A flight to Miami.

37. (A) Make reservations for his flight sooner.
    (B) Spend his vacation somewhere else.
    (C) Read a travel book.
    (D) Stay at a different hotel.

PART C

Directions: This part of the test consists of several talks, each given by a single speaker. After each of these talks there are a number of questions. You will hear each talk and question only once, and the questions are *not* written out.

When you have heard the question, read the four answer choices and select the *one*—(A), (B), (C), or (D)—that best answers the question based on what is directly stated or on what can be inferred. Then fill in the space on your answer sheet that matches the letter of the answer that you have selected.

Here is an example.

You will hear:

M1: Students, this evening we'll have a chance to observe a phenomenon that we've discussed several times in class. Tonight, there will be a lunar eclipse. As we've said, when an eclipse of the moon occurs, the earth passes between the sun and the moon. Therefore, the shadow of the earth moves across the surface of the moon and obscures it. Because you won't be looking at the sun, it is not necessary to use the special lenses and filters that you need when observing a solar eclipse. You can observe a lunar eclipse with your unaided eye or with a telescope and photograph it with an ordinary camera. So if the weather's not cloudy tonight, go out and take a look at this eclipse of the moon. I'm sure you'll find it interesting.

Now here is a sample question.

You will hear:

M2: In what course is this lecture probably being given?

You will read:

(**A**) Philosophy.
(**B**) Meteorology.
(**C**) Astronomy.
(**D**) Photography.

The lecture concerns a lunar eclipse, a topic that would typically be discussed in an astronomy class. The choice that best answers the question "In what course is this lecture probably being given?" is (C), "Astronomy." You should fill in (C) on your answer sheet.

Sample Answer

  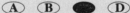

Here is another sample question.

You will hear:

M2: According to the speaker, which of the following occurs during a lunar eclipse?

You will read:

(**A**) The earth's shadow moves across the moon.
(**B**) Clouds block the view of the moon.
(**C**) The moon moves between the earth and the sun.
(**D**) The sun can be observed without special equipment.

From the lecture, you learn that a lunar eclipse occurs when the earth moves between the sun and the moon and the shadow of the earth passes across the moon. The choice that best answers the question "According to the speaker, which of the following occurs during a lunar eclipse?" is (A), "The earth's shadow moves across the moon." Don't forget: During actual exams, taking notes or writing in your test book is *not* permitted.

Sample Answer

38. (A) In the home of an art collector.
    (B) In a restaurant.
    (C) In a museum.
    (D) In a private art gallery.

39. (A) Not all of it is folk art.
    (B) Most of it was made for this event.
    (C) All of it was created for display.
    (D) Some of it has been in previous exhibits.

40. (A) It is still brightly colored.
    (B) It was used to advertise a restaurant.
    (C) It is less than a hundred years old.
    (D) It once hung in front of a bootmaker's shop.

41. (A) Unpopular.
    (B) Charming.
    (C) Complex.
    (D) Disturbing.

42. (A) There are no signatures on the signs.
    (B) The plaques haven't been put on the wall yet.
    (C) The signatures are too faded to read.
    (D) The sign painters needed to conceal their identities.

43. (A) To present an award.
    (B) To say goodbye to Professor Callaghan.
    (C) To explain computer models.
    (D) To welcome a new college president.

44. (A) An administrator.
    (B) A faculty member.
    (C) A chancellor of the college.
    (D) A graduate student.

45. (A) Computer science.
    (B) History.
    (C) Economics.
    (D) Physics.

46. (A) Two years.
    (B) Four years.
    (C) Six years.
    (D) Eight years.

47. (A) He greatly influenced Emily Dickinson.
    (B) His poetry was similar to Emily Dickinson's.
    (C) He and Emily Dickinson were very influential poets.
    (D) He and Emily Dickinson became good friends.

48. (A) For her unusual habits.
    (B) For her success as a poet.
    (C) For her personal wealth.
    (D) For her eventful life.

49. (A) Their titles.
    (B) Their great length.
    (C) Their range of subject matter.
    (D) Their economy.

50. (A) None.
    (B) About 10.
    (C) Around 50.
    (D) Over 1,700.

THIS IS THE END OF SECTION 1: LISTENING.

STOP WORK ON SECTION 1.

Section 2

This section tests your ability to recognize grammar and usage suitable for standard written English. It is divided into two parts, each with its own directions.

SENTENCE COMPLETION

Directions: Items in this part are incomplete sentences. Following each of these sentences, there are four words or phrases. You should select the *one* word or phrase—(A), (B), (C), or (D)—that best completes the sentence. Then fill in the space on your answer sheet that matches the letter of the answer that you have selected.

Example I

Pepsin _____ an enzyme used in digestion.

(A) that
(B) is
(C) of
(D) being

This sentence should properly read "Pepsin is an enzyme used in digestion." You should fill in choice (B) on your answer sheet.

Sample Answer

Ⓐ ● Ⓒ Ⓓ

Example II

_____ large natural lakes are found in the state of South Carolina.

(A) There are no
(B) Not the
(C) It is not
(D) No

This sentence should properly read "No large natural lakes are found in the state of South Carolina." You should fill in choice (D) on your answer sheet. As soon as you understand the directions, begin work on this part.

Sample Answer

Ⓐ Ⓑ Ⓒ ●

1. _____ a blend of the actual note sounded and related tones called overtones.

   (A) Musical tones consist of every
   (B) All musical tones consisting of
   (C) It consists of all musical tones
   (D) Every musical tone consists of

2. _____, all animals need oxygen, water, food, and the proper range of temperatures.

   (A) To survive
   (B) Their survival
   (C) Surviving
   (D) They survive

3. Billie Holiday's rough _____ emotional voice made her stand out as a jazz singer.

   (A) so
   (B) but
   (C) nor
   (D) still

4. The Breed Test, _____ method of counting bacteria in fresh milk, was developed by R. S. Breed in Geneva, New York, in 1925.

   (A) which, as a
   (B) is a
   (C) it is a
   (D) a

5. _____ a liquid changes to a solid, heat is given off.

   (A) That
   (B) Sometimes
   (C) Whenever
   (D) From

6. Completed in 1756, Nassau Hall is the oldest building now _____ on the campus of Princeton University.

   (A) standing
   (B) it stands
   (C) has stood
   (D) stood

7. The one person most responsible for making New York City a center of furniture design in the early nineteenth century _____ cabinetmaker Duncan Phyfe.

   (A) was the hardworking
   (B) through his hard work
   (C) he was hardworking
   (D) by working hard, the

8. Candles _____ from beeswax burn with a very clean flame.

   (A) are made
   (B) making
   (C) which make
   (D) made

9. Hydroponics is the cultivation of plants _____ soil.

   (A) not having
   (B) without
   (C) a lack of
   (D) do not have

10. _____ a language family is a group of languages with a common origin and similar vocabulary, grammar, and sound systems.

    (A) What linguists call
    (B) It is called by linguists
    (C) Linguists call it
    (D) What do linguists call

11. In the eighteenth century, the town of Bennington, Vermont, was famous for _____ pottery.

    (A) it made
    (B) its
    (C) the making
    (D) where its

12. _____ bacterial infection is present in the body, the bone marrow produces more white blood cells than usual.

    (A) A
    (B) That a
    (C) If a
    (D) During a

13. Anyone who has ever pulled weeds from a garden _____ roots firmly anchor plants to the soil.

    (A) is well aware that
    (B) well aware
    (C) is well aware of
    (D) well aware that

14. So thick and rich _____ of Illinois that early settlers there were unable to force a plow through it.

(A) as the soil
(B) the soil was
(C) was the soil
(D) the soil

15. _____ because of the complexity of his writing, Henry James never became a popular author, but his works are admired by critics and other writers.

(A) It may be
(B) Perhaps
(C) Besides
(D) Why is it

ERROR IDENTIFICATION

Directions: The items in this part have four underlined words or phrases. You must identify the *one* underlined expression—(A), (B), (C), or (D)—that must be changed for the sentence to be correct. Then fill in the space on your answer sheet that matches the letter of the answer that you have selected.

Example I

Lenses may to have either concave or convex shapes.
        A   **B** **C**   **D**

This sentence should read "Lenses may have either concave or convex shapes." You should therefore select choice (A).

Sample Answer

●   Ⓑ   Ⓒ   Ⓓ

Example II

When painting a fresco, an artist is applied paint directly to the damp plaster of a wall.
  A   **B**   **C**   **D**

This sentence should read "When painting a fresco, an artist applies paint directly to the wet plaster of a wall." You should therefore select (B). As soon as you understand the directions, begin work on this part.

Sample Answer

Ⓐ   ●   Ⓒ   Ⓓ

16. A rattlesnake has a spot between one's eyes
                            ——————— ———
                               A   B
    that is sensitive to heat.
         —————————   ————
             C   D

17. Improvements in people's health are
    ———————————
         A
    due in part to advances in medical care and
    ——————   ——————————
       B   C
    better sanitary.
    ——————————
         D

18. In 1792, a corporation constructed a
    ———   —————————
     A   B
    60-miles toll road from Philadelphia to
    ——————————   ————
        C   D
    Lancaster, Pennsylvania.

19. Insects appeared on Earth before long the
            ——————— ——   ——————————
               A   B   C
    earliest mammals.
    ————————————
         D

20. All of Agnes Repplier's writings, even those
    ———   ——————————
     A   B
    on the most serious subjects, show her
    ———————————————
           C
    sense of humorous.
            ————————
               D

21. Fungi are the most important decomposers
             ————————————————————
                        A
    of forest soil just like bacteria are the chief
    ————————   ————————   ————
        B   C   D
    decomposers of grassland soil.

22. Halifax Harbor in Nova Scotia is one of
                               ——
                               A
    the most safe harbors in the world.
    —————————   ——————   ——————
         B   C   D

23. Ballpoint pens require a tiny,
                   ———————
                      A
    perfectly round ball for its tips.
    ———————— ————   ————
        B   C   D

24. Since the 1930s, the archaeology has
    —————   ——————————————
      A   B
    become a precise science with strict
             ——————————
                 C
    rules and procedures.
    ————————————
         D

25. Interstate Highway 80 is so an important
                          —— ——————————
                          A   B
    road that it is sometimes referred to as
    ——————   ——————————
       C   D
    "America's Main Street."

26. John Jay, a diplomat and statesman, first
                    ——————
                      A
    entered public live in 1773.
    ——————— —————— ———
       B   C   D

27. Mount Hood in Oregon is a center for
                      ——
                       A
    alpine sports such as skiing, climbing, and
    ——————   ——————— —————————
       B   C
    hikes.
    ————
     D

28. The chameleon's able to change color to
                    ————————
                       A
    match its surroundings is shared by quite
    ————————————————   —————————
          B   C
    a few lizards.
    ——————————
        D

29. Florence Sabin is recognized not only for
                     ———————————   ————
                          A   B
    her theoretical research in anatomy and
                                —————————
                                    C
    physiology and for her work in public
    ——————————
        D
    health.

30. The top layer of the ocean stores as much
    ————————   ———
        A   B
    heat as does all the gases in the
             ——————
                C
    atmosphere.
    ——————————
         D

31. Almost lemons grown in the United States
    ——————   —————
       A   B
    come from farms in Florida and California.
    ————   —————
      C   D

32. Hair is made of the same basic material
    ————
     A
    as both the nails, claws, and hooves of
    ——————   ——————————
       B   C
    mammals are made of.
    ——————————————
            D

33. Not until geologists began to study exposed
                          ——————   ————————
                            A   B
    rocks in ravines and on mountainsides
                        ——————————————
                             C
    they did discover many of the earth's
    —————————
        D
    secrets.

34. The water of the Gulf Stream may be

    as much as 20 percentage warmer than the
    ——————————   —————————— ——————
        A   B   C
    surrounding water.
    ——————————
         D

35. Mathematics have taken centuries
　　　　　　　　 A
to develop the methods that we now use in
　 B 　　 **C** 　　　　　 **D**
arithmetic.

36. One of the most beautiful botanical gardens
　　　　　　　 A 　　　　　　　 **B**
in the United States is the wildly and lovely
　　　　　　　　　　　 C
Magnolia Gardens near Charleston, South
　　　　　　　　 D
Carolina.

37. Benthic organisms are those that live on or
　　　　　　　　　　　 A 　　　　　 **B**
in a bottom of a body of water.
　 C 　　 **D**

38. It has been known since the eighteenth
　　 A 　　　　　　 **B**
century that the adrenal glands are essential
　　　　　　　　　　　　 C
of life.
　 D

39. The making of leather goods from animal
　　 A 　　　　　 **B**
skins is one of the soonest accomplish-
　 C 　　　　　　 **D**
ments of humankind.

40. Married customs differ greatly from society
　 A 　　　　　 **B** 　 **C**
to society.
　 D

THIS IS THE END OF SECTION 2.

IF YOU FINISH BEFORE THE TIME LIMIT, CHECK YOUR WORK ON SECTION 2 ONLY.

DO NOT READ OR WORK ON ANY OTHER SECTION OF THE TEST.

Section 3

This section of the test measures your ability to comprehend written materials.

Directions: This section contains several passages, each followed by a number of questions. Read the passages and, for each question, choose the *one* best answer—(A), (B), (C), or (D)—based on what is stated in the passage or on what can be inferred from the passage. Then fill in the space on your answer sheet that matches the letter of the answer that you have selected.

Read the Following Passage

Line   Like mammals, birds claim their own territories. A bird's territory may be small or large. Some birds claim only their nest and the area right around it, while others claim far larger territories that include their feeding areas. Gulls, penguins, and other waterfowl nest in huge colonies, but even in the biggest colonies, each male and his mate have small territories of their own
5   immediately around their nests.

       Male birds defend their territory chiefly against other males of the same species. In some cases, a warning call or threatening pose may be all the defense needed, but in other cases, intruders may refuse to leave peacefully.

Example I

What is the main topic of this passage?

(A) Birds that live in colonies
(B) Birds' mating habits
(C) The behavior of birds
(D) Territoriality in birds

The passage mainly concerns the territories of birds. You should fill in (D) on your answer sheet.

Sample Answer

Example II

According to the passage, male birds defend their territory primarily against which of the following?

(A) Female birds
(B) Birds of other species
(C) Males of their own species
(D) Mammals

The passage states that "Male birds defend their territory chiefly against other males of the same species." You should fill in (C) on your answer sheet. As soon as you understand the directions, begin work on this section.

Sample Answer

QUESTIONS 1–10

Line   Cooperation is the common endeavor of two or more people to perform a task or reach a jointly
cherished goal. Like competition and conflict, there are different forms of cooperation, based on
group organization and attitudes.

      In the first form, known as primary cooperation, group and individual fuse. The group contains
5   nearly all of each individual's life. The rewards of the group's work are shared with each member.
There is an interlocking identity of individual, group, and task performed. Means and goals become
one, for cooperation itself is valued.

      While primary cooperation is most often characteristic of preliterate societies, secondary
cooperation is characteristic of many modern societies. In secondary cooperation, individuals devote
10 only part of their lives to the group. Cooperation itself is not a value. Most members of the group
feel loyalty, but the welfare of the group is not the first consideration. Members perform tasks so that
they can *separately* enjoy the fruits of their cooperation in the form of salary, prestige, or power.
Business offices and professional athletic teams are examples of secondary cooperation.

      In the third type, called tertiary cooperation or accommodation, latent conflict underlies the
15 shared work. The attitudes of the cooperating parties are purely opportunistic; the organization is
loose and fragile. Accommodation involves common means to achieve antagonistic goals; it breaks
down when the common means cease to aid each party in reaching its goals. This is not, strictly
speaking, cooperation at all, and hence the somewhat contradictory term *antagonistic cooperation* is
sometimes used for this relationship.

1. What is the author's main purpose in the first paragraph of the passage?

  (A) To explain how cooperation differs from competition and conflict

  (B) To show the importance of group organization and attitudes

  (C) To offer a brief definition of cooperation

  (D) To urge readers to cooperate more often

2. The word *cherished* in line 2 is closest in meaning to

  (A) prized.
  (B) agreed on.
  (C) defined.
  (D) set up.

3. The word *fuse* in line 4 is closest in meaning to

  (A) react.
  (B) unite.
  (C) evolve.
  (D) explore.

4. Which of the following statements about primary cooperation is supported by information in the passage?

  (A) It was confined to prehistoric times.

  (B) It is usually the first stage of cooperation achieved by a group of individuals attempting to cooperate.

  (C) It is an ideal that can never be achieved.

  (D) It is most commonly seen among people who have not yet developed reading and writing skills.

5. According to the passage, why do people join groups that practice secondary cooperation?

  (A) To experience the satisfaction of cooperation

  (B) To get rewards for themselves

  (C) To associate with people who have similar backgrounds

  (D) To defeat a common enemy

6. Which of the following is an example of the third form of cooperation as it is defined in the fourth paragraph?

   (A) Students form a study group so that all of them can improve their grades.
   (B) A new business attempts to take customers away from an established company.
   (C) Two rival political parties temporarily work together to defeat a third party.
   (D) Members of a farming community share work and the food that they grow.

7. Which of the following is NOT given as a name for the third type of cooperation?

   (A) Tertiary cooperation
   (B) Accommodation
   (C) Latent conflict
   (D) Antagonistic cooperation

8. The word *fragile* in line 16 is closest in meaning to

   (A) inefficient.
   (B) easily broken.
   (C) poorly planned.
   (D) involuntary.

9. As used throughout the passage, the term *common* is closest in meaning to which of the following?

   (A) Ordinary
   (B) Shared
   (C) Vulgar
   (D) Popular

10. Which of the following best describes the overall organization of the passage?

   (A) The author describes a concept by analyzing its three forms.
   (B) The author compares and contrasts two types of human relations.
   (C) The author presents the points of view of three experts on the same topic.
   (D) The author provides a number of concrete examples and then draws a conclusion.

QUESTIONS 11–22

Line   The first scientific attempt at coaxing moisture from a cloud was in 1946, when scientist Vincent
Schaefer dropped 3 pounds of dry ice from an airplane into a cloud and, to his delight, produced
snow. The success of the experiment was modest, but it spawned optimism among farmers and
ranchers around the country. It seemed to them that science had finally triumphed over weather.

5   Unfortunately, it didn't work out that way. Although there were many cloud-seeding operations
during the late 1940s and the 1950s, no one could say whether they had any effect on precipitation.
Cloud seeding, or weather modification as it came to be called, was clearly more complicated than
had been thought. It was not until the early 1970s that enough experiments had been done to
understand the processes involved. What these studies indicated was that only certain types of clouds

10   are amenable to seeding. One of the most responsive is the winter orographic cloud, formed when
air currents encounter a mountain slope and rise. If the temperature in such a cloud is right, seeding
can increase snow yield by 10 to 20 percent.
          There are two major methods of weather modification. In one method, silver iodide is burned
in propane-fired ground generators. The smoke rises into the clouds where the tiny silver-iodide

15   particles act as nuclei for the formation of ice crystals. The alternate system uses airplanes to deliver
dry-ice pellets. Dry ice does not provide ice-forming nuclei. Instead, it lowers the temperature near
the water droplets in the clouds so that they freeze instantly—a process called spontaneous nucleation. Seeding from aircraft is more efficient but more expensive.
          About 75 percent of all weather modification in the United States takes place in the Western

20   states. With the population of the West growing rapidly, few regions of the world require more
water. About 85 percent of the waters in the rivers of the West comes from melted snow. As one
expert put it, the water problems of the future may make the energy problems of the 1970s seem
like child's play to solve. That's why the U.S. Bureau of Reclamation, along with state governments,
municipal water districts, and private interests such as ski areas and agricultural cooperatives, is

25   putting increased effort into cloud-seeding efforts. Without consistent and heavy snowfalls in the
Rockies and Sierras, the West would literally dry up. The most intensive efforts to produce precipitation was during the West's disastrous snow drought of 1976–77. It is impossible to judge the
efficiency of weather modification based on one crash program, but most experts think that such
hurry-up programs are not very effective.

11. What is the main subject of the passage?

    (A) The scientific contributions of Vincent
        Schaefer
    (B) Developments in methods of increas-
        ing precipitation
    (C) The process by which snow crystals
        form
    (D) The effects of cloud seeding

12. The word *spawned* in line 3 is closest in
    meaning to

    (A) intensified.
    (B) reduced.
    (C) preceded.
    (D) created.

13. After the cloud-seeding operations of the
    late 1940s and the 1950s, the farmers and
    ranchers mentioned in the first paragraph
    probably felt

    (A) triumphant.
    (B) modest.
    (C) disappointed.
    (D) optimistic.

14. Which of the following can be inferred
    from the passage about the term *weather
    modification*?

    (A) It is not as old as the term *cloud
        seeding*.
    (B) It has been in use since at least 1946.
    (C) It refers to only one type of cloud
        seeding.
    (D) It was first used by Vincent Schaefer.

15. According to the passage, winter orographic clouds are formed

    (A) on relatively warm winter days
    (B) over large bodies of water
    (C) during intense snow storms
    (D) when air currents rise over mountains

16. To which of the following does the word *they* in line 17 refer?

    (A) Water droplets
    (B) Clouds
    (C) Ice-forming nuclei
    (D) Airplanes

17. When clouds are seeded from the ground, what actually causes ice crystals to form?

    (A) Propane
    (B) Silver-iodide smoke
    (C) Dry-ice pellets
    (D) Nuclear radiation

18. Clouds would most likely be seeded from airplanes when

    (A) it is important to save money.
    (B) the process of spontaneous nucleation cannot be employed.
    (C) the production of precipitation must be efficient.
    (D) temperatures are lower than usual.

19. About what percentage of the western United States' water supply comes from run-off from melted snow?

    (A) 10 percent
    (B) 20 percent
    (C) 75 percent
    (D) 85 percent

20. What does the author imply about the energy problems of the 1970s?

    (A) They were caused by a lack of water.
    (B) They took attention away from water problems.
    (C) They may not be as critical as water problems will be in the future.
    (D) They were thought to be minor at the time but turned out to be serious.

21. The author mentions *agricultural cooperatives* (line 24) as an example of

    (A) state government agencies.
    (B) private interests.
    (C) organizations that compete with ski areas for water.
    (D) municipal water districts.

22. It can be inferred from the passage that the weather-modification project of 1976–77 was

    (A) put together quickly.
    (B) a complete failure.
    (C) not necessary.
    (D) easy to evaluate.

Questions 23–30

Line The biological community changes again as one moves from the city to the suburbs. Around all cities
is a biome called the "suburban forest." The trees of this forest are species that are favored by man,
and most of them have been deliberately planted. Mammals such as rabbits, skunks, and opossums
have moved in from the surrounding countryside. Raccoons have become experts at opening garbage
5   cans, and in some places even deer wander suburban thoroughfares. Several species of squirrel get
along nicely in suburbia, but usually only one species is predominant in any given suburb—fox
squirrels in one place, red squirrels in another, gray squirrels in a third—for reasons that are little
understood. The diversity of birds in the suburbs is great, and in the South, lizards thrive in gardens
and even houses. Of course, insects are always present.
10   There is an odd biological sameness in these suburban communities. True, the palms of Los
Angeles are missing from the suburbs of Boston, and there are species of insects in Miami not found
in Seattle. However, over wide stretches of the United States, ecological conditions in suburban
biomes vary much less than do those of natural biomes. Further, unlike the natural biomes, the urban
and suburban communities exist in spite of, not because of, the climate.

23. If there was a preceding paragraph to this passage it would most likely be concerned with which of the following topics?

   (A) The migration from cities to suburbs
   (B) The biological community in urban areas
   (C) The mammals of the American countryside
   (D) The history of American suburbs

24. The author implies that the mammals of the "suburban forest" differ from most species of trees there in which of the following ways?

   (A) They were not deliberately introduced.
   (B) They are considered undesirable by humans.
   (C) They are represented by a greater number of species.
   (D) They have not fully adapted to suburban conditions.

25. The word *thoroughfares* in line 5 is closest in meaning to

   (A) neighborhoods.
   (B) lawns.
   (C) open spaces.
   (D) streets.

26. Which of the following conclusions about squirrels is supported by information in the passage?

   (A) The competition among the three species is intense.
   (B) Fox squirrels are more common than gray or red squirrels.
   (C) Two species of squirrels seldom inhabit the same suburb.
   (D) The reasons why squirrels do well in the suburbs are unknown.

27. The word *thrive* in line 8 is closest in meaning to

   (A) remain.
   (B) flourish.
   (C) reproduce.
   (D) survive.

28. The word *odd* in line 10 is closest in meaning to

   (A) unusual.
   (B) appropriate.
   (C) unforgettable.
   (D) expected.

29. Which of the following best expresses the main idea of the second paragraph of the passage?

    (A) Biological communities in East Coast suburbs differ greatly from those on the West Coast.
    (B) The suburban forest occupies an increasingly large segment of the American landscape.
    (C) Suburbs in the United States have remarkably similar biological communities.
    (D) Natural biomes have been studied more than suburban biomes.

30. What does the author imply about the effect of climate on the suburban biome?

    (A) It is more noticeable than the effect of climate on the urban biome.
    (B) It is not as important as it once was.
    (C) It depends on the location of the biome.
    (D) It is not as dramatic as the effect of climate on natural biomes.

Questions 31–39

Line   Deep within the earth there seethes a vast cauldron called Hot Dry Rock, or HDR, that observers
believe could make the United States and other nations practically energy independent. HDR is a
virtually limitless source of energy that generates neither pollution nor dangerous wastes.

5   The concept, now being tested at the Los Alamos National Laboratory in New Mexico, is quite
simple, at least in theory. Two adjacent wells are punched several miles into the earth to reach this
subterranean furnace. Water is pumped down one well to collect inside the Hot Dry Rock, creating a
pressurized reservoir of superheated liquid. This is then drawn through the other well to the surface,
and there the water's accumulated load of heat energy is transferred to a volatile liquid that, in turn,
drives an electric power-producing turbine.

10   David Duchane, HDR program manager at Los Alamos, believes that an economically competitive, 1-megawatt plant of this type will be up and running in around two decades. A small prototype
station will be built in half that time, but Duchane dreams an even grander dream. "We could build
an HDR plant near the seacoast," he says. "Could you imagine pumping seawater down to where it
heats up well above its boiling point? Then you bring it to the surface to make electrical energy, and

15   you turn some into vapor to get as much pure water as you need."

31. What is the main idea of the passage?

(A) Despite certain advantages, there are
many drawbacks involved in the use
of Hot Dry Rock.

(B) Hot Dry Rock is a potentially important energy source.

(C) By drilling deep wells in the ground,
researchers at Los Alamos discovered
Hot Dry Rock.

(D) Hot Dry Rock power plants are more
useful if they are built near the
seacoast.

32. Which of the following terms is NOT used
in the passage to refer to Hot Dry Rock?

(A) A vast cauldron (line 1)

(B) A virtually limitless source of power
(line 3)

(C) Subterranean furnace (line 6)

(D) A pressurized reservoir (line 7)

33. The word *adjacent* in line 5 is closest in
meaning to

(A) up-and-down.

(B) deep.

(C) advanced.

(D) side-by-side.

34. The second paragraph of the passage
implies that the concept of utilizing Hot
Dry Rock as an energy source

(A) might be difficult to put into practice.

(B) is hard for nonscientists to understand.

(C) is theoretically possible but techno-
logically impractical.

(D) may involve unknown dangers.

35. The word *there* in line 8 refers to

(A) a place deep inside the earth.

(B) a place near the seacoast.

(C) Los Alamos National Laboratory.

(D) the surface of the earth.

36. The power-producing turbine in the Hot
Dry Rock power plant described in the
second paragraph is actually driven by

(A) electricity.

(B) volatile liquid.

(C) superheated water.

(D) Hot Dry Rock.

37. According to David Duchane, how long will
it probably take to build a small prototype
Hot Dry Rock power station?

(A) Two years

(B) Four years

(C) Ten years

(D) Twenty years

38. What is the *grander dream*, mentioned in
line 12?

(A) The opportunity for the United States
to become energy independent

(B) The chance to generate power
without increasing pollution

(C) The possibility of obtaining pure
water from seawater while generating
electricity

(D) The hope that scientists can continue
their research on Hot Dry Rock

39. The word *some* in line 15 refers to

(A) seawater.

(B) electrical energy.

(C) water vapor.

(D) pure water.

QUESTIONS 40–50

Line The brilliant light, crystalline air, and spectacular surroundings have long drawn people to the tiny New Mexican town of Taos. Today, the homes of some of those who have settled there during Taos' 300-year history have been restored and are open to the public. Along with the churches and art galleries, these residences make up a part of the unique cultural heritage of Taos.

5   Representing the Spanish Colonial era is the meticulously restored hacienda of Don Antonio Severino Martinez. He moved his family to Taos in 1804 and transformed a simple cabin into a huge, imposing fortress. Its twenty-one rooms and two courtyards now house a living museum where visitors can watch potters and weavers at work. The American territorial era is represented by two houses: the home of the explorer and scout Kit Carson, located off Taos Square, and that of Charles
10 Bent, a trader who later became governor of the New Mexico territory. Carson's house was built in 1843, Bent's three years later.

      In the twentieth century, Taos, like its bigger sister Santa Fe to the south, blossomed into a center for artists and artisans. One of the first artists to move there was Ernest Blumenschein, who is known for his illustrations, including those for the works of Jack London and other bestselling
15 authors. In 1898, while on a Denver-to-Mexico City sketching tour, Blumenschein's wagon broke down near Taos. He walked into town carrying his broken wheel, looked around, and decided to stay. His rambling, twelve-room house is furnished as it was when he lived there. Not far from the Blumenschein house is the home of another artist, Russian-born painter Nicolai Fechin, who moved to Taos in the 1920s. He carved and decorated the furniture, windows, gates, and fireplaces himself,
20 transforming the interior of his adobe house into that of a traditional country house in his homeland. A few miles north of town is the Millicent Rogers Museum, the residence of a designer and collector who came to Taos in 1947. An adobe castle, it contains a treasure trove of Native American and Hispanic jewelry, pots, rugs, and other artifacts.

40. The passage mainly discusses which aspect of Taos?

(A) Its famous families
(B) Events from its 300-year history
(C) Its different architectural styles
(D) Its historic houses

41. The word *meticulously* in line 5 is closest in meaning to

(A) tastefully.
(B) privately.
(C) carefully.
(D) expensively.

42. The word *imposing* in line 7 is closest in meaning to

(A) striking.
(B) complex.
(C) threatening.
(D) antiquated.

43. According to the passage, the home of Don Antonio Severino Martinez is now a(n)

(A) fortress.
(B) art gallery.
(C) museum.
(D) simple cabin.

44. According to the passage, what were Charles Bent's two occupations?

(A) Merchant and politician
(B) Artist and artisan
(C) Explorer and scout
(D) Potter and weaver

45. Charles Bent's house was probably built in

(A) 1804.
(B) 1840.
(C) 1843.
(D) 1846.

46. The town of Santa Fe is probably referred to as Taos's *bigger sister* (line 12) because it

(A) is older.
(B) has a larger population.
(C) is more famous.
(D) has more artists.

47. The word *works* in line 14 is used in the context of this passage to mean

(A) books.
(B) factories.
(C) designs.
(D) paintings.

48. According to the passage, what was Ernest Blumenschein's original destination when he went on a sketching tour in 1898?

(A) Denver
(B) Santa Fe
(C) Mexico City
(D) Taos

49. The author implies that the interior of Nicolai Fechin house is decorated in what style?

(A) Spanish colonial
(B) American territorial
(C) Native American
(D) Traditional Russian

50. Which of the following people is NOT mentioned as a resident of Taos?

(A) Nicolai Fechin
(B) Jack London
(C) Ernest Blumenschein
(D) Millicent Rogers

THIS IS THE END OF SECTION 3.

IF YOU FINISH BEFORE THE TIME LIMIT, CHECK YOUR WORK ON SECTION 3 ONLY.

DO NOT READ OR WORK ON ANY OTHER SECTION OF THE TEST.

Practice Test 5

Section 1

LISTENING

This section tests your ability to comprehend spoken English. It is divided into three parts, each with its own directions. During actual exams, you are *not* permitted to turn the page during the reading of the directions or to take notes at any time.

PART A

Directions: Each item in this part consists of a brief conversation involving two speakers. Following each conversation, a third voice will ask a question. You will hear the conversations and questions only once, and they will *not* be written out.

When you have heard each conversation and question, read the four answer choices and select the one—(A), (B), (C), or (D)—that best answers the question based on what is directly stated or on what can be inferred. Then fill in the space on your answer sheet that matches the letter of the answer that you have selected.

Here is an example.

You will hear:

M1: Do you think I should lean this chair against the wall or put it somewhere else?

F1: Over by the window, I'd say.

M2: What does the woman think the man should do?

You will read:

(**A**) Open the window.
(**B**) Move the chair.
(**C**) Leave the room.
(**D**) Take a seat.

From the conversation you find out that the woman thinks the man should put the chair over by the window. The best answer to the question "What does the woman think the man should do?" is (B), "Move the chair." You should fill in (B) on your answer sheet.

Sample Answer

 Ⓐ ● Ⓒ Ⓓ

1. (A) He picked these strawberries himself.
   (B) He chose the freshest strawberries.
   (C) The strawberries were displayed outside Bailey's market.
   (D) The market had just sold the last strawberries.

2. (A) He's the worst lecturer they've ever heard.
   (B) He gave one of his standard lectures.
   (C) His article was the worst they've ever read.
   (D) His lectures are generally better.

3. (A) Ate breakfast quickly.
   (B) Came late to an appointment.
   (C) Skipped breakfast.
   (D) Waited in line.

4. (A) What kind it is.
   (B) Where he bought it.
   (C) How much it cost.
   (D) What color it is.

5. (A) She'd like to watch it, but she hasn't.
   (B) She didn't find it enjoyable.
   (C) She tried to understand it, but she couldn't.
   (D) She doesn't know when it comes on.

6. (A) Go skiing some other day.
   (B) Take their lunch with them.
   (C) Buy sandwiches at the ski lodge.
   (D) Eat at an expensive restaurant.

7. (A) Botany.
   (B) Mathematics.
   (C) Acting.
   (D) Astronomy.

8. (A) She wrote them herself.
   (B) She thinks they're sentimental.
   (C) She sings them with feeling.
   (D) She knows them from memory.

9. (A) Take a taxi.
   (B) Stay at another hotel.
   (C) Ask the driver for directions.
   (D) Walk to the hotel.

10. (A) Windows.
    (B) Dishes.
    (C) Eyeglasses.
    (D) Automobiles.

11. (A) That Dean Metzger will have a reception.
    (B) That the reception will be held tonight.
    (C) That the reception will be at seven.
    (D) That Dean Metzger's reception has been canceled.

12. (A) He's not very good at math.
    (B) He's taking two advanced classes.
    (C) He doesn't remember seeing the woman in class.
    (D) He found the class too easy.

13. (A) He never seems to have any plans.
    (B) She was disappointed with his planning.
    (C) She enjoyed the event that he planned.
    (D) He will do all the planning in the future.

14. (A) He had an accident because of his nervousness.
    (B) He seemed very jumpy last night.
    (C) He was upset because he'd almost had an accident.
    (D) He was nervous about acting in the play last night.

15. (A) Professor Dixon asked his students to wait outside.
    (B) The weather isn't very good today.
    (C) Professor Dixon's class is meeting outside today.
    (D) The class was suddenly canceled.

16. (A) He's changed his mind.
    (B) He's taking statistics a second time.
    (C) He considered it briefly.
    (D) He finally decided to take economics.

17. (A) He hasn't seen many operas.
    (B) Tickets for the opera don't cost much.
    (C) He didn't attend the opera yesterday.
    (D) The opera wasn't as good as others.

18. (A) Listen to music.
    (B) Address a letter.
    (C) Get his hair cut.
    (D) Send a package.

19. (A) He and his roommate are alike.
    (B) He is a helpful person.
    (C) He always comes late to dinner.
    (D) His roommate likes him a lot.

20. (A) It was sad.
    (B) It was believable.
    (C) It was boring.
    (D) It was funny.

21. (A) In room 301.
    (B) Next door to room 301.
    (C) On another floor.
    (D) In another building.

22. (A) He didn't think she would attend.
    (B) She was the last person to come into the meeting.
    (C) She didn't think the meeting would last long.
    (D) He thought she would be late.

23. (A) Who Marie is.
    (B) Where the newspaper is.
    (C) What picture was in the paper.
    (D) Why Marie's picture appeared.

24. (A) She knew the traffic would be heavy.
    (B) She was sure that the flight would be late.
    (C) She told the man to leave earlier.
    (D) She just returned from Boston herself.

25. (A) He's sorry it's going out of business.
    (B) He doesn't know when it's open.
    (C) It has moved to another location.
    (D) It's not a very good restaurant.

26. (A) He wanted a large hamburger.
    (B) He ordered a small drink, not a large one.
    (C) He didn't call the waiter.
    (D) He thinks the drink looks small.

27. (A) Do some work in the yard.
    (B) Play softball.
    (C) Go to a bookstore.
    (D) Buy some wood.

28. (A) She didn't need to practice.
    (B) She was feeling much better.
    (C) She didn't belong to the choir anymore.
    (D) She was too sick to go out.

29. (A) She has no information about it.
    (B) There was an announcement about it on the radio.
    (C) Someone told her about it.
    (D) She read about it somewhere.

30. (A) He will stay at the Sherman Hotel.
    (B) The Buckley House is preferable.
    (C) A decision must be made soon.
    (D) He doesn't have to attend the conference.

PART B

Directions: This part of the test consists of extended conversations between two speakers. After each of these conversations there are a number of questions. You will hear each conversation and question only once, and the questions are *not* written out.

When you have heard the questions, read the four answer choices and select the *one*—(A), (B), (C), or (D)—that best answers the question based on what is directly stated or on what can be inferred. Then fill in the space on your answer sheet that matches the letter of the answer that you have selected.

Don't forget: During actual exams, taking notes or writing in your test book is *not* permitted.

31. (A) Go to a meeting of the fencing club.
   (B) Watch a fencing match.
   (C) Review for an exam.
   (D) Attend a physical education class.

32. (A) Speed.
   (B) Concentration.
   (C) Strength.
   (D) Agility.

33. (A) Both are fast-moving sports.
   (B) Both depend on good tactics.
   (C) Both provide a lot of exercise.
   (D) Both require a lot of training.

34. (A) Required textbooks.
   (B) Used books.
   (C) Books on a "suggested readings" list.
   (D) Children's books.

35. (A) At the beginning.
   (B) After three weeks.
   (C) Around the middle.
   (D) Near the end.

36. (A) $40.
   (B) $80.
   (C) $120.
   (D) $160.

37. (A) If a student has written a note in it.
   (B) If it was purchased at another store.
   (C) If a professor decides to use another text.
   (D) If it is more than a year old.

PART C

Directions: This part of the test consists of several talks, each given by a single speaker. After each of these talks there are a number of questions. You will hear each talk and question only once, and the questions are *not* written out.

When you have heard the question, read the four answer choices and select the *one*—(A), (B), (C), or (D)—that best answers the question based on what is directly stated or on what can be inferred. Then fill in the space on your answer sheet that matches the letter of the answer that you have selected.

Here is an example.

You will hear:

M1: Students, this evening we'll have a chance to observe a phenomenon that we've discussed several times in class. Tonight, there will be a lunar eclipse. As we've said, when an eclipse of the moon occurs, the earth passes between the sun and the moon. Therefore, the shadow of the earth moves across the surface of the moon and obscures it. Because you won't be looking at the sun, it is not necessary to use the special lenses and filters that you need when observing a solar eclipse. You can observe a lunar eclipse with your unaided eye or with a telescope and photograph it with an ordinary camera. So if the weather's not cloudy tonight, go out and take a look at this eclipse of the moon. I'm sure you'll find it interesting.

Now here is a sample question.

You will hear:

M2: In what course is this lecture probably being given?

You will read:

(**A**) Philosophy.
(**B**) Meteorology.
(**C**) Astronomy.
(**D**) Photography.

The lecture concerns a lunar eclipse, a topic that would typically be discussed in an astronomy class. The choice that best answers the question "In what course is this lecture probably being given?" is (C), "Astronomy." You should fill in (C) on your answer sheet.

Sample Answer

Here is another sample question.

You will hear:

M2: According to the speaker, which of the following occurs during a lunar eclipse?

You will read:

(**A**) The earth's shadow moves across the moon.
(**B**) Clouds block the view of the moon.
(**C**) The moon moves between the earth and the sun.
(**D**) The sun can be observed without special equipment.

From the lecture, you learn that a lunar eclipse occurs when the earth moves between the sun and the moon and the shadow of the earth passes across the moon. The choice that best answers the question "According to the speaker, which of the following occurs during a lunar eclipse?" is (A), "The earth's shadow moves across the moon." Don't forget: During actual exams, taking notes or writing in your test book is *not* permitted.

Sample Answer

38. (A) A professor.
(B) An architecture student.
(C) A professional architect.
(D) An interior designer.

39. (A) Auto tires.
(B) A solar-powered generator.
(C) Straw and mud.
(D) A water pump.

40. (A) Visited an Earthship.
(B) Interviewed the inventor.
(C) Built an Earthship himself.
(D) Read books about Earthships.

41. (A) A room in an Earthship.
(B) A large Earthship.
(C) A group of Earthships.
(D) A small Earthship.

42. (A) A photograph.
(B) An architectural design.
(C) An architectural model.
(D) A book of plans.

43. (A) Once.
(B) Twice.
(C) Three times.
(D) Four times.

44. (A) The heaviest kite.
(B) The kite with the most unusual shape.
(C) The kite that flies the highest.
(D) The funniest kite.

45. (A) Only engineering students.
(B) Only young children.
(C) Any Central State University student.
(D) Anyone who wants to enter.

46. (A) Saturday at the commons.
(B) Saturday on top of the Engineering Tower.
(C) Sunday at the commons.
(D) Sunday at the stadium.

47. (A) Potluck dinners.
(B) A Native American ceremony.
(C) Marriage customs.
(D) The economy of the Pacific Northwest.

48. (A) Only the Kwakiutl tribe.
(B) All Native American tribes.
(C) Only tribes in British Columbia.
(D) All the tribes in the Pacific Northwest.

49. (A) To receive valuable gifts.
(B) To celebrate his birthday.
(C) To improve his social position.
(D) To taste different dishes.

50. (A) They cost the host so much money.
(B) The guests had to have potlatches in turn.
(C) The guests brought money and valuables.
(D) The host's children had to have similar ceremonies.

THIS IS THE END OF SECTION 1.

STOP WORK ON SECTION 1.

DO NOT READ OR WORK ON ANY OTHER SECTION OF THE TEST.

Section 2

This section tests your ability to recognize grammar and usage suitable for standard written English. It is divided into two parts, each with its own directions.

SENTENCE COMPLETION

Directions: Items in this part are incomplete sentences. Following each of these sentences, there are four words or phrases. You should select the *one* word or phrase—(A), (B), (C), or (D)—that best completes the sentence. Then fill in the space on your answer sheet that matches the letter of the answer that you have selected.

Example I

Pepsin _____ an enzyme used in digestion.

(A) that
(B) is
(C) of
(D) being

This sentence should properly read "Pepsin is an enzyme used in digestion." You should fill in (B) on your answer sheet.

Sample Answer

Ⓐ ● Ⓒ Ⓓ

Example II

_____ large natural lakes are found in the state of South Carolina.

(A) There are no
(B) Not the
(C) It is not
(D) No

This sentence should properly read "No large natural lakes are found in the state of South Carolina." You should fill in (D) on your answer sheet. As soon as you understand the directions, begin work on this part.

Sample Answer

Ⓐ Ⓑ Ⓒ ●

1. Indian summer is a period of mild weather _____ during the autumn.

   (A) occurs
   (B) occurring
   (C) it occurs
   (D) is occurring

2. Bacteria may be round, _____, or spiral.

   (A) rod shapes
   (B) in the shape of rods
   (C) like a rod's shape
   (D) rod-shaped

3. _____ of his childhood home in Hannibal, Missouri, provided Mark Twain with the inspiration for two of his most popular novels.

   (A) Remembering
   (B) Memories
   (C) It was the memories
   (D) He remembered

4. Most of the spices and many of the herbs _____ today originate from plants native to tropical regions.

   (A) using
   (B) use of
   (C) in use
   (D) are used

5. _____ many improvements made to highways during the nineteenth century, but Americans continued to depend on water routes for transportation.

   (A) Despite the
   (B) There were
   (C) However
   (D) Though there were

6. There are believed _____ over 300 species of trees in El Yunque rain forest in Puerto Rico.

   (A) to be
   (B) being
   (C) they are
   (D) there are

7. First performed in 1976, _____.

   (A) William Lane wrote the one-character play *The Belle of Amherst* about the life of Emily Dickinson
   (B) the life of Emily Dickinson was the subject of the one-character play *The Belle of Amherst* by William Lane
   (C) William Lane's one-character play *The Belle of Amherst* was about the life of Emily Dickinson
   (D) there was only one character in William Lane's play *The Belle of Amherst* about the life of Emily Dickinson

8. Minnesota's thousands of lakes _____ over 4,000 square miles.

   (A) that cover
   (B) covering
   (C) are covered
   (D) cover

9. Mushrooms have no vascular tissue, they reproduce by means of spores, and they _____ chlorophyll.

   (A) lack
   (B) no
   (C) without
   (D) not have

10. _____ get older, the games they play become increasingly complex.

    (A) Children
    (B) Children, when they
    (C) As children
    (D) For children to

11. _____ is the ancestor of most types of domestic ducks is well documented.

    (A) That the mallard
    (B) The mallard
    (C) Because the mallard
    (D) The mallard that

12. Rarely _____ last longer than an hour.

    (A) do tornados
    (B) tornados
    (C) tordados that
    (D) tornados do

13. Adobe bricks tend to crumble if _____ to excessive moisture or cold.

    (A) they expose
    (B) exposed
    (C) are exposed
    (D) to be exposed

14. _____ play *Alison's House*, the author Susan Glaspell won a Pulitzer Prize in 1931.

    (A) Her
    (B) By her
    (C) It was her
    (D) For her

15. _____ type of insects that pollinate plants.

    (A) Not only are the bees
    (B) Bees are not the only
    (C) Not the only bees are
    (D) Bees are not only the

ERROR IDENTIFICATION

Directions: The items in this part have four underlined words or phrases. You must identify the *one* underlined expression—(A), (B), (C), or (D)—that must be changed for the sentence to be correct. Then fill in the space on your answer sheet that matches the letter of the answer that you have selected.

Example I

Lenses may to have either concave or convex shapes.
  A   B   C   D

This sentence should read "Lenses may have either concave or convex shapes." You should therefore select choice (A).

Sample Answer

● Ⓑ Ⓒ Ⓓ

Example II

When painting a fresco, an artist is applied paint directly to the damp plaster of a wall.
  A   B   C   D

This sentence should read "When painting a fresco, an artist applies paint directly to the wet plaster of a wall." You should therefore select choice (B). As soon as you understand the directions, begin work on this part.

Sample Answer

Ⓐ ● Ⓒ Ⓓ

16. Machines <u>used</u> to harvest tree crops,
            A
<u>such as</u> cherries and almonds, can be
 B
classified <u>both</u> as shakers <u>or</u> as pickup
       C   **D**
machines.

17. An extended family consists <u>not only</u> of
                       A
parents and <u>children</u> but also of <u>others</u>
        B   **C**
relatives, such as grandparents and
<u>unmarried</u> aunts and uncles.
 D

18. Draft horses <u>are</u> the <u>tallest</u>, most <u>powerful</u>,
          A   **B**   **C**
and <u>heavy</u> group of horses.
     D

19. The <u>sculptor</u> John Rogers produced many
     A
<u>replica</u> of <u>his</u> bronze <u>statues</u>.
  B   **C**   **D**

20. Archaeological sites are sometimes <u>revealed</u>
        A
<u>when</u> the <u>construction</u> of roads
  B   **C**
<u>and buildings</u>.
    D

21. Acting teacher Stella Adler <u>played</u> a
      A   **B**
pivotal role in the <u>develop</u> of the <u>Method</u>
  C   **D**
School of acting.

22. Medical students must <u>learning</u> both the
                 A
<u>theory</u> and the <u>practice</u> of <u>medicine</u>.
  B   **C**   **D**

23. The first <u>recorded</u> use of natural gas to <u>light</u>
        A   **B**
street lamps <u>it</u> was in <u>the</u> town of Freder-
       C   **D**
ick, New York, in 1825.

24. Quinine, cinnamon, and other <u>useful</u>
                    A
substances <u>are</u> all derived <u>of</u> the
       B   **C**
<u>bark</u> of trees.
 D

25. Although the social sciences <u>different</u> a
                      A
great deal <u>from</u> one another, they share a
    B   **C**
common interest in human <u>relationships</u>.
                 D

26. Admiral Grace Hopper <u>created</u> the
               A
computer language COBOL, <u>which</u> is used
             B
<u>primary</u> for scientific <u>purposes</u>.
  C   **D**

27. Unlike competitive <u>running</u>, race walkers
            A
<u>must always</u> keep some portion of <u>their</u>
     B   **C**
feet in contact <u>with</u> the ground.
         D

28. Henry David Thoreau's book *Walden: A Life*
in the Woods is <u>a</u> record of <u>his</u> <u>simply</u>
          A   **B** **C**
existence in a cabin on Walden Pond.
     D

29. A promissory note is a <u>written agreement</u>
                    A
<u>to pay</u> a certain sum of money <u>at some</u>
  B   **C**
<u>time future</u>.
    D

30. Mario Pei helped <u>provide</u> the world <u>with</u> a
              A   **B**
popular <u>understand</u> of <u>linguistics</u>.
     C   **D**

31. Even <u>though</u> they are among <u>the smallest</u>
    A   **B**
carnivores, weasels will attack animals <u>that</u>
                        C
are <u>double</u> their size.
    D

32. Wilson Alwyn Bentley was a Vermont
farmer <u>who</u> <u>took</u> over 6,000 <u>close-up</u>
    A   **B**   **C**
photographs of snowflakes during <u>the</u>
                    D
lifetime.

33. New York City <u>surpassed</u> the other Atlantic
          A
seaports in <u>partly</u> because it <u>developed</u> the
      B   **C**
best transportation links <u>with</u> the interior of
                 D
the country.

34. All of mammals, dolphins are undoubtedly
     A   B
among the friendliest to humans.
  C   D

35. Harmonize, melody, and rhythm are
      A   B
important elements in most forms of music.
              C   D

36. When babies are around fifteen months old,
     A
they can pick up objects and put
  B   C
themselves into small containers.
    D

37. Loblolly pines, chiefly found in the South-
         A
eastern United States, has strong wood used
           B
as lumber and for paper pulp.
  C   D

38. All root vegetables grow underground, and
     A   B
not all vegetables that grow underground
                    C
are roots.
  D

39. Tiny pygmy shrews breathe ten
                A
times as fast as humans beings.
  B   C   D

40. Before diamonds can be used as jewels,
     A   B
they must be cut and polish.
    C   D

THIS IS THE END OF SECTION 2.

IF YOU FINISH BEFORE THE TIME LIMIT, CHECK YOUR WORK ON SECTION 2 ONLY.

DO NOT READ OR WORK ON ANY OTHER SECTION OF THE TEST.

Section 3

This section of the test measures your ability to comprehend written materials.

Directions: This section contains several passages, each followed by a number of questions. Read the passages and, for each question, choose the *one* best answer—(A), (B), (C), or (D)—based on what is stated in the passage or on what can be inferred from the passage. Then fill in the space on your answer sheet that matches the letter of the answer that you have selected.

Read the Following Passage

Line   Like mammals, birds claim their own territories. A bird's territory may be small or large. Some birds claim only their nest and the area right around it, while others claim far larger territories that include their feeding areas. Gulls, penguins, and other waterfowl nest in huge colonies, but even in the biggest colonies, each male and his mate have small territories of their own

5   immediately around their nests.

Male birds defend their territory chiefly against other males of the same species. In some cases, a warning call or threatening pose may be all the defense needed, but in other cases, intruders may refuse to leave peacefully.

Example I

What is the main topic of this passage?

(A) Birds that live in colonies
(B) Birds' mating habits
(C) The behavior of birds
(D) Territoriality in birds

The passage mainly concerns the territories of birds. You should fill in (D) on your answer sheet.

Sample Answer

Ⓐ Ⓑ Ⓒ ⬤

Example II

According to the passage, male birds defend their territory primarily against which of the following?

(A) Female birds
(B) Birds of other species
(C) Males of their own species
(D) Mammals

The passage states that "Male birds defend their territory chiefly against other males of the same species." You should fill in (C) on your answer sheet. As soon as you understand the directions, begin work on this section.

Sample Answer

Ⓐ Ⓑ ⬤ Ⓓ

Questions 1–12

Line   Galaxies are not evenly distributed throughout the universe. A few are found alone, but almost all are
grouped in formations termed *galactic clusters*. These formations should not be confused with stellar
clusters, globular clusters of stars that exist within a galaxy. The size of galactic clusters varies
enormously, with some clusters containing only a dozen or so members and others containing as
5   many as 10,000. Moreover, galactic clusters themselves are part of larger clusters of clusters, termed
superclusters. It is surmised that even clusters of superclusters are possible.

Our galaxy, the Milky Way, is part of a galactic cluster called the Local Group, which has
twenty members and is typical in terms of the types of galaxies it contains. There are three large
spiral galaxies: Andromeda, the largest galaxy in the group; the Milky Way, the second-largest galaxy;
10   and the Triangulum Spiral, the third largest. There are also four medium-sized spiral galaxies, including the Large Cloud of Magellan and the Small Cloud of Magellan. There are four regular elliptical
galaxies; the remainder are dwarf ellipticals. Other than our own galaxy, only Andromeda and the
Clouds of Magellan can be seen with the naked eye, and the Clouds are visible only from the
Southern Hemisphere.

15   In the vicinity of the Local Group are several clusters, each containing around twelve members.
The nearest cluster rich in members is the Virgo Cluster, which contains thousands of galaxies of all
types. Like most large clusters, it emits X rays. The Local Group, the small neighboring clusters, and
the Virgo Cluster form part of a much larger cluster of clusters—the Local Supercluster.

The existence of galactic clusters presented a riddle to scientists for many years—the "missing
20   mass" problem. Clusters are presumably held together by the gravity generated by their members.
However, measurements showed that the galaxies did not have enough mass to explain their
apparent stability. Why didn't these clusters disintegrate? It is now thought that galaxies contain great
amounts of "dark matter," which cannot be directly observed but that generates gravitational pull.
This matter includes gas, dust, burnt-out stars, and even black holes.

1. Which of the following does the passage mainly discuss?

   (A) Clusters and superclusters of galaxies
   (B) An astronomical problem that has never been solved
   (C) A recent development in astronomy
   (D) The incredible distance between galaxies

2. The word *evenly* in line 1 is closest in meaning to

   (A) uniformly.
   (B) predictably.
   (C) relatively.
   (D) paradoxically.

3. What conclusion can be made about galaxies that are not found in clusters?

   (A) They have never been observed.
   (B) They are larger than other galaxies.
   (C) They are not actually galaxies but parts of galaxies.
   (D) They are outnumbered by galaxies that do occur in clusters.

4. The word *globular* in line 3 is closest in meaning to

   (A) immense.
   (B) spherical.
   (C) dense.
   (D) brilliant.

5. The author would probably characterize the existence of clusters of superclusters as

   (A) impossible.
   (B) surprising.
   (C) theoretical.
   (D) certain.

6. According to the passage, in what way is the Local Group typical of galactic clusters?

   (A) In its size
   (B) In the number of galaxies it contains
   (C) In its shape
   (D) In the types of galaxies that make it up

7. In the Local Group, which of the following types of galaxies are most numerous?

   (A) Large spirals
   (B) Medium-sized spirals
   (C) Regular ellipticals
   (D) Dwarf ellipticals

8. All of the following are visible from somewhere on Earth without a telescope EXCEPT

(A) the Clouds of Magellan.
(B) Andromeda.
(C) the Triangulum Spiral.
(D) the Milky Way.

9. According to the passage, the Local Group and the Virgo Cluster have which of the following in common?

(A) Both are rich in galaxies.
(B) Both emit X rays.
(C) Both are part of the same supercluster.
(D) Both are small clusters.

10. The word *riddle* in line 19 is closest in meaning to

(A) tool.
(B) puzzle.
(C) theory.
(D) clue.

11. Which of the following is NOT true about the *dark matter* mentioned in line 23?

(A) It is impossible to observe directly.
(B) It may include black holes.
(C) It helps explain the "missing mass" problem.
(D) It is found in the space between galaxies.

12. As used throughout the passage, the word *members* refers to

(A) stars.
(B) galaxies.
(C) scientists.
(D) clusters.

Questions 13–24

Line The Roman alphabet took thousands of years to develop, from the picture writing of the ancient
Egyptians through modifications by Phoenicians, Greeks, Romans, and others. Yet in just a dozen
years, one man, Sequoyah, invented an alphabet for the Cherokee people. Born in eastern Tennessee,
Sequoyah was a hunter and a silversmith in his youth, as well as an able interpreter who knew
5   Spanish, French, and English.

Sequoyah wanted his people to have the secret of the "talking leaves," as he called the books of
white people, and so he set out to design a written form of Cherokee. His chief aim was to record
his people's ancient tribal customs. He began by designing pictographs for every word in the
Cherokee vocabulary. Reputedly his wife, angry at him for his neglect of garden and house, burned
10   his notes, and he had to start over. This time, having concluded that picture-writing was cumbersome, he made symbols for the sounds of the Cherokee language. Eventually he refined his system to
eighty-five characters, which he borrowed from the Roman, Greek, and Hebrew alphabets. He
presented this system to the Cherokee General Council in 1821, and it was wholeheartedly approved.
The response was phenomenal. Cherokees who had struggled for months to learn English lettering in
15   school picked up the new system in days. Several books were printed in Cherokee, and in 1828, a
newspaper, the *Cherokee Phoenix*, was first published in the new alphabet. Sequoyah was acclaimed
by his people.

In his later life, Sequoyah dedicated himself to the general advancement of his people. He went
to Washington, D.C., as a representative of the Western tribes. He helped settle bitter differences
20   among Cherokee after their forced movement by the federal government to the Oklahoma territory in
the 1830s. He died in Mexico in 1843 while searching for groups of lost Cherokee. A statue of
Sequoyah represents Oklahoma in the Statuary Hall in the Capitol building in Washington, D.C.
However, he is probably chiefly remembered today because sequoias, the giant redwood trees of
California, are named for him.

13. The passage is mainly concerned with

(A) the development of the Roman alphabet.
(B) the accomplishments of Sequoyah.
(C) the pictographic system of writing.
(D) Sequoyah's experiences in Mexico.

14. According to the passage, how long did it take to develop the Cherokee alphabet?

(A) Twelve years
(B) Twenty years
(C) Eighty-five years
(D) Thousands of years

15. There is NO indication in the passage that, as a young man, Sequoyah

(A) served as an interpreter.
(B) made things from silver.
(C) served as a representative in Washington.
(D) hunted game.

16. According to the passage, Sequoyah used the phrase *talking leaves* (line 6) to refer to

(A) redwood trees.
(B) books.
(C) symbols for sounds.
(D) newspapers.

17. What was Sequoyah's main purpose in designing a Cherokee alphabet?

(A) To record Cherokee customs
(B) To write books in Cherokee
(C) To write about his own life
(D) To publish a newspaper

18. The word *cumbersome* in line 10 is closest in meaning to

(A) awkward.
(B) radical.
(C) simplistic.
(D) unfamiliar.

19. In the final version of the Cherokee alphabet system, each of the characters represents a

(A) word.
(B) picture.
(C) sound.
(D) thought.

20. All of the following were mentioned in the passage as alphabet systems that Sequoyah borrowed from EXCEPT

(A) Egyptian.

(B) Roman.

(C) Hebrew.

(D) Greek.

21. The word *wholeheartedly* in line 13 is closest in meaning to

(A) unanimously.

(B) enthusiastically.

(C) immediately.

(D) ultimately.

22. According to the passage, a memorial statue of Sequoyah is located in

(A) Oklahoma.

(B) Mexico.

(C) Tennessee.

(D) Washington, D.C.

23. Why does the author mention the giant redwood trees of California in the passage?

(A) Sequoyah took his name from those trees.

(B) The trees inspired Sequoyah to write a book.

(C) Sequoyah was born in the vicinity of the redwood forest.

(D) The trees were named in Sequoyah's honor.

24. The author begins to describe the Cherokees' reaction to the invention of a written language in

(A) lines 2-3.

(B) lines 7-8.

(C) lines 14-17.

(D) lines 18-19.

QUESTIONS 25–32

Line For a long time, amphibians were confused with reptiles. Like reptiles, they have three-chambered
hearts and are cold-blooded. Some amphibians, such as salamanders, are even shaped like lizards.
However, unlike reptiles, amphibians never have claws on their toes or scales on their bodies.
Furthermore, the eggs of amphibians lack shells, so they must be laid in water or moist places.

5   Amphibians were the first creatures to spend sizable amounts of their lives on land. The larvae
of most amphibians, such as frog tadpoles, are born with gills and live in water. However, their gills
disappear as they develop lungs. Most retain the ability to breathe through the moist surface of their
skin. This comes in handy when they hibernate in the bottom mud of lakes and ponds during the
coldest months. They take in the small amount of oxygen they need through their skin. Some

10 amphibians undergo what is known as a "double metamorphosis," changing not only from gill
breathers to lung breathers but also from vegetarians to insectivores.

         Although the amphibian class is rather small in number of species, it shows great diversity.
There are three major types. The caecilians of the tropics are long, legless, burrowing creatures.
Caudate amphibians, such as newts and salamanders, mostly have long tails and stubby legs. Salien-

15 tians, which include both frogs and toads, are tailless as adults and have powerful hind legs. Toads
differ from frogs primarily in that they have dry, warty skin.

25. The author's main purpose in writing the passage is to

 (A) define and describe amphibians.
 (B) contrast different types of amphibians.
 (C) trace the development of amphibians from larvae to adults.
 (D) explain how amphibians differ from other creatures.

26. According to the passage, which of the following is NOT a characteristic of amphibians?

 (A) They have three-chambered hearts.
 (B) They lay eggs without shells.
 (C) They have claws on their toes.
 (D) They are cold-blooded.

27. As used in line 3, the term *scales* is closest to which of the following in meaning?

 (A) Devices used to measure weight
 (B) Plates covering the bodies of certain animals
 (C) Sounds made by various animals
 (D) Proportions between different sets of dimensions

28. According to the passage, the term *double metamorphosis* (line 10) refers to the fact that amphibians

 (A) first breathe through their gills, then through their lungs, then through their skin.
 (B) change both the shape of their bodies and the way in which they lay eggs.
 (C) first live in the water, then on land, then in mud in the bottom of ponds and lakes.
 (D) change both their methods of breathing and their feeding habits.

29. It can be inferred from the passage that amphibians' ability to breathe through their skin is especially useful during the

 (A) summer.
 (B) fall.
 (C) winter.
 (D) spring.

30. All of the following are identified in the passage as amphibians EXCEPT

 (A) newts.
 (B) salamanders.
 (C) caecilians.
 (D) lizards.

31. The word *stubby* in line 14 is closest in meaning to

 (A) long and thin.
 (B) undeveloped.
 (C) thick and short.
 (D) powerful.

32. In line 16, the word *they* refers to

 (A) toads.
 (B) tails.
 (C) adults.
 (D) frogs.

QUESTIONS 33–44

Line   The first animated film, *Humorous Phases of Funny Faces*, was made in 1906 by newspaper
illustrator James Blackton. He filmed faces that were drawn on a blackboard in progressive stages. In
New York City, Winsor McCay exhibited his most famous films, *Little Nemo* (1910) and *Gertie the
Dinosaur* (1914). His films featured fluid motion and characters with individual personalities. For the
5   first time, characters drawn of lines seemed to live on the screen. In 1914, John R. Bray streamlined
the animation process, using assembly-line techniques to turn out cartoons.

By 1915, film studios began producing cartoon series. The Pat Sullivan studio produced the
series featuring Felix the Cat. He became one of the most beloved characters of the silent-film era.
The Max Fleischer studio produced series starring Ko-Ko the Clown and, later, Betty Boop and
10   Popeye.

The first cartoon with sound was *Steamboat Willie* (1928), which introduced Mickey Mouse.
This film was produced by Walt Disney, the most famous of American animators. His early success
enabled Disney to train his animators in anatomy, acting, drawing, and motion studies. The results of
this are apparent in *Snow White and the Seven Dwarfs* (1937), the first full-length animated feature.
15   It became an instant success, and still remains popular. Other important Disney films followed.

Warner Brothers' studio challenged Disney for leadership in the field with cartoons starring
Bugs Bunny, Daffy Duck, and other characters. These films were faster-paced and featured slapstick
humor. In the 1950s, a group of animators splintered off from Disney and formed United Production
of America, which rejected Disney's realism and employed a bold, modernistic approach.
20   In the 1950s, children's cartoons began to be broadcast on Saturday morning television and,
later, in prime time. Among the most successful were those made by William Hanna and Joseph
Barbera, such as those featuring Yogi Bear and the Flintstones.

The full-length animated film became popular again in the 1980s and 1990s. Producer Steven
Spielberg released his first animated film, *An American Tail* (1986), and Disney began a series of
25   remarkable annual hits with *The Little Mermaid* (1989). *Who Framed Roger Rabbit?* (1988), a joint
production of Spielberg and Disney, blurred the lines between live action and animation. Animation
returned to prime-time television with the Fox Network's *The Simpsons*. Animators had experimented with computer animation as early as the 1950s, but *Toy Story* (1995) was the first full-length
film to be entirely computer animated. These developments promise to bring about the most exciting
30   era in animation since its heyday.

33. What does the passage mainly discuss?

   (A) The history of animated film
   (B) The life of Walt Disney
   (C) The development of one animated
          cartoon
   (D) The use of computers in animation

34. It can be inferred from the passage that the
characters in *Little Nemo* and *Gertie the
Dinosaur*

   (A) were first drawn on a blackboard.
   (B) were part of a cartoon series.
   (C) seemed to have their own personalities.
   (D) did not look as lifelike as Blackton's
          characters.

35. The word *streamlined* in line 5 is closest in
meaning to

   (A) simplified.
   (B) revolutionized.
   (C) bypassed.
   (D) invented.

36. The word *he* in line 8 refers to

   (A) Pat Sullivan.
   (B) Felix the Cat.
   (C) Max Fleischer.
   (D) Ko-Ko the Clown.

37. What can be inferred from the passage
about animated films produced before
1928?

   (A) They were not very popular.
   (B) They were longer than later movies.
   (C) They were not drawn by hand.
   (D) They were silent films.

38. According to the passage, the film *Snow White and the Seven Dwarfs*

    (A) showed the benefits of training the Disney animators.

    (B) was the first movie produced by Walt Disney.

    (C) was the last movie Disney made before his death.

    (D) did not become successful until many years later.

39. The phrase *splintered off from* in line 18 is closest in meaning to

    (A) competed with.

    (B) broke away from.

    (C) merged with.

    (D) released from.

40. The author does NOT specifically mention characters produced by

    (A) Walt Disney.

    (B) Hanna and Barbera.

    (C) United Productions of America.

    (D) Warner Brothers.

41. The phrase *blurred the lines* in line 26 is closest in meaning to

    (A) eliminated the distinctions.

    (B) obscured the issues.

    (C) answered the questions.

    (D) emphasized the problems.

42. The first experiments with computer animation took place during the

    (A) 1950s.

    (B) 1960s.

    (C) 1980s.

    (D) 1990s.

43. Which of the following is closest in meaning to the word *heyday* in line 30?

    (A) Beginning

    (B) Decline

    (C) Prime

    (D) Rebirth

44. Where in the passage does the author first mention animation on television?

    (A) Line 7

    (B) Line 11

    (C) Lines 20–21

    (D) Lines 26–27

QUESTIONS 45-50

Line Fog is a cloud in contact with or just above the surface of land or sea. It can be a major environmental hazard. Fog on highways can cause chain-reaction accidents involving dozens of cars. Delays and shutdowns at airports can cause economic losses to airlines and inconvenience to thousands of travelers. Fog at sea has always been a danger to navigation. Today, with supertankers carrying vast
5   quantities of oil, fog increases the possibility of catastrophic oil spills.

The most common type of fog, radiation fog, forms at night, when moist air near the ground loses warmth through radiation on a clear night. This type of fog often occurs in valleys, such as California's San Joaquin Valley. Another common type, advection fog, results from the movement of warm, wet air over cold ground. The air loses temperature to the ground and condensation sets in.
10   This type of fog often occurs along the California coast and the shores of the Great Lakes. Advection fog also forms when air associated with a warm ocean current blows across the surface of a cold current. The thick fogs of the Grand Banks off Newfoundland, Canada, are largely of this origin, because here the Labrador Current comes in contact with the warm Gulf Stream.

Two other types of fog are somewhat more unusual. Frontal fog occurs when two fronts of
15   different temperatures meet, and rain from the warm front falls into the colder one, saturating the air. Steam fog appears when cold air picks up moisture by moving over warmer water.

45. The first paragraph focuses on which aspect of fog?

(A) Its dangers
(B) Its composition
(C) Its beauty
(D) Its causes

46. The word *catastrophic* in line 5 is closest in meaning to

(A) accidental.
(B) inevitable.
(C) unexpected.
(D) disastrous.

47. According to the article, fog that occurs along the California coast is generally

(A) radiation fog.
(B) advection fog.
(C) frontal fog.
(D) steam fog.

48. It can be inferred from the passage that the Labrador Current is

(A) cold.
(B) weak.
(C) polluted.
(D) warm.

49. The author organizes the discussion of the different types of fog according to

(A) their geographic locations.
(B) their relative density.
(C) the types of problems they cause.
(D) their relative frequency.

50. The author of the passage is probably an expert in the field of

(A) physics.
(B) economics.
(C) transportation.
(D) meteorology.

THIS IS THE END OF SECTION 3.

IF YOU FINISH BEFORE THE TIME LIMIT, CHECK YOUR WORK ON SECTION 3 ONLY.

DO NOT READ OR WORK ON ANY OTHER SECTION OF THE TEST.

Writing Section/TWE

INTRODUCTION

The Writing Section/TWE differs from the rest of the TOEFL Test in that it is **productive**. Instead of choosing one of four answer choices, you must write your own short essay. It consists of a single essay topic; there is no choice as to what to write about. You have 30 minutes in which to write an essay based on the topic. A typical answer is about 200 to 300 words long and is divided into four or five paragraphs.

The most common type of topic asks you to write a contrast/opinion essay. In this type of essay, you must contrast two points of view, then defend one of those positions. Another type of essay asks you to select some development, invention, or phenomenon and explain its importance. Essay topics that ask you to interpret the information given in a graph or chart are no longer given.

RED ALERT

TEN KEYS TO WRITING THE ESSAY

Key #1
Budget your time carefully.

You have only a half hour in which to complete your work. You should use your time more or less as shown below:

Reading and thinking about the topic	2-3 minutes
Planning and taking notes	2-3 minutes
Writing the essay	20 minutes
Checking the essay	3-5 minutes

As with all parts of the TOEFL test, be familiar with the directions for the writing section so that you don't have to waste time reading them.

Key #2
Read the question carefully.

You must write on the topic exactly as it is given, so be sure that you understand it. If you write about another topic, you won't receive a score at all. If you don't completely address the topic, you will receive a lower score.

Key #3
Brainstorm!

Before you begin to write, spend a minute or two "brainstorming." Think about the topic and the best way to approach it. Remember: there is no "correct" answer for the writing section questions. You can choose to support any position as long as you can adequately support your choice. Jot down any ideas you have while you're brainstorming.

Key #4
Plan your essay before you write.

You don't have to write out a formal outline with Roman numerals, capital letters, and so on. However, you *should* make some notes. By following your notes, you can organize your essay *before* you write, leaving you free to concentrate on the task of writing.

When making notes, don't worry about writing complete, grammatical sentences; use abbreviations if possible. The point of taking notes is to simply get your ideas down on paper as quickly as possible.

Key #5
Be sure your handwriting is as clear and legible as possible.

Handwriting that is hard to read may unconsciously prejudice the readers who are grading your essay. Be sure your handwriting is not too small or too large.

Key #6
Follow a clear, logical organization.

All essays should consist of three basic parts: an **introductory paragraph**, a **body** that consists of two or three paragraphs, and a **concluding paragraph**. You need to include all of these elements in your essay. The introduction states the main idea of the essay in one sentence called the **thesis statement** and may provide some background about that idea. The body develops the main idea brought up in the introduction.

Specific examples are given to make the thesis statement seem stronger and more believable to the reader. The conclusion evaluates and summarizes the material that is in the body. It provides the reader with a sense of closure—the feeling that the essay is really finished, not that the writer simply ran out of time.

The exact plan of organization you use depends on the type of topic you are given. The following patterns could be used for the two main types of topics commonly given. Of course, these are not the only patterns that could be used in writing essays, but they are effective plans for organizing your ideas.

TOPIC TYPE A: CONTRAST/OPINION

Introduction: Paragraph 1: Present the two sides of the issue; give a brief amount of background information.

Body: Paragraph 2: Discuss the negative side of the issue; give examples.

Paragraph 3: Discuss the positive side of the issue; give examples.

Conclusion: Paragraph 4: Express your own opinion about the issue; give specific reasons for your decision.

TOPIC TYPE B: EXPLAIN THE IMPORTANCE OF A DEVELOPMENT, INVENTION, OR PHENOMENON

Introduction: Paragraph 1: Explain what development you have chosen to write about and why.

Body: Paragraph 2: Discuss one aspect of why this development is important; give examples.

Paragraph 3: Discuss another aspect of why this development is important; give examples.

Conclusion: Paragraph 4: Summarize the points made in Paragraphs 2 and 3.

Key #7

Use concrete examples and specific reasons.

Whenever you make a general statement, you should support it with specific examples. Don't just say, "Computers are important to modern business." Give specific examples of how computers can benefit businesses. If you state an opinion, give reasons. Don't just say, "I believe television is harmful to children." Explain exactly why you think television hurts children.

Key #8

Use signal words to indicate transitions.

Signal words can be used to join paragraph to paragraph and sentence to sentence. These words make your essay clearer and easier to follow. Some of these expressions and their meanings are given below.

Expressions Used to List Points, Examples, or Reasons

First example or reason
> First . . .
> The first example is . . .
> The first reason it . . .

Additional examples or reasons
> Second, . . . (Third, Fourth)
> A second (third, fourth) example is that . . .
> Another example is . . .
> Another reason is . . .
> In addition, . . .
> Furthermore, . . .
> Moreover, . . .

Final examples or reasons
> Finally, . . .

To give individual examples
> For example, . . .
> For instance, . . .
> To give a specific example, . . .
> *X* is an example of *Y*.

To show contrast
> However, . . .
> On the other hand, . . .
> Nevertheless, . . .

To show a conclusion
> Therefore, . . .
> Consequently, . . .

To show similarity
> Likewise, . . .
> Similarly, . . .

To begin a concluding paragraph
> In conclusion, . . .
> In summary, . . .

Examples of the Use of Signal Words

I agree with the idea of stricter gun control for a number of reasons. *First*, statistics show that guns are not very effective in preventing crime. *Second*, accidents involving guns occur frequently. *Finally*, guns can be stolen and later used in crimes.

I believe that a good salary is an important consideration when looking for a career. *However,* the nature of the work is more important to me. *Thus*, I would not accept a job that I did not find rewarding.

For me, the reasons for living in an urban area are stronger than the reasons for living in a rural community. *Therefore*, I agree with those people who believe it is an advantage to live in a big city.

Key #9

Use a variety of sentence types.

Good writing in English consists of a more or less equal balance between short, simple sentences consisting of only one clause and longer sentences containing two or more clauses. Therefore, make an effort to use sentences of various lengths.

You should also vary sentence structures. Begin some sentences with prepositional phrases or subordinate clauses.

Examples of various sentence types

Instead of . . .

I agree with this idea for several reasons.

Try . . .

For several reasons, I agree with this idea.

Instead of . . .

I support Idea A even though Idea B has some positive attributes.

Try . . .

Even though Idea B has some positive attributes, I support Idea A.

Key #10

Check your essay for errors.

Allow a few minutes to proofread the essay. However, don't make any major changes at this time. Don't cross out long sections or try to add a lot of new material. Look for obvious errors in punctuation, spelling, and capitalization as well as common grammatical mistakes: subject-verb agreement, wrong tense, incorrect use of plurals, incorrect word forms, and so on. If you have ever taken a writing class in English, look at the corrections the teacher made on your papers to see what types of mistakes you commonly make, and look for these.

FOUR PRACTICE WRITING SECTION/TWE TESTS

The following exams are similar to actual writing sections. Time yourself carefully while taking these practice tests. You can use the scoring information on page 157 to estimate your score. If you are taking an English course, you may want to ask your English teacher to score your test and to make recommendations for improving your essay.

PRACTICE WRITING SECTION/TWE—30 MINUTES

1. When you are ready, go to the next page and carefully read the essay prompt.

2. Before you begin writing, think about the prompt. You will probably want to make some notes to organize your thoughts. Use only the space marked NOTES to write notes or an outline.

3. Write on only one topic. If you do not write on the topic given, you will not receive a score.

4. Your essay should be clear and precise. Support your ideas with facts. The quality of your writing is more important than the quantity, but you will probably want to write more than one paragraph.

5. Begin your essay on the first line of the essay page. Use the next page if you need to. Write as neatly as possible. Don't write in large letters. Don't skip lines or leave large margins.

6. Check your essay after you have finished. Give yourself enough time to read over your essay and make minor revisions before the end of the exam.

7. After 30 minutes, stop writing and put your pencil down.

PRACTICE WRITING SECTION/TWE 1

Some people believe that it is more advantageous to study at a small college or university. Others take the opposite view, that a large college or university offers better educational opportunities. Discuss these two positions. Tell which one you agree with, and explain your decision.

NOTES

Use this space for essay notes only. Write the final version of your essay on the next two pages.

Name: _____

Write your essay here.

_____

_____

_____

_____

_____

_____

_____

_____

_____

_____

_____

_____

_____

_____

_____

_____

_____

_____

_____

_____

_____

_____

_____

_____

_____

144

PRACTICE WRITING SECTION/TWE 2

One reason that a job is desirable is a good salary. Choose one other factor that you think is important in choosing a job. Give specific reasons for your choice.

NOTES

Use this space for essay notes only. Write the final version of your essay on the next two pages.

Name: _____

Write your essay here.

_____

_____

_____

_____

_____

_____

_____

_____

_____

_____

_____

_____

_____

_____

_____

_____

_____

_____

_____

_____

_____

_____

_____

PRACTICE WRITING SECTION/TWE 3

The use of modern technology has had significant effects on many fields. For example, the use of modern communication devices and computers has practically revolutionized the banking industry. Select another industry, profession, or field of study that has been influenced by modern technology. Give specific examples of the effects technology has had on that field.

NOTES

Use this space for essay notes only. Write the final version of your essay on the next two pages.

_____

_____

_____

_____

_____

_____

_____

_____

_____

_____

_____

_____

_____

_____

_____

_____

_____

_____

_____

Name: _____

Write your essay here.

_____

_____

_____

_____

_____

_____

_____

_____

_____

_____

_____

_____

_____

_____

_____

_____

_____

_____

_____

_____

_____

_____

_____

_____

150

PRACTICE WRITING SECTION/TWE 4

Some people believe that all schoolchildren of a certain age should be educated together. Others take the position that children should be separated into groups, depending on their skills and abilities. Discuss both positions. Tell which one you agree with, and explain why.

NOTES

Use this space for essay notes only. Write the final version of your essay on the next two pages.

_____

_____

_____

_____

_____

_____

_____

_____

_____

_____

_____

_____

_____

_____

_____

_____

_____

_____

_____

_____

_____

Name: _____

Write your essay here.

_____

_____

_____

_____

_____

_____

_____

_____

_____

_____

_____

_____

_____

_____

_____

_____

_____

_____

_____

_____

_____

_____

SCORING THE PRACTICE TESTS

The level of difficulty varies slightly from one TOEFL Test to another. ETS uses a statistical process called "test equating" to adjust each set of scores. The chart given below can be used only to determine a range of scores. ETS, of course, reports your score as a single number, not as a range.

After completing each test, obtain a raw score for each of the three sections by counting the number of correct answers in the three sections. Then look at the score conversion chart to determine the range of scaled scores for each section. Add the three low scores from the range of scores for each section, then the three high scores. Multiply both totals by 10 and divide by 3. Your "actual" TOEFL score will lie somewhere in that range of numbers.

For example, suppose that you had 32 correct answers in Listening, 29 in Structure, and 37 in Reading:

	Raw Score (number correct)	Range of Scaled Scores (from conversion chart)
Section 1	32	49–50
Section 2	29	50–52
Section 3	37	53–54

49 + 50 + 53 = 152
50 + 52 + 54 = 156

152 × 10 = 1,520 ÷ 3 = 507
156 × 10 = 1,560 ÷ 3 = 520

Your score on the practice test would be between 507 and 520.

SCORE CONVERSION CHART I
PRACTICE TESTS 1, 2, 4, AND 5

SECTION 1		SECTION 2		SECTION 3	
RAW SCORES	RANGE OF SCALED SCORES	RAW SCORES	RANGE OF SCALED SCORES	RAW SCORES	RANGE OF SCALED SCORES
48–50	65–68	39–40	64–68	48–50	65–67
45–47	57–64	36–38	60–64	45–47	57–64
42–44	55–57	34–35	57–59	42–44	56–57
39–41	54–55	31–33	53–56	39–41	55–56
36–38	52–54	29–30	50–52	36–38	53–54
33–35	50–52	27–28	49–50	33–35	51–52
30–32	49–50	24–26	48–49	30–32	50–51
27–29	47–48	21–23	46–48	27–29	48–49
24–26	45–47	18–20	43–45	24–26	46–47
21–23	44–45	15–17	39–42	21–23	44–45
18–20	42–44	12–14	36–38	18–20	42–44
15–17	39–41	9–11	32–35	15–17	39–41
12–14	36–38	6–8	28–32	12–14	36–38
9–11	33–36	3–5	24–27	9–11	33–36
6–8	29–32	0–2	20–23	6–8	29–32
3–5	25–28			3–5	25–28
0–2	23–24			0–2	21–24

SCORE CONVERSION CHART II
PRACTICE TEST 3 (LONG FORM)

SECTION 1		SECTION 2		SECTION 3	
RAW SCORES	**RANGE OF SCALED SCORES**	**RAW SCORES**	**RANGE OF SCALED SCORES**	**RAW SCORES**	**RANGE OF SCALED SCORES**
77-80	64-68	58-60	64-68	72-75	65-67
72-76	59-63	54-57	59-63	69-70	61-64
68-71	57-58	50-53	56-58	65-68	58-60
63-67	54-56	45-49	53-55	61-64	56-57
59-62	52-53	41-44	50-52	57-60	54-55
54-58	50-51	36-40	48-49	53-56	53-54
50-53	49-50	32-35	45-47	50-52	51-52
45-49	47-48	27-31	43-44	46-49	49-50
41-44	46-47	23-26	40-42	42-45	47-48
36-40	44-45	18-22	36-39	40-42	45-46
32-35	42-43	14-17	31-35	36-40	43-45
27-31	40-41	9-13	26-30	32-35	40-42
23-26	37-39	5-8	23-25	27-31	38-39
18-22	33-36	0-4	20-22	23-26	35-37
14-17	31-35			18-22	33-34
9-13	26-30			14-17	31-32
5-8	24-25			9-13	27-30
0-4	22-23			5-8	23-26
				0-4	20-22

PERSONAL SCORE RECORD

Practice Test 1			
Section 1 Range of Scores	Section 2 Range of Scores	Section 3 Range of Scores	Total Range of Scores

Practice Test 2			
Section 1 Range of Scores	Section 2 Range of Scores	Section 3 Range of Scores	Total Range of Scores

Practice Test 3			
Section 1 Range of Scores	Section 2 Range of Scores	Section 3 Range of Scores	Total Range of Scores

Practice Test 4			
Section 1 Range of Scores	Section 2 Range of Scores	Section 3 Range of Scores	Total Range of Scores

Practice Test 5			
Section 1 Range of Scores	Section 2 Range of Scores	Section 3 Range of Scores	Total Range of Scores

SCORING THE
PRACTICE WRITING SECTION/TWE TESTS

ETS uses a scoring system similar to the one given below to score essays. You can use this chart to estimate your score when you take the Practice Writing Sections. If you are taking an English course, you may want to ask your teacher to "score" the exam for you, and to make recommendations for improving your essay.

Score   **Explanation of Score**

6 Strongly indicates the ability to write a well-organized, well-developed, and logical essay. Specific examples and details support the main ideas. All the elements of the essay are unified and cohesive. A variety of sentence structures are used successfully, and sophisticated vocabulary is employed. Grammatical errors are infrequent, but a few minor mistakes may occur.

5 Indicates the ability to write an organized, developed, and logical essay. The main ideas are adequately supported by examples and details. Sentence structure may be less varied than that of a level 6 essay, and vocabulary less sophisticated. Some grammatical errors will appear.

4 Indicates a moderate ability to write an acceptable essay. Although main ideas may be adequately supported, weaknesses in organization and development will be apparent. Sentence structure and vocabulary may lack sophistication or be used inappropriately. Grammatical errors may be frequent.

3 Indicates some minimal ability in writing an acceptable essay, but involves serious weaknesses in organization and development. Significant sentence structure and vocabulary problems occur, and there are frequent grammatical errors that sometimes make the writer's ideas difficult to comprehend.

2 Indicates the inability to write an acceptable essay. Organization and development are weak or nonexistent. Lacks unity and cohesion. Few if any specific details may be given in support of the writer's ideas. If details are given, they may seem inappropriate. Significant and frequent errors in grammar occur throughout the essay. The writer may not have fully understood the essay topic.

1 Strongly indicates the inability to write an acceptable essay. No apparent development or organization. Sentences may be brief and fragmentary and unrelated to one another. Significant grammatical errors occur throughout the essay and make it difficult to understand any of the author's ideas. The writer may have completely misunderstood the essay topic.

OFF Did not write on the topic assigned.

NR Did not write the essay.

The average Writing Section score is between 3.5 and 4.0. The Writing Section is scored separately from the rest of the test and has no effect on your overall TOEFL score.

PERSONAL SCORE RECORD:
PRACTICE ESSAYS

Practice Essay 1 _____

Practice Essay 2 _____

Practice Essay 3 _____

Practice Essay 4 _____

Practice Tests
Answer Keys
and Transcripts

Practice Test 1

Answer Key

1.	C	11.	B	21.	A	31.	B	41.	B
2.	D	12.	B	22.	B	32.	D	42.	D
3.	C	13.	D	23.	B	33.	A	43.	C
4.	A	14.	A	24.	C	34.	D	44.	A
5.	B	15.	D	25.	D	35.	B	45.	C
6.	B	16.	C	26.	A	36.	C	46.	D
7.	D	17.	A	27.	C	37.	A	47.	B
8.	C	18.	D	28.	B	38.	A	48.	D
9.	A	19.	D	29.	C	39.	A	49.	C
10.	C	20.	C	30.	A	40.	B	50.	B

PART A

TRANSCRIPT*

1. M1: I can't find those photographs I just had developed.
   F1: I think I saw them on the piano.
   M2: What does the woman mean?

2. F2: Fred sure was angry.
   M1: I'll say. He left without saying goodbye to anyone.
   M2: What does the man say about Fred?

3. M1: What an uncomfortable-looking chair.
   F1: Well, it may look that way—but just try it out!
   M2: What does the woman imply?

4. M1: So, where are the rose gardens? Didn't you say they were here on the west side of the park?
   F2: No, no. I said they were on the *east* side.
   M2: What does the woman mean?

5. F2: George, is Linda leaving tonight?
   M1: I *think* that's what she said.
   M2: What does George say about Linda?

6. M1: Two weeks' work down the drain!
   F1: Oh no! Your experiment wasn't successful?
   M2: What is learned about the man from this conversation?

7. F1: I see Carrie's riding her bike again. Did she fix it herself?
   M1: I think she got her brother to do it.
   M2: What does the man believe about Carrie?

---

* Note: M1 = first male voice   M2 = second male voice   F1 = first female voice   F2 = second female voice

8. M1: Did the band play for about 2 hours?
    F1: No. This time, the concert was over in an hour and a half.
    M2: How long did the concert last?

9. F2: Maybe you could get a ride to campus with Peggy tomorrow.
    M1: Oh, Peggy no longer drives to class.
    M2: What does the man say about Peggy?

10. M1: Swimming is good exercise.
    F1: Of course. And so is dancing.
    M2: What does the woman mean?

11. M1: I need to go out. Is it still raining?
    F1: Yes, but it's starting to let up a little.
    M2: What does the woman mean?

12. M1: Then you and Robert finished your project on time?
    F2: Yes, no thanks to Robert!
    M2: What does the woman imply?

13. F2: I just heard that Professor Hendrix is retiring at the end of the semester.
    F1: Too bad. I was hoping to take his chemistry course next semester.
    M2: What is learned about Professor Hendrix from this conversation?

14. M1: I'd like some flowers delivered to Hillcrest Hospital.
    F1: Certainly. If you step over here, I'll show you some arrangements.
    M2: What is the man going to do?

15. M1: My watch isn't running.
    F2: Why not have the jeweler around the corner fix it?
    M2: What does the woman suggest the man do?

16. M1: Just think, in another couple of days, I'll be in Montreal.
    F1: How will you get around once you get there?
    M2: What does the woman ask the man?

17. F1: I'm exhausted. I can't wait for the weekend to get here.
    M1: Need a little rest, do you?
    M2: What does the man mean?

18. F2: Diane is always saying she loves to go ice-skating.
    M1: Yes, but when's the last time you actually saw her out on the ice?
    M2: What does the man imply about Diane?

19. M1: I'd like to return this sweater because it's too small. I don't have the receipt with me, though.
    F2: You could exchange the sweater for another size. But if you don't have the receipt, I won't be able to give you your money back.
    M2: What does the woman tell the man?

20. M1: Have you ever eaten at the Fisherman's Grotto?
    F1: Have I? I never go to the beach without stopping there.
    M2: What does the woman mean?

21. M1: Brenda, will you play that song you wrote?
    F1: Only if you accompany me on the guitar.
    M2: What does Brenda want the man to do?

22. M1: I'm planning to clean up the kitchen this afternoon.
    F2: Shouldn't you clean the rest of your apartment while you're at it?
    M2: What does the woman tell the man?

23. F2: That was a great play, wasn't it?
M1: Yeah, the cast was wonderful. I could hardly believe they weren't professional actors.
M2: What does the man mean?

24. F1: There are only a few drops left in the can. I guess we'll have to buy some in the morning.
M1: Well, we can finish up this job tomorrow. Let's just wash out our brushes for now.
M2: What will they probably buy in the morning.

25. F1: Jim, can I have one of those bananas you bought?
M1: Sorry, they're still not ripe enough.
M2: What does Jim mean?

26. F2: The students in Professor Murray's class think that the test he gave was unfair.
F1: A few of them do, anyway.
M2: What can be inferred from this conversation?

27. M1: John sure knows some good places to eat, doesn't he?
F2: Yeah, when it comes to finding great restaurants, John wrote the book.
M2: What does the woman say about John?

28. M1: Look at my face! I got sunburned again yesterday.
F2: Maybe next time you'll remember to wear your hat when you're working in the garden.
M2: What does the woman think the man should do?

29. F1: Were any of the windows unlocked?
M1: Not one of them.
M2: What does the man mean?

30. F2: Harry, what's your new roommate like?
M1: Well, for one thing, he's very outgoing.
M2: What does Harry say about his roommate?

PART B

Questions 31–34: Listen to a conversation on a college campus.

M1: Excuse me, I'm trying to find my way to Reynolds Hall.
F1: Reynolds Hall? I don't think I know where that is.
M1: I'm looking for an exhibit of graduate student paintings. The campus newspaper said it was in Reynolds Hall.
F1: Oh, now I know where you mean. Everyone on campus just calls that the Art Building.
M1: So how do I get there?
F1: Go straight ahead until you come to the main library. You'll see a walkway leading off to the left. Go that way, and then past the Chemistry Building . . .
M1: Let's see . . . to the library, take the walkway to the right . . .
F1: No, to the left.
M1: To the left, and past the Chemistry Building . . .
F1: That's right, and then you'll cross a little service road. Walk just a little bit farther and there's the Art Building. You can't miss it because there's a big abstract metal sculpture right in front of it.
M1: I think I've got it.
F1: I hope you enjoy the exhibit. Usually the graduate student exhibits are very interesting, and I've heard this one is especially good.
M1: Actually, the main reason I'm going is that my sister has a couple of paintings in the show. I wanted to take a look at them.

31. M2: Why was the woman at first confused when the man asked her for directions?

32. M2: According to the woman, what is directly in front of the Art Building?

33. M2: What can be inferred from the conversation about the man's sister?

34. M2: What is the woman's attitude toward the man?

Questions 35–38: Listen to a conversation in an astronomy class.

M1: Professor Carmichael, I'd like to ask a question. You just said that, according to Einstein, nothing can go faster than the speed of light. Is that right?

F2: Yes, Ted, that's what Einstein said, and most scientists agree with him.

M1: Then does that mean that we could never build spaceships to go to other stars?

F2: Well, let's think about it. Do you remember how far it is to the nearest star?

M1: Umm . . . I think you said a few days ago that it's about four light years.

F2: About that. And how fast does light travel?

M1: Around 186,000 miles per second.

F2: Yes, and a light-year is the distance light travels in a YEAR! Imagine that! A light-year is the equivalent of almost 6 trillion miles.

M1: But what if we built a ship that could go ALMOST as fast as light. Then we could get to the closest star in four or five years.

F2: That's true in theory. Unfortunately, there are no spaceships that can even approach the speed of light. Even if we built ships that are MUCH faster than the rockets we have today, it would probably take hundreds or thousands of years to get to the closest stars. How could you carry enough fuel to last that long? We'd need a completely different method of powering spaceships.

M1: So you're saying that you don't think people will ever be able to travel to the stars?

F2: Well, I don't want to say never, Ted. Who knows what kinds of scientific breakthroughs there will be? But I think for the foreseeable future, there will only be starships in science fiction movies and books.

35. M2: What had Professor Carmichael been talking about when Ted asked her a question?

36. M2: If a ship could travel almost as fast as light, how long would it take to get to the closest star?

37. M2: According to Professor Carmichael, what must be developed before ships can travel to the closest stars?

38. M2: How does Professor Carmichael characterize travel to other stars?

PART C

Questions 39–41: Listen to a talk given at a newspaper office.

F2: Good afternoon, ladies and gentlemen, and welcome to the *Daily Gazette* Building. As I'm sure you're aware from your journalism classes, large newspapers are divided into a number of areas, all of them important to the success of the overall operation. We'll be visiting three important departments today. We'll begin our tour with a visit to the Circulation Department, which is responsible for distributing the paper all over the city. Then we'll move to the Editorial Department. In that department, there's the City Desk, which is responsible for gathering and reporting local news. The National Desk and the International Desk are there, too, and various feature desks. Since you're probably most interested in that part of our operation, we'll be spending most of our time there, and you'll have a chance to chat with some of our reporters. Finally, we'll visit the Production Department, where the newspaper is printed. Please step this way.

39. M2: Whom is the speaker addressing?

40. M2: Where will the people listening to this talk go first?

41. M2: According to the speaker, what type of work is done at the City Desk?

Questions 42–46: Listen to part of a talk about a special student program.

M1: Good evening. For you who don't know me, I'm Professor Mackenzie of the School of Architecture here at Hunt University. I've been involved with "Semester Afloat" for some years now, so I've been asked to give this introductory talk about the program. So, what is "Semester Afloat"? It's an educational program that is held aboard an ocean-going ship, the SS *Apollo*. There are three programs you can sign up for—one in the eastern Mediterranean, one in the western Mediterranean, and one in Southeast Asia. You'll have the opportunity to see some unforgettable sights. There are many social activities, and you'll make lasting friendships during the semester you spend on the ship, but tonight I want to talk mainly about the academic program. The SS *Apollo* is a floating university. The faculty is recruited from the top universities in North America. There's an excellent library aboard. You'll study the history, language, art, and architecture of the countries that you visit. I, myself, have taught courses in historical architecture during two eastern Mediterranean programs, and I can tell you, those classes are unlike any classes you can take here at Hunt or anywhere else. For example, last semester I gave a lecture about Greek temple design one morning, and that afternoon, I took my class out to see several Greek temples for themselves. Oh, and of course, for all the classes you take, you'll receive academic credit at almost any university in the United States. Now, I have a lot more information about this program for you, but before I go on, I want to introduce two students who took part in "Semester Afloat" last semester, and you can ask them any questions you like.

42. M2: What aspect of the "Semester Afloat" program does Professor Mackenzie's talk focus on?

43. M2: What did Professor Mackenzie teach during the "Semester Afloat" programs?

44. M2: With which of these "Semester Afloat" programs was Professor Mackenzie associated?

45. M2: What does Professor Mackenzie say about "Semester Afloat" classes?"

46. M2: Whom will Professor Mackenzie introduce to the audience next?

Questions 47–50: Listen to a talk about olympic speed skating.

F1: Speed skating has been a Winter Olympic event for many years, but in recent years, conditions on the ice tracks used by speed skaters have gotten better. Until the most recent Winter Olympics, speed-skating events were held outdoors. Conditions on outdoor ice tracks vary from hour to hour, depending on the weather. On indoor tracks, conditions can be controlled, giving all skaters an equal opportunity to skate at the top of their form. On indoor tracks, a constant temperature of 20° Fahrenheit can be maintained. This is important because if the ice is too cold, it forms frost, slowing down the skaters, and it chips easily. If the temperature is too high, the ice begins to melt. Also, ice tracks today are made with extremely pure water. Minerals in water make ice soft, and soft ice doesn't provide enough resistance for skates. Recent improvements in making and maintaining ice will almost certainly lead to new world records in speed skating in the near future.

47. M2: What aspect of speed skating does the speaker primarily discuss?

48. M2: What does the speaker imply about speed skaters who competed before the most recent Winter Olympics?

49. M2: According to the speaker, what happens to ice that contains too many minerals?

50. M2: What prediction does the speaker make about the near future?

SECTION 2: STRUCTURE

Answer Key

1. **B**	11. **B**	21. **A**	31. **B**
2. **B**	12. **C**	22. **B**	32. **C**
3. **A**	13. **B**	23. **D**	33. **A**
4. **C**	14. **A**	24. **A**	34. **B**
5. **A**	15. **D**	25. **C**	35. **D**
6. **D**	16. **B**	26. **C**	36. **C**
7. **C**	17. **D**	27. **D**	37. **B**
8. **A**	18. **C**	28. **C**	38. **A**
9. **D**	19. **C**	29. **C**	39. **C**
10. **A**	20. **D**	30. **B**	40. **C**

EXPLANATION: ERROR IDENTIFICATION

16. The correct answer is (B). The past participle *written* should be used in place of the present participle *writing*. The past participle is used to reduce (shorten) a relative clause with a passive verb. *In an essay written in 1799* is a short way to say *In an essay that was written in 1779*.

17. The correct answer is (D). A singular pronoun (*itself*) must be used because the pronoun refers to a singular noun phrase (*a metallic object*).

18. The correct answer is (C). An adverb (*abruptly*) must be used in place of the adjective *abrupt* because this word is used to modify a verb (*occurs*).

19. The correct answer is (C). The preposition *of* has been omitted from the phrase *by means of*.

20. The correct answer is (D). A plural verb form (*bounce*) is required because the subject of the clause (*sound waves*) is plural.

21. The correct answer is (A). The correct word form is *carpenter*. (*Carpentry* refers to the field; *carpenter* refers to a person who works in that field.)

22. The correct answer is (B). The relative pronoun *who* is used to refer to people. The pronoun *which* should be used to refer to inanimate things.

23. The correct answer is (D). A possessive adjective (*her*) should be used in place of *the* to indicate that this is the career of a particular person (*Mary Gardner*).

24. The correct answer is (A). The correct word order is *the sky is*. (The expression *when the sky is clear* is an adverb clause, not a direct question; therefore, the word order is subject + verb, not verb + subject as in direct questions.)

25. The correct answer is (C). The correct word pattern is *both . . . and*.

26. The correct answer is (C). To be parallel with the other verbs in the series (*makes* and *lines*) another full verb (*closes*) is needed in place of the *-ing* form *closing*.

27. The correct answer is (D). The noun *loss* should be used in place of the verb *lost*.

28. The correct answer is (C). The verb *made* should be used in place of the verb *done*; the verb means "constructed" in this sentence.

29. **The correct answer is (C).** To be parallel with the other items in the series (*status* and *love*), the noun *wealth* should be used in place of the adjective *wealthy*.

30. **The correct answer is (B).** The singular verb *is* should be used in place of the plural verb *are* to agree with the singular subject *coloring*. (The nouns *red, orange,* and *brown* are adjectives modifying the subject, but are not subjects themselves.)

31. **The correct answer is (B).** The word *also* cannot be used by itself to connect parts of a sentence; *and* or *and also* should be used.

32. **The correct answer is (C).** The verb *ripen* must be used in place of the adjective *ripe*.

33. **The correct answer is (A).** The correct preposition is *Since*. (This is indicated by the use of the present perfect verb form *have devoted*.)

34. **The correct answer is (B).** In a passive verb phrase, a past participle (*found*) must be used rather than the simple form of the verb (*find*).

35. **The correct answer is (D).** The correct form is *another*.

36. **The correct answer is (C).** The correct verb form is *took place*.

37. **The correct answer is (B).** *Machinery* is properly a noncount noun and cannot be pluralized; the plural-count noun *machines* is correct.

38. **The correct answer is (A).** The word *many* must be used in place of *much* before a plural noun such as *people*. (Although the noun *people* does not end in the letter *-s*, it is still a plural word.)

39. **The correct answer is (C).** The correct word order is *almost entirely*.

40. **The correct answer is (C).** The adjective *native* is followed by the preposition *to*. (However, the noun *native* is often used with the preposition *of*; for example, "She's a native of Texas.")

SECTION 3: READING

Answer Key

1.	D	11.	D	21.	B	31.	A	41.	C
2.	C	12.	C	22.	C	32.	C	42.	A
3.	A	13.	B	23.	B	33.	D	43.	A
4.	D	14.	A	24.	C	34.	C	44.	A
5.	A	15.	A	25.	D	35.	D	45.	C
6.	B	16.	B	26.	A	36.	B	46.	D
7.	C	17.	C	27.	D	37.	B	47.	B
8.	B	18.	A	28.	B	38.	C	48.	D
9.	D	19.	B	29.	A	39.	B	49.	A
10.	B	20.	D	30.	C	40.	D	50.	B

EXPLANATION: READING

1. **The correct answer is (D).** The passage deals with the medical uses of optical fibers.

2. **The correct answer is (C).** The passage states that optical fibers "have opened a window into the living tissues of the body" (line 2) and that with the use of this technology, "physicians can look into the lungs, intestines, and other areas that were formerly inaccessible" lines 4–5.

3. **The correct answer is (A).** *Formerly* means *previously*.

4. **The correct answer is (D).** The reference is to the physicians in line 4.

5. **The correct answer is (A).** According to the passage, "the illuminating bundle, carries light to the tissues" (line 7).

6. **The correct answer is (B).** The word *cores* is closest in meaning to *centers*.

7. **The correct answer is (C).** Lines 11–13 state that "During the last five years improved methods of fabricating optical fibers have led to . . . an increase in the number of fibers."

8. **The correct answer is (B).** In the context of the passage, *resolution* means *sharpness* (the sharpness of the image).

9. **The correct answer is (D).** Whether fiber-optics techniques are easy to teach to doctors is not mentioned. Choices (A), (B), and (C) are all mentioned in the last paragraph.

10. **The correct answer is (B).** A basic description of the fiberscope—"[it] consists of two bundles of fibers"—is provided in line 6.

11. **The correct answer is (D).** The passage primarily deals with Alice Walker's book *The Color Purple* and with critical and popular reaction to the book.

12. **The correct answer is (C).** *The Color Purple* is a novel and thus a work of fiction.

13. **The correct answer is (B).** The word *vividly* means *graphically, distinctly*.

14. **The correct answer is (A).** *Drudgery* means *hard work*—it is usually low-paying, uninteresting work as well.

15. **The correct answer is (A).** Lines 9–10 indicate that eighteenth-century novelists used the epistolary style; in other words, their books told their stories through the use of letters. Line 12 says that Alice Walker also used this style in *The Color Purple*.

16. The correct answer is (B). The author says that "Celie, like William Faulkner's character Dilsey, does not simply survive, but prevails" (line 14). The two characters are alike in that way.

17. The correct answer is (C). The word *prevail* means *triumph, succeed, win*.

18. The correct answer is (A). The author uses a number of positive terms in connection with the novel, such as "vividly narrates" (line 2) and "special flavor" (line 8). The author mentions that the novel was attacked by some critics but balances that by saying that it was praised by others, that it was a bestseller, and that it won some important literary awards (lines 4-7). All in all, the author's attitude is admiring.

19. The correct answer is (B). According to the first paragraph, the changing colors of the blossoms tell insects which blossoms are full of pollen. Since the insects do not have to visit each blossom, they can gather pollen more efficiently.

20. The correct answer is (D). The word *woo* means *attract, allure*.

21. The correct answer is (B). The reference is to an insect.

22. The correct answer is (C). The word *hue* means *color, shade*.

23. The correct answer is (B). The word *Thus* means *therefore, consequently*.

24. The correct answer is (C). A flower on the lantana plant "starts out . . . as yellow" (line 9) but "turns orange on the second day and red on the third" (lines 11-12).

25. The correct answer is (D). The word *triggering* means *activating, stimulating*.

26. The correct answer is (A). According to the passage, "a flower starts out on the first day as yellow" (line 9) and "insects visited the yellow flowers at least 100 times more than would be expected from haphazard visitation" (lines 14-15). Clearly, the flowers are most attractive to the insects on the first day.

27. The correct answer is (D). Lines 15-17 indicate that the purpose of the experiments was to show that insects were responding to colors rather than to other stimuli, such as the scent (smell) of the nectar.

28. The correct answer is (B). The word *haphazard* means *random, arbitrary*.

29. The correct answer is (A). Lines 18-19 say that "In other types of plants, blossoms change from white to red, others from yellow to red, and so on." This indicates that these plants follow a variety of color-change sequences.

30. The correct answer is (C). According to the passage, the phenomenon has been seen in "74 families of plants" (line 19).

31. The correct answer is (A). The passage begins "The 1960s, however, saw a rising dissatisfaction with the Modernist movement." This indicates that the previous paragraph contained a description of Modernism because this paragraph challenges the concepts of Modernism.

32. The correct answer is (C). The word *highlighting* means *emphasizing, featuring*.

33. The correct answer is (D). The reference is to Modernist structures (line 5).

34. The correct answer is (C). The passage states that the Modernist movement's "failings were exposed" in the two books mentioned in the first paragraph, indicating that both Jacobs and Venturi were critical of Modernism.

35. The correct answer is (D). According to the second paragraph, the event that signaled the beginning of post-Modernism was the demolition of Modernist buildings in St. Louis in 1972.

36. The correct answer is (B). Venturi's design for the Brant-Johnson house in Vail, Colorado, "owes something to the Italian Renaissance" (lines 14-15).

37. The correct answer is (B). The word *disciple* means *follower, pupil*.

38. The correct answer is (C). Lines 17–18 indicates that these two buildings "incorporate historical souvenirs." This means that they include architectural features from the past that would generally not be associated with skyscrapers.

39. The correct answer is (B). Line 21 says that "[this building is the] most complete instance of historical accuracy."

40. The correct answer is (D). The main topic of the passage is nineteenth-century model communities. Choice (A) is not mentioned; choice (B) is too general; choice (C) is too specific.

41. The correct answer is (C). The author states that "many nineteenth-century reformers hoped to bring about reform through education . . ." (line 1). However, these are not the "communitarian reformers" on whom the passage focuses.

42. The correct answer is (A). Line 6 say that "A number of religious groups, most notably the Shakers, practiced communal living."

43. The correct answer is (A). The word *impetus* means *stimulus, motivation*.

44. The correct answer is (A). The word *thriving* means *prospering, flourishing*.

45. The correct answer is (C). Lines 14–16 say that Fourier's theories influenced Americans through the writings of Albert Brisbane and that Fourierism involved self-sufficient associations called "phalanxes."

46. The correct answer is (D). According to line 18, Hawthorne was "an early member of the latter" ("the latter" refers to Brook Farm).

47. The correct answer is (B). According to lines 18–19, "Noyes founded the most enduring . . . of the utopian communities, the Oneida Community" (*enduring* means *long lasting*).

48. The correct answer is (D). The word *oddest* (the superlative form of the adjective "odd") means *strangest, most unusual*.

49. The correct answer is (A). The author begins the concluding sentence (the last sentence of the passage) with the phrase "needless to say . . . ," which means *obviously*.

50. The correct answer is (B). The author presents an overview of the concept of model communities in the first paragraph and specific examples of this concept (New Harmony, Brook Farm, and the Oneida Community) in the second.

Practice Test 2

SECTION 1: LISTENING

Answer Key

1.	C	11.	D	21.	D	31.	B	41.	B
2.	C	12.	A	22.	B	32.	C	42.	A
3.	A	13.	C	23.	B	33.	A	43.	B
4.	D	14.	B	24.	B	34.	D	44.	C
5.	B	15.	A	25.	D	35.	D	45.	B
6.	C	16.	B	26.	C	36.	A	46.	D
7.	A	17.	C	27.	D	37.	D	47.	B
8.	B	18.	D	28.	C	38.	A	48.	A
9.	D	19.	A	29.	C	39.	A	49.	D
10.	B	20.	C	30.	A	40.	C	50.	C

PART A

TRANSCRIPT*

1. F1: Have you seen my suitcase?
    M2: I kept tripping over it, so I put it in the closet.
    F2: What does the man mean?

2. F1: That's all you're having for dinner?
    M1: I had a late lunch.
    F2: What does the man imply?

3. M2: I thought Mary Ann would have a hard time getting used to college life.
    M1: Were you ever wrong!
    F2: What is learned from this conversation about Mary Ann?

4. F1: George, don't feel so bad. It's not your fault your brother failed that class.
    M2: I don't know. I could have encouraged him to study more.
    F2: How does George feel?

5. M1: Pamela made quite a few mistakes in the laboratory.
    F1: Well, she wouldn't have if she hadn't been in such a hurry to get finished.
    F2: What does the woman say about Pamela?

6. F1: Excuse me, I'm trying to get to the courthouse, and I think I'm going the wrong way. Should I have turned left on Monroe Street?
    M2: No, no you're all right. Just keep going straight on Fourth Avenue until you get to the Post Office, and turn left there.
    F2: What is the woman's destination?

7. F1: Mitch and Lynn must have a lot in common since they're both economics majors.
    M2: Oh, I didn't realize that Mitch was an economics major too.
    F2: What does the man imply?

---

* Note: M1 = first male voice   M2 = second male voice   F1 = first female voice   F2 = second female voice

8. M1: I've got to call Tony right away.

    F1: Yeah? How come?

    F2: What does the woman ask the man?

9. F2: So, did you have a busy afternoon, Emory?

    M1: Well, I watered the tomatoes and corn, and I did some weeding.

    F2: What did Emory do this afternoon?

10. M2: Whom should we ask to introduce the guest speaker?

    F1: What about Professor Welch?

    F2: What does the woman imply about Professor Welch?

11. M2: Would you like milk or sugar in your coffee?

    F1: Neither, thank you.

    F2: What does the woman want?

12. F1: Did you find that movie exciting?

    M1: Exciting! To put it mildly!

    F2: What does the man say about the movie?

13. F1: Doug, are you looking forward to moving this weekend?

    M1: Well, there are a couple of other ways I'd rather spend my weekend!

    F2: What does Doug mean?

14. M2: I won't be able to come to rehearsal this evening.

    F1: Arthur can't either. Maybe we should call it off.

    F2: What does the woman mean?

15. F1: There's plenty of lemonade. Have another glass.

    M1: Thanks, I believe I will.

    F2: What will the man probably do?

16. F1: Do you know where Dean Nicholson's office is?

    M2: There's a directory in the entrance way.

    F2: What does the man imply about Dean Nicholson's office?

17. F2: Hotel rooms along the beach must be very expensive.

    M1: Not now. During the off-season, they're dirt cheap.

    F2: What does the man say about the hotel rooms?

18. M1: Hi Nora. I was just walking over to the cafeteria for lunch. Care to join me?

    F1: I can't. I've got to go to a meeting. It's in the same building as the cafeteria though.

    F2: What will Nora probably do?

19. M2: If we hurry, we'll be at the stadium in half an hour.

    F1: At best.

    F2: What does the woman mean?

20. F1: Joan is *not* what I'd call easygoing.

    M1: I know. People find it hard to believe that she's my sister.

    F2: What does the man imply?

21. F1: That sure is a catchy song.

    M1: You're telling me. The melody's been running through my head all week.

    F2: What can be concluded about the song?

22. F1: This stamp you found is pretty rare. I'd like to have one like it myself.

    M1: Oh, an expert, are you?

    F2: What does the man say about the woman?

23. M1: This schedule says we have to attend an orientation session before we can register.
M2: Look at it again. That's just for new students.
F2: What can be inferred about these two speakers?

24. F1: How's your research project coming, Mike?
M2: So far, so good.
F2: What does Mike mean?

25. F1: I won't be able to take a vacation this summer. I have to work.
M1: Guess we're in the same boat.
F2: What can be inferred about the two speakers?

26. M1: Professor Phillips's class seems pretty interesting.
F1: I couldn't agree with you more!
F2: What does the woman mean?

27. M2: Mind if I take your picture?
F1: No, not at all.
F2: What does the woman mean?

28. M1: I'm going to buy Julie a book of poems. I know she loves poetry.
F1: But you can't just get her any book of poems!
F2: What does the woman imply about Julie?

29. M2: We need to discuss our presentation some time in the next few days.
F1: Fine. How about over lunch today?
F2: When does the woman want to talk about the presentation?

30. M1: I drove my motorcycle to work today. It was a great day for a ride.
F1: Oh, you mean you *did* buy that motorcycle after all!
F2: What had the woman assumed?

PART B

Questions 31–34: Listen to a conversation between two friends.

F1: Tim, did you get your ticket for the concert Friday?
M1: I tried to. I stopped by the ticket office on the way back from campus, but they wouldn't take my check.
F1: Why not?
M1: The cashier said I didn't have enough identification with me; a student ID card wasn't enough. He said I needed a driver's license, too.
F1: What happened to yours? Did you lose it, or just forget to bring it with you?
M1: I don't have one. You know me. I ride my bicycle everywhere I go, so why do I need a driver's license?
F1: You could still get an official identification card from the state and use that to cash checks.
M1: Where do I get one of those?
F1: At the same place you get a driver's license, the Bureau of Motor Vehicles.
M1: Is that office downtown?
F1: No, it's out on Southland Parkway, next to the Midvale Shopping Mall.
M1: What do you think I'll need to do to get one?
F1: Just bring some official document that has your date of birth on it. You could use a passport, for example.
M1: I'll ride out there tomorrow.
F1: Good idea. And I'll tell you what, Tim—if you promise to cash a check as soon as you can, I'll let you borrow some money, and you can go get that ticket.

31. F2: According to the conversation, why was Tim unable to buy the ticket?

32.   F2:   According to the woman, where is the Bureau of Motor Vehicles?

33.   F2:   What does the woman suggest Tim bring when he goes to the Bureau of Motor Vehicles?

34.   F2:   What does the woman offer to do for Tim?

Questions 35–38: Listen to a conversation at a student health clinic.

     F1:   The doctor should be able to see you in a few minutes. I just need some information from you first. What seems to be the problem?

     M2:   Well, as you can see, I've got a rash on my hands and arms. I think it might be some kind of allergic reaction. My roommate just got a new cat. Maybe I'm allergic to cats.

     F1:   Hmm. Usually, allergies to animals don't cause rashes on your hands.

     M2:   Well, maybe I'm allergic to some kind of food, or . . .

     F1:   When did your rash first develop?

     M2:   On Monday. By Tuesday, it was worse, and on Tuesday night I could hardly sleep.

     F1:   Tell me, have you been out in the woods lately?

     M2:   Out in the woods? I went hiking Saturday. Why? Oh, I get it. You think my rash might be caused by poison ivy, right?

     F1:   Well, it *looks* like that. The doctor can tell you for sure. Do you know if you came in contact with poison ivy?

     M2:   No, but then I have no idea what poison ivy looks like.

     F1:   It grows in clusters of three leaves, and the leaves are waxy looking.

     M2:   Well, if I *do* have poison ivy, what can the doctor do for me?

     F1:   He can prescribe a lotion that will relieve the itching. But if I were you, I'd go to the library and look for some color photos of poison ivy, and try to avoid it the next time you go into the woods.

35.   F2:   What is the probable relationship between the two speakers?

36.   F2:   According to the conversation, when did the man go hiking?

37.   F2:   What does the woman believe is the probable source of the man's problem?

38.   F2:   What does the woman suggest that the man do?

PART C

Questions 39–41: Listen to a talk given by a tour guide.

     F1:   Welcome back to your Northwest Holidays tour bus. I hope you enjoyed your visit to Redwood National Park. We'll be leaving the park in just a few more minutes and heading for Tall Trees Lodge, where we'll spend the night.

        I want to tell you a little about tomorrow's destination—Crater Lake National Park. Crater Lake is located in an extinct volcano. A cone-shaped island, Wizard Island, seems to float on its surface. One of the first things you'll notice when we get there is the deep-blue color of the water of the lake. The water will be that color whether the sky is clear or cloudy. Once it was thought that the color was due to an unusual mineral content, but chemical analysis showed no such thing. It's now believed that the lake water is so clear and deep that it separates and reflects the blue rays of sunlight and absorbs the other colors.

        Oh, and here's another interesting fact about Crater Lake. It has neither an outlet nor an inlet, yet it maintains almost exactly the same level of water, with only slight variations from season to season and year to year. Somehow, gains from snow and rain are perfectly balanced by losses from evaporation and seepage.

        We should be arriving at Crater Lake early tomorrow afternoon. We'll be spending the rest of the day in the park, and then on to our next stop, the city of Portland, Oregon. For now, sit back and relax, and we'll be at our hotel in about 20 minutes.

39. F2: Where does this conversation take place?

40. F2: According to the speaker, which of the following makes the water of Crater Lake appear to be such an intense shade of blue?

41. F2: What does the speaker say about the water level of Crater Lake?

Questions 42–46: Listen to a lecture given in a U.S. history course.

M2: Good morning, students. Today we'll be continuing to talk about the development of rapid communications in the United States. No discussion of communications is complete without a mention of a particularly dramatic means of delivering the mail: the Pony Express. It was founded in 1860, the year before the Civil War, to carry mail from St. Joseph, Missouri, to the gold fields of California. Racing across Nebraska, Wyoming, Utah, and Nevada, these horsemen covered 2,000 miles in ten days. Every 10 miles, there was a relay station where a fresh horse waited. Each man rode a total of five relays—that's 50 miles!—before he was replaced by a fresh rider. The riders galloped summer and winter, day and night, through rain and wind and snow. Now, let me read to you from a newspaper advertisement that was used to recruit Pony Express riders: "Wanted . . . thin, wiry young fellows—preferably orphans." Can you imagine yourself answering an ad for a job where orphans were preferred! That should give you some idea of the nature of the work. Only eighteen months after the Pony Express was founded, the transcontinental telegraph was opened and put the company out of business. It had been losing money anyway. In its day, though, it provided an extremely useful service. Any questions before we go on?

42. F2: What has the class been studying?

43. F2: According to the speaker, what was the final destination of Pony Express riders?

44. F2: According to the speaker, how many miles did each rider cover before being replaced by another rider?

45. F2: The speaker would probably use which of the following words to describe the work of Pony Express riders?

46. F2: According to the speaker, which of the following caused the end of the Pony Express?

Questions 47–50: Listen to a talk given at a meeting of the drama club.

M1: As president of the University Drama Club, I'd like to welcome all our members. Today we have a special guest speaker, Molly Quinn. Molly was a member of the Drama Club herself when she was a student here, and she went on to great success. First, she won parts in several New York plays, and then she made guest appearances on a number of television shows. Most recently, she completed work on her first role in a feature movie. She also hopes to start directing soon; she told me that she might try to get a start by directing television commercials. Molly is going to talk to us today about getting into the acting profession, but before we hear from her, I want to remind everyone that next weekend the Drama Department is holding tryouts for parts in the play *A Doll's House,* so mark that on your calendars. Given her own experience, I'm sure Molly would agree that appearing in campus plays is a great way to learn the basics of acting. Now, let's give Molly a big welcome!

47. F2: What is the speaker's primary purpose in giving the talk?

48. F2: When is this talk being given?

49. F2: According to the speaker, what is Molly Quinn's most recent accomplishment?

50. F2: The speaker implies that Molly Quinn did which of the following when she was a student?

SECTION 2: STRUCTURE

Answer Key

1. A	11. B	21. A	31. C
2. B	12. C	22. C	32. A
3. A	13. B	23. B	33. C
4. D	14. C	24. D	34. A
5. C	15. D	25. D	35. D
6. D	16. A	26. A	36. D
7. A	17. D	27. D	37. C
8. B	18. D	28. C	38. B
9. C	19. C	29. C	39. A
10. A	20. D	30. B	40. B

EXPLANATION: ERROR IDENTIFICATION

16. **The correct answer is (A).** Before a plural count noun (such as *superstitions*) the word *many* must be used. (*Much* is used before noncount nouns.)

17. **The correct answer is (D).** The participle *illuminated* is needed in place of the noun *illumination*.

18. **The correct answer is (D).** The plural pronoun *them* should be used to refer to the plural noun *joints*.

19. **The correct answer is (C).** The word *percentage* must be used if there is no preceding number ("the *percentage* is growing" but "fifteen *percent*").

20. **The correct answer is (D).** The word *ago* is used unnecessarily; the phrase should read *for over 5,000 years*.

21. **The correct answer is (A).** The adjective form, *outer*, is required.

22. **The correct answer is (C).** The comparative form of a two-syllable adjective ending in -*y* (such as *easy*) is -*ier*; *more* is not used; *easier* is therefore the correct form.

23. **The correct answer is (B).** The correct word order is preposition + relative pronoun (*in which*).

24. **The correct answer is (D).** A noun (*warmth*) must be used in place of the adjective *warm*.

25. **The correct answer is (D).** In this sentence, *editorial* is the first word of a compound noun (*editorial staffs*) and should not be pluralized.

26. **The correct answer is (A).** The past tense (*began*) should be used in place of the past participle *begun*. (By itself, a past participle such as *begun* can never serve as a main verb.)

27. **The correct answer is (D).** The word *as* has been omitted; the phrase should read *such as rayon*.

28. **The correct answer is (C).** The subject and verb of the second clause, *it is*, are missing; the phrase should read *but it is not*.

29. **The correct answer is (C).** The correct word order is *much too*. (Or the word *much* may be omitted.)

30. The correct answer is (B). The noun *economics* is required in place of the adjective *economic*.

31. The correct answer is (C). The correct word order is adjective + *enough*: *smooth enough*.

32. The correct answer is (A). *Whatever* should replace *however*.

33. The correct answer is (C). The correct form is *other*. (*Another* is not usually used before plural nouns such as *types*.)

34. The correct answer is (A). The noun *depth* is needed in place of the adjective *deep*.

35. The correct answer is (D). The correct pattern is *from . . . to*.

36. The correct answer is (D). The word *it* is used unnecessarily and should be omitted. (The subject of that clause is the relative pronoun *that*.)

37. The correct answer is (C). The word *relatively* cannot be used with an intensifying modifier such as *very*; the word *very* should be omitted.

38. The correct answer is (B). The adjective *formal* should replace the adverb *formally*.

39. The correct answer is (A). The word *sunshine* is a noncount noun and cannot be pluralized.

40. The correct answer is (B). The article *the* should be omitted: *by hand*.

SECTION 3: READING

Answer Key

1. **D**	11. **B**	21. **C**	31. **B**	41. **C**
2. **A**	12. **A**	22. **A**	32. **C**	42. **D**
3. **C**	13. **A**	23. **D**	33. **A**	43. **A**
4. **B**	14. **D**	24. **C**	34. **D**	44. **B**
5. **D**	15. **B**	25. **B**	35. **B**	45. **C**
6. **A**	16. **C**	26. **D**	36. **B**	46. **C**
7. **A**	17. **A**	27. **D**	37. **C**	47. **D**
8. **B**	18. **D**	28. **A**	38. **A**	48. **C**
9. **C**	19. **A**	29. **C**	39. **B**	49. **A**
10. **D**	20. **B**	30. **D**	40. **B**	50. **C**

EXPLANATION: READING

1. **The correct answer is (D).** Choice (A) is only a detail; there is no comparison between clippers and steamships, so choice (B) is not correct; there is no mention of shipbuilding techniques in the passage, so choice (C) is not correct; the best answer is choice (D).

2. **The correct answer is (A).** The word *swiftest* means *fastest, quickest*.

3. **The correct answer is (C).** The passage says that "most were constructed in the shipyards of New England."

4. **The correct answer is (B).** In the context of the passage, a vessel is a ship.

5. **The correct answer is (D).** Line 6 states that "clippers took gold seekers from the East Coast to the West."

6. **The correct answer is (A).** The second paragraph indicates that clippers were "built for speed" (line 8) and that other considerations, such as operating costs, choice (B), and cargo capacity, choice (C), were sacrificed for this purpose (lines 8-9). A large crew, choice (D), was necessary for the speedy operation of clippers (lines 11-12).

7. **The correct answer is (A).** The word *slanted* means *tilted, angled*.

8. **The correct answer is (B).** According to the passage, clipper ships "sometimes (used) skysails and moonrakers," indicating that clipper ships did not always use these sails.

9. **The correct answer is (C).** According to lines 14-15, this record was held by the clipper ship *Lightning*.

10. **The correct answer is (D).** The *Cutty Sark* was a British tea clipper, and according to the passage, these ships were "composites" (line 18); in other words, they were built with iron frames and wooden planking.

11. **The correct answer is (B).** Choices (A), (C), and (D) are all discussed in the final paragraph; there is no mention of competition with British ships.

12. **The correct answer is (A).** The passage ends with a mention of the end of the age of sail; it is logical that the next paragraph will concern the beginnings of the next age, that of ships powered by steam.

13. **The correct answer is (A).** The passage primarily discusses Ralph Earl's career. There is no comparison between Earl's art and that of Gainsborough's, choice (B); there is no specific reference to Earl's influences, choice (C); there is no description of the art scene in New York City in the late eighteenth century, choice (D).

14. **The correct answer is (D).** It is mentioned in several points in the passage that Earl painted portraits, choice (A); in the first paragraph, it is mentioned that Earl painted landscapes, choice (B), and scenes from the battles of Lexington and Concord, choice (C); there is no evidence that he painted pictures of fruit and flowers—still lifes, choice (D).

15. **The correct answer is (B).** According to the passage, Earl went to London "to study with Benjamin West" (line 4), so West must have been Earl's teacher.

16. **The correct answer is (C).** In the context of the passage, *outstanding* means *unpaid*.

17. **The correct answer is (A).** The word *itinerant* means *traveling, wandering*.

18. **The correct answer is (D).** The phrase *sprang from the same roots* means *having the same general background*.

19. **The correct answer is (A).** In the third paragraph, the author discusses the "counterpoint" (contrast) between "the severity of the couple" and "the relative luxury of the Ellsworth's interior furnishings."

20. **The correct answer is (B).** According to the passage, *Reclining Hunter* is an anomaly (something uncharacteristic or unusual) because it "uncharacteristically shows Earl's wit (humor)." This indicates that most of Earl's paintings were more serious than this one.

21. **The correct answer is (C).** The reference is to the "well-dressed gentleman"—that is, the hunter.

22. **The correct answer is (A).** The author mentions a number of positive qualities in the passage about Earl; for example, "his uncommon technical skills." No negative attributes are mentioned.

23. **The correct answer is (D).** The passage discusses the phenomenon of sparks on the moon and offers an explanation for this phenomenon.

24. **The correct answer is (C).** According to the first line of the passage, the sparks of light have been seen "for centuries" (hundreds of years).

25. **The correct answer is (B).** The word *sporadically* means *occasionally*.

26. **The correct answer is (D).** According to the passage, evidence for the theory is provided when the rocks are "fractured in the lab" (line 8).

27. **The correct answer is (D).** The reference is to the lunar rocks.

28. **The correct answer is (A).** In the context of the passage, *stray* means *loose* or *escaped* (from the rocks).

29. **The correct answer is (C).** The passage explains that thermal cracking is caused by "a sudden change in temperature" (line 11). Choice (C) is the best example of this.

30. **The correct answer is (D).** There is no mention in the passage that gas pressure can fracture lunar rocks.

31. **The correct answer is (B).** The passage mainly deals with guyots—one feature of the undersea world.

32. **The correct answer is (C).** The word *conceal* means *hide, obscure*.

33. **The correct answer is (A).** According to line 4, Harry H. Hess discovered guyots while serving "on a ship equipped with a fathometer," implying that this device was used in the discovery.

34. The correct answer is (D). Lines 5-6 state that Guyot "served on the faculty of Princeton University for thirty years."

35. The correct answer is (B). Lines 6-7 state that guyots "have been found in every ocean but the Arctic."

36. The correct answer is (B). According to lines 7-8, "like offshore canyons, guyots present a challenge to oceanographic theory." Guyots are not necessarily found near continental shelves, choice (A); there is no evidence that offshore canyons are of volcanic origin, choice (C), or that they were ever above the surface of the sea, choice (D).

37. The correct answer is (C). Line 11 states that "most lie between 3,200 feet and 6,500 feet."

38. The correct answer is (A). Rubble is rough, broken fragments (pieces) of stone or other material.

39. The correct answer is (B). According to lines 11-12, "their tops are not really flat but slope upward to a low pinnacle at the center." Choice (B) best depicts this description.

40. The correct answer is (B). According to the passage, the two processes were the depression of the sea floor beneath the volcanoes and rising level of the sea (lines 15-16).

41. The correct answer is (C). Lines 16-17 indicate that the sea level rose "especially when the last Ice Age ended, some 8,000 to 11,000 years ago."

42. The correct answer is (D). The passage primarily concerns the effort by women to secure the right to vote; choices (A) and (B) are mentioned only as details, and there is little discussion of the effect of the Nineteenth Amendment, choice (C).

43. The correct answer is (A). The phrase *in earnest* means *seriously, earnestly*.

44. The correct answer is (B). According to the passage, the National Women's Suffrage Association worked "on the federal level" (lines 3-4), while the American Women's Suffrage Association worked "through state legislation" (lines 4-5).

45. The correct answer is (C). Lines 6-7 indicate that Wyoming enfranchised women in 1869 "while still a territory."

46. The correct answer is (C). The phrase *most astute* means *most clever, most wise*.

47. The correct answer is (D). According to lines 11-12, Alice Paul founded the National Women's Party.

48. The correct answer is (C). In the context of the passage, *province* refers to the sphere of activities of a certain group—in this case, men's jobs.

49. The correct answer is (A). Since both of the newly enfranchised women and the men voted for Harding (lines 20-21) the clear implication is that Harding was elected.

50. The correct answer is (C). The author mentions the growth of women in the workforce in line 15.

Practice Test 3

Answer Key

1. C	11. B	21. D	31. A	41. D	51. D	61. A	71. D
2. A	12. D	22. A	32. D	42. C	52. B	62. B	72. B
3. A	13. C	23. C	33. B	43. B	53. C	63. B	73. C
4. C	14. D	24. C	34. A	44. A	54. B	64. C	74. C
5. D	15. D	25. B	35. C	45. B	55. A	65. C	75. A
6. B	16. B	26. D	36. D	46. A	56. D	66. C	76. B
7. C	17. D	27. A	37. A	47. D	57. A	67. B	77. C
8. B	18. A	28. B	38. B	48. D	58. C	68. D	78. D
9. C	19. A	29. C	39. C	49. A	59. A	69. C	79. D
10. A	20. B	30. C	40. D	50. C	60. C	70. C	80. A

PART A

TRANSCRIPT*

1. **M1:** Why did it take them so long to fix your car?
   F1: Well, for one thing, they had to remove the engine.
   M2: What does the woman mean?

2. **F2:** So Patrick, now that your final exams are over, what are you going to do?
   M1: I plan to take it easy for a couple of weeks or so.
   M2: What does Patrick tell the woman?

3. **F1:** I'm going to ask Greg to help me learn this computer program.
   M1: Greg's pretty busy now. But I know a thing or two about this program myself.
   M2: What does the man imply?

4. **M1:** How often does the bus go to Springsdale?
   F2: Only twice a day.
   M2: What does the woman mean?

5. **M1:** Professor Cassini, can we write our term paper on any topic we like?
   F1: As long as you talk it over with me first.
   M2: What is learned from this conversation?

6. **F2:** I just found an old photo of this dormitory.
   M1: It looks so different!
   M2: What can be inferred from this conversation?

7. **M1:** I saw Rudy in chemistry class, and boy, he looked upset.
   F1: Yeah? I wonder how come.
   M2: What would the woman like to know about Rudy?

---

* Note: M1 = first male voice   M2 = second male voice   F1 = first female voice   F2 = second female voice

8. F1: Why isn't Patty going to the party tonight?
F2: Oh, you know Patty; she hates loud parties.
M2: What can be inferred about Patty?

9. F2: You can either change planes in Chicago or Denver.
M1: You mean there's no direct flight from New York to Phoenix?
M2: Where does the man want to go?

10. M1: Cindy, did you like that movie you saw last night?
F1: Oh yes, but you know what? Halfway through it, I realized I'd seen it years before.
M2: What does Cindy tell the man?

11. F2: Ted used to ask so many questions in Professor Beasley's class.
F1: Yeah, and then, for some reason, he just stopped asking her anything.
M2: What do the speakers say about Ted?

12. F2: So Harry, were you able to solve the puzzle?
M1: Yes, but I'll tell you, it's a lot harder than it looks.
M2: What does Harry tell the woman?

13. M1: Kelly, I thought you were going skiing this weekend.
F1: I was hoping to, but that plan fell through.
M2: What does Kelly tell the man?

14. F2: How's your cold, Ron?
M1: It's gone from bad to worse, I'm afraid.
M2: What does Ron mean?

15. F1: I picked up a few flowers for the dinner party.
M1: A few! The dining room looks like a florist shop!
M2: What does the man imply about the woman?

16. F1: I wasn't in class the day Professor Mitchie gave out the schedule. Can I see yours?
M1: Oh, sure. But he told us that there are a couple of mistakes on it.
M2: What does the man mean?

17. F1: Now, this one shows the view right out of my hotel room.
F2: Wow! It looks just like a postcard!
M2: What are the speakers probably doing?

18. M1: Steve left us some directions for finding the campground.
F2: I saw them, and if these are the best directions we can get, we'll never find it!
M2: What does the woman imply?

19. F1: You're wearing that old blue jacket to the theater tonight?
M1: What else?
M2: What does the man mean?

20. M1: Walter told me that he was late because he had a flat tire.
F2: That's a likely story!
M2: What does the woman mean?

21. M1: I'm sorry, Laura, but something's come up. I won't be able to meet with you today.
F1: Well, how about the same time tomorrow. We can meet at that new coffee shop on Fourteenth Street because this place will be closed then.
M2: What does Laura mean?

22. M2: How did you get that big dent in your door?
F1: I have no idea. Yesterday, I went into the shopping mall, and when I came back out to the parking lot, there it was.
M2: What are the speakers discussing?

23. F1: I heard you're taking an advanced physics class. How's it going?
    M1: I'm out of my depth, I'm afraid.
    M2: What does the man mean?

24. F2: Hope you can make it to the dinner tonight. We're serving fish and salad and some fresh corn from my garden.
    M1: Oh, you decided to have fish after all.
    M2: What had the man assumed?

25. F1: What's the matter, Rob?
    M1: I just locked my keys in my car and I have to be at work in half an hour.
    M2: What is Rob's problem?

26. M1: Kathy, I want to hang this new picture. Do you have a hammer I can borrow?
    F2: No. But you could use this old shoe.
    M2: What does Kathy suggest the man do with the shoe?

27. M1: I can't decide which of these two articles would be more useful to read.
    F1: As far as I'm concerned, you can't go wrong.
    M2: What does the woman mean?

28. F2: I'd love to be up in the mountains where it's cool.
    M1: So you're not enjoying our weather this month?
    M2: What can be inferred from the man's remark?

29. F1: I just got some change from the change machine upstairs.
    M1: Oh, so someone finally fixed that?
    M2: What had the man originally assumed before talking to the woman?

30. M1: This is a great restaurant. You can get anything you want here.
    F2: Anything except good service!
    M2: What is the woman's opinion of the restaurant?

31. M1: You know, at first, I didn't realize what a comedian Howard is!
    F1: Oh, I know. He fools a lot of people!
    M2: How would the speakers describe Howard?

32. M1: I'm having a lot of trouble writing this paper.
    F2: If I were you, I'd go back to the drawing board.
    M2: What does the woman suggest the man do?

33. F1: What delicious salad!
    M1: How about another helping?
    M2: What does the man ask the woman about the salad?

34. F1: I didn't know you were interested in geology, Sam.
    M1: Well, it's a requirement to take at least one science course, and geology seemed like the easiest one.
    M2: Why is Sam taking the geology course?

35. F2: Have you ever seen a professional basketball game?
    M1: Only on television.
    M2: What does the man mean?

36. F1: Connie asked you a lot of questions, didn't she?
    M1: Yeah, she sure did, and I'd like to know what she was driving at.
    M2: What does the man wonder about Connie?

37. F1: Well, we found something nice for Jill. Now what about Allen?
    M1: Let's stop by the sporting goods store and get an archery target. Allen loves archery.
    M2: What are these two probably doing?

38. F2: Gary, do you know when the work on that new road will be done?
M1: The sooner the better, as far as I'm concerned.
M2: What does Gary say about the new road?

39. M1: I had to wait 3 hours to see the doctor.
F1: Oh, come on, Jim! I just heard you tell your roommate that you had a 2-hour wait!
M2: What does the woman imply about Jim?

40. F1: Andy sure has a hot temper, doesn't he?
F2: He does fly off the handle easily.
M2: What do the speakers say about Andy?

41. M1: Professor Pottinger, you'll be giving your lecture on the causes of the Civil War next week, right?
F1: The week after, actually.
M2: What does Professor Pottinger say about the lecture?

42. F2: See you later. I'm going to the bank to deposit my check.
M1: Oh, Marie, I really need some laundry detergent. If I give you some money, do you think you can pick up some on the way back?
M2: What does the man ask Marie to do?

43. F1: What did you say when you were introduced to the author?
M1: To tell you the truth, I was so tongue-tied, I could hardly say a word to her.
M2: What does the man mean?

44. M1: Are you going to buy that car you looked at this afternoon?
F2: Well, maybe. It's got a lot of miles on it. But I need a car with a lot of room and it sure has that.
M2: What does the woman like about the car?

45. M1: Look at these photos I took. They're terrible! I've got to try another camera.
F1: Or take some photography lessons!
M2: What does the woman imply?

46. M1: That was a difficult passage to translate.
F2: I'll say. Even David had trouble with this one!
M2: What does the woman imply about David?

47. F1: What kind of music would you like to hear?
M1: Well, I haven't heard any good jazz for a while.
M2: What does the man imply?

48. M1: Who was that woman you were talking to at the party?
F2: Oh, that was Wendy Donovan. She was my roommate's best friend in high school.
M2: How does the woman know Wendy Donovan?

49. M1: Did you see that notice from the landlord?
F1: Yes, and I could hardly believe my eyes!
M2: What does the woman say about the notice?

50. M1: Alice, what would you say if I told you that I asked a few more people to join our study group?
F2: Oh, I wouldn't mind a bit!
M2: What does Alice mean?

PART B

Questions 51–54: Listen to a conversation between two friends.

F1: Kirk, I understand your jazz band is going to play at the Student Center Ballroom. I just saw a poster advertising the event, and I called to tell you I'll be there.

M1: Oh, thanks, but I'm not in that band anymore. In fact, I'm not in a group at all right now.

F1: That's too bad; you're such a talented musician. Why did you leave the group?

M1: I just couldn't be a full-time student and still rehearse with the band every night. I missed a couple of practice sessions during my midterm exams, and I thought I'd better quit before the bandleader fired me.

F1: Say, you know my friend Charlie, don't you? He plays saxophone and trumpet, and he and some of his friends are getting a band together. I bet they could use a good drummer.

M1: I wouldn't have time for that, either.

F1: Oh, I don't think they'll practice very often. Charlie and his friends are all students, too.

M1: Do they plan to perform?

F1: No, I don't think so. They just enjoy playing jazz. Here, I'll give you his number, and you can get in touch with him.

51. M2: What prompted the woman to call the man?

52. M2: The man implies that he left the band for which of the following reasons?

53. M2: What role did the man probably play in the band?

54. M2: What does the woman suggest that the man do in order to contact her friend?

Questions 55–58: Listen to a telephone conversation.

(RING . . . RING . . . SOUND OF PHONE BEING PICKED UP.)

M1: Hello, *Campus Daily,* advertising department. This is Mark speaking.

F2: Hi. I'm calling to place a couple of ads.

M1: Sure. Under what classification?

F2: Well, I'd like one in the "Roommates Wanted" section.

M1: All right. And how would you like your ad to read?

F2: It should read "Female roommate wanted for pleasant, sunny two-bedroom apartment on Elliewood Avenue, three blocks from campus. Share rent and utilities. Available September first. Call between 5 and 9 p.m. and ask for Cecilia."

M1: Fine. And what about your other ad?

F2: That one I'd like under "Merchandise for Sale," and I'd like it to read "Matching blue sofa and easy chair for sale, excellent condition, $350 or best offer. Call between 5 and 9 p.m. and ask for Cecilia." Did you get all that?

M1: Uh huh. You'll want your phone number on these, right?

F2: Oh sure. Thanks for reminding me. It's 555-6792.

M1: And how long do you want these ads to run?

F2: For a week, I guess. How much would that be?

M1: Let's see—it's $5.00 a week per line. Your two ads will both take up three lines, so that's $15 per ad.

55. M2: Where does Mark work?

56. M2: Which of the following is Cecilia trying to find?

57. M2: Which of the following did Cecilia initially forget to tell Mark?

58. M2: What is the total amount that the woman has to spend for the two advertisements?

Questions 59-63: Listen to a conversation between two friends.

M1: Hi, Shelly! How was your vacation?

F1: Great! I went to New Orleans.

M1: Really? Why did you decide to go there?

F1: Well, I have a cousin who lives there. She's been trying to get me to take a vacation down there for a long time, and so finally, she talked me into it.

M1: How did you get there?

F1: Well, at first I was going to drive, but my cousin said parking is a big problem there, so I flew. Once I was there, I took buses and streetcars.

M1: I've seen some pictures of New Orleans. The architecture there is really interesting, isn't it?

F1: Yeah, it's incredible, especially in the French Quarter and in the Garden District where my cousin lives. And I love the spicy food there, and the music, of course. My cousin took me to some great little restaurants and jazz clubs.

M1: How was the weather when you were there?

F1: That's about the only thing I *didn't* enjoy. It was really hot and sticky.

M1: Wasn't New Orleans originally a French city?

F1: Yes, the French founded it. And then the king of France gave it to the king of Spain, and later the French took it over again. And then the French sold it to the United States along with the rest of the Louisiana Purchase.

M1: I remember reading in a history book about the battle of New Orleans. That was during the War of 1812, wasn't it?

F1: Right. The Americans under Andrew Jackson fought a battle with the British near there. In fact, Jackson Square in the French Quarter is named after him.

M1: Well, it sure sounds like you had a great time.

F1: Oh, I sure did. And I plan to go back there next spring for the Mardi Gras festival!

59. M2: What are these people primarily discussing?

60. M2: According to the conversation, how did the woman get to New Orleans?

61. M2: What was one aspect of New Orleans that the woman did NOT enjoy?

62. M2: Which of the following groups originally founded New Orleans?

63. M2: According to the woman, what role did Andrew Jackson play in the history of New Orleans?

PART C

Questions 64–67: Listen to part of a lecture given in a class of film students.

M1: Class, today we're going to continue our discussion of special genres of film. In our last class, we talked about Westerns, and saw some excerpts from some of those movies, such as *High Noon* and *Duel in the Sun.* Today we'll shift our attention to science fiction films. Most people think of science fiction as a fairly modern genre, but in fact, one of the first commercial films ever made was about a trip to the moon. In the 1930s there were some excellent prophetic films about the future, including *Things to Come,* which is based on a story by the famous author H. G. Wells. The so-called "Golden Age" of science fiction movies took place in the 1950s when hundreds of such films were made. Some of these turned out to be unforgettable classics. Some of these, frankly, were awful films, and the only reason we watch them today is that they seem quaint and sometimes unintentionally funny, with their low-budget special effects and wooden dialogue.

A renaissance in science fiction films took place in the late 1970s when George Lucas released his first *Star Wars* film. It had a fast pace, interesting characters, and, finally, special effects came of age. It was wildly popular then and remains popular now, and many similar films have followed.

Now, I think you'll find your homework for this weekend rather enjoyable. The Paramount Theater is holding a science fiction film festival over the weekend. They're showing a dozen films, all made during the "Golden Age" of science fiction. They're showing some of the real classics, including my personal favorite, *The Day the Earth Stood Still,* as well as some movies that have seldom been seen since they were first released back in the 1950s. I'd like all of you to attend at least two or three of these films and be prepared to talk about your reactions to them in class on Monday.

64. M2: What is the main topic of this lecture?

65. M2: According to the speaker, which of the following is a Western film?

66. M2: What can be inferred about the movies being shown this weekend at the Paramount Theater?

67. M2: What does the speaker ask the audience to be ready to do on Monday?

Questions 68–71: Listen to a talk about hydrogen-fueled vehicles.

F2: It's the goal of nearly all automakers to produce a car that causes no air pollution at all—a zero-emission vehicle, or ZEV. Some states have even mandated that manufacturers make ZEVs available by a certain deadline. So far, most research has been done on electric cars, but such battery operated cars have certain disadvantages. The biggest drawback is that electric cars must have their batteries recharged every 100 miles or so. Recently, engineers have completed some encouraging research on the use of hydrogen as a fuel. They believe that vehicles with internal combustion engines can become ZEVs if they switch from gasoline to hydrogen. When hydrogen is mixed with oxygen and burned, it produces no toxic fumes, only water vapor. However, because it is such a volatile gas, engines burning hydrogen are always backfiring. The engineers learned that if rotary engines are used instead of conventional piston-driven engines, there is no backfiring, just smooth acceleration. Some people wonder if hydrogen-fueled cars would be safe. As it turns out, they are safer than gasoline-fueled cars. That's because they don't store free hydrogen in tanks. The hydrogen is bound to metal, and released as needed. The main problem with hydrogen is that there's simply not enough available. If hydrogen-fueled cars become popular, there will be a need to build hundreds of massive hydrogen-producing plants.

68. M2: How does the speaker probably feel about the development of hydrogen-fueled cars?

69. M2: According to the speaker, researchers trying to develop zero-emission vehicles have concentrated until recently on which of the following?

70. M2: According to the speaker, hydrogen-fueled cars produce which of the following?

71. M2: According to the speaker, which of the following is the primary problem with large-scale use of hydrogen-fueled cars?

Questions 72–75: Listen to a talk about parrots.

F1: First off, I'd like to clear up a couple of popular misconceptions about parrots. For one thing, they do not all have brilliant, colorful plumage. In fact, some are quite plain-looking birds with dull-colored feathers. Another misconception is that parrots all live in hot tropical forests. In fact, some species live high in the mountains. One species, the kea parrot, lives near the highland glaciers of New Zealand. The only type of climate that parrots cannot tolerate is an extremely dry one. There are 816 types of parrots, and all of them can speak at least a few words when kept as pets. The champion talker is the gray parrot, which can learn two or three hundred words. Parrots also have remarkable singing skills. Among us humans, the ability to sing exactly on key is called perfect pitch, and only one out of about 500 of us have it. All parrots are born with this knack. Parrots also have a perfect sense of rhythm, never missing a beat.

72. M2: What is the speaker's first purpose in giving this talk?

73. M2: Which of the following environments would be least favorable for parrots?

74. M2: What does the speaker say about the gray parrot?

75. M2: What ability are all parrots born with?

Questions 76–80: Listen to part of a classroom lecture.

M2: Today, class, we're going to talk about the traditional homes of the Innuit people of the Arctic. The Innuit—or Eskimos, as they are sometimes called—generally had two homes, one for summer and one for winter. During the summer, they usually lived in tents made of either canvas or animal skin. The Innuit built three types of winter homes, depending on where they lived. In northern Alaska, where driftwood is plentiful, most winter homes were domes of wood covered with earth. In Labrador and Greenland, winter homes were generally constructed of flat stones. Only in the Central Canadian Arctic did they generally build houses of snow. Canadians of European descent called these igloos, but to the Innuit, any kind of house is called an igloo. To make a snow house, the Innuit stacked blocks of wind-packed ice in a rising spiral of ever-smaller circles. They filled in the cracks with loose snow. A skilled Innuit could build a snow house in around 2 hours. The Innuit are the only people who built such domes without support underneath. Heat from a lamp warmed the house, while the bitter outside air prevented it from melting. An Innuit family ate and slept on a platform of packed snow covered with furs. The snow house also featured an entrance tunnel that was lower than the floor. This served as a trap for cold outside air. There was also a small opening in the roof, covered with seal skin, that could be opened to let out stale air and ventilate the house. Today, almost all Innuit live in permanent all-year housing, but they sometimes build these wonderful, traditional houses of snow, and a few even continue to live in them.

76. M1: Which of the following was used by the Innuit as the main material for a summer house?

77. M1: Where were snow houses the main form of winter house?

78. M1: What does the word *igloo* mean to an Innuit?

79. M1: What was one unique feature of the snow houses built by the Innuit?

80. M1: How was seal skin used in snow houses?

SECTION 2: STRUCTURE

Answer Key

Sentence Completion

1. C	6. D	11. B	16. A	21. D
2. C	7. C	12. D	17. A	22. C
3. B	8. A	13. D	18. B	23. A
4. C	9. D	14. B	19. D	
5. A	10. C	15. D	20. C	

Error Identification

24. A	32. D	40. A	47. B	54. C
25. B	33. C	41. A	48. B	55. A
26. C	34. B	42. B	49. A	56. C
27. B	35. D	43. B	50. D	57. D
28. A	36. A	44. C	51. D	58. A
29. B	37. B	45. D	52. B	59. B
30. C	38. D	46. A	53. D	60. A
31. C	39. C			

EXPLANATION: ERROR IDENTIFICATION

24. **The correct aqnswer is (A).** The word *like* must be used in place of *alike*. (The correct patterns are "Like A, B . . ." and "A and B are alike.")

25. **The correct answer is (B).** The full passive verb *are needed* should be replaced by a past participle (*needed*) or by a relative clause (*that are needed*).

26. **The correct answer is (C).** The plural possessive *their* must be used in place of *its* because it refers to the plural noun phrase *blind snakes*.

27. **The correct answer is (B).** The verb *do* should be used in place of *make*.

28. **The correct answer is (A).** The word *so* is required in place of *too*. (The correct pattern is *so* + adjective + *that* clause.)

29. **The correct answer is (B).** A main verb (*include*) must be used in place of the participle. (Used alone, an -*ing* form can never serve as a main verb.)

30. **The correct answer is (C).** An adverb (*efficiently*) is needed rather than the noun *efficiency*.

31. **The correct answer is (C).** The plural form, *thousands*, is required.

32. **The correct answer is (D).** To be parallel with the other items in the series (*beaten, melted*, and *pured*) another past participle (*drawn*) is required.

33. **The correct answer is (C).** The adjective *high* is needed in place of the noun *height*. (The phrase *in height* could also be used to correct the sentence.)

34. **The correct answer is (B).** The present perfect tense (*have worn*) is required in place of the past tense (*wore*). (The present perfect is usually used in sentences that contain the expression *since* + time word.)

35. **The correct answer is (D).** The noun *use* is needed in place of the gerund *using*.

36. **The correct answer is (A).** The definite article *the* cannot be used before a fraction; the phrase should correctly read *one third* or *a third*.

37. The correct answer is (B). A comparative form (*more beautiful*) is needed in place of the superlative (*most beautiful*).

38. The correct answer is (D). The noun *biography* should be used in place of the adjective *biographical*.

39. The correct answer is (C). The singular verb *has* must be used to agree with the subject. (After the phrase *each of the* + plural noun, a singular verb is always used.)

40. The correct answer is (A). The word *because* must be used before a clause. (*Because of* is used only before a noun phrase.)

41. The correct answer is (A). Before a noun phrase (*Martha Graham's first dance lesson*) the word *after* must be used rather than *afterwards*.

42. The correct answer is (B). The word *to* has been omitted; the phrase should read *due to the*.

43. The correct answer is (B). In this sentence, the preposition *for* must be used after *responsible*. (It is possible to use *responsible to* + person).

44. The correct answer is (C). The singular pronoun *it* should replace the pronoun *they* because the pronoun refers to the singular phrase *Costume jewelry*.

45. The correct answer is (D). In order to be parallel with the other words in the series (*scientific practices* and *superstitions*) a noun (*beliefs*) is needed in place of the verb *believes*.

46. The correct answer is (A). The noun *sculptures* should be used in place of the noun *sculptors*. (A *sculptor* is a person who makes a *sculpture*.)

47. The correct answer is (B). The relative pronoun *who* is properly used to refer only to a person; the relative pronouns *that* or *which* should be used to refer to a profession.

48. The correct answer is (B). The word *apples* should not be pluralized; it is part of a compound noun. (*Apple and pear trees* means *apple trees and pear trees*.)

49. The correct answer is (A). The preposition *at* is unnecessary and should be omitted.

50. The correct answer is (D). At the end of a clause, this phrase should be *as well*, not *as well as*. (The correct patterns are *A as well as B*, and *A and B as well*.)

51. The correct answer is (D). The adverb *suddenly* is needed in place of the adjective *sudden*.

52. The correct answer is (B). The preposition *by* is omitted; the phrase should read *formed by the. . . .*

53. The correct answer is (D). The reflexive pronoun *themselves* should be used in place of the personal pronoun *them*.

54. The correct answer is (C). The definite article *the* has been omitted; the phrase should correctly read *the course of*.

55. The correct answer is (A). The correct word order is adverb + participle (*widely spaced*).

56. The correct answer is (C). The noun *loss* should be used in place of the verb/participle *lost*.

57. The correct answer is (D). Before a noun (*distortions*) the negative word *no* should be used in place of *not*.

58. The correct answer is (A). In this sentence, the verb *takes* should be used in place of the verb *is*. (The correct pattern is *it* + *takes* + time period + infinitive.)

59. The correct answer is (B). The singular pronoun *that* should be used, because it refers to the singular noun phrase *fossil record*.

60. The correct answer is (A). The word *as* should be used in place of *that*. (*As* in this sentence means *in the way that . . .*)

SECTION 3: READING

Answer Key

1. C	11. D	21. A	31. A	41. A	51. D	61. D
2. A	12. C	22. B	32. C	42. C	52. B	62. D
3. B	13. A	23. C	33. C	43. A	53. B	63. C
4. D	14. D	24. C	34. C	44. C	54. D	64. D
5. A	15. B	25. C	35. B	45. B	55. A	65. C
6. B	16. C	26. A	36. B	46. A	56. B	66. A
7. C	17. D	27. B	37. D	47. D	57. C	67. D
8. A	18. A	28. B	38. C	48. B	58. A	68. C
9. D	19. A	29. C	39. A	49. C	59. D	69. A
10. B	20. B	30. B	40. D	50. A	60. C	70. B

EXPLANATION: READING

1. **The correct answer is (C).** There is no mention in the passage that lighthouses are used as weather stations to report bad weather to sailors. The other functions of lighthouses are given in lines 1–2.

2. **The correct answer is (A).** The reference is to *mariners* (*sailors*) in line 1.

3. **The correct answer is (B).** The word *prominent* is closest in meaning to *conspicuous*.

4. **The correct answer is (D).** According to the passage, a characteristic is a "distinctive pattern of light" (line 4).

5. **The correct answer is (A).** According to lines 8–9, "a group-occulting signal consists of a fixed light with two or more periods of darkness at regular intervals."

6. **The correct answer is (B).** A catoptric apparatus is one "in which metal is used to reflect the light" (line 11).

7. **The correct answer is (C).** There is no specific example provided for a lighthouse with day-marker patterns. There *are* examples of a lighthouse in the shape of a pyramid (the Bastion Lighthouse), a lighthouse made of steel (American Shoal Lighthouse), and a lighthouse that resembles a house on a platform (Race Rock Light).

8. **The correct answer is (A).** The word *tapering* means *becoming narrower*.

9. **The correct answer is (D).** According to lines 17–18, "Where lighthouses might be confused in daylight, they can be distinguished by day-marker patterns." It is logical that lighthouses would be confused in daylight because they have similar structures.

10. **The correct answer is (B).** The author said that, in the past, "lighthouse keepers put in hours of tedious work maintaining the lights." Today, however, humans supply "only occasional maintenance."

11. **The correct answer is (D).** There is no information to support choice (A); the passage says that the number of lighthouses has declined greatly since 1900. There is no information about the number of lighthouses in any single country other than the United States, so choice (B) could not be correct. Nor is there information about choice (C)—the specific numbers of functioning lighthouses or lighthouses that have been converted into historical monuments. There is information to support choice (D); there were 1,500 lighthouses in the United States in 1900, more than the 1,400 lighthouses existing outside the United States today.

12. **The correct answer is (C).** The passage compares the scientific accomplishments and methodologies of Luther Burbank and George Washington Carver. The products created by the two scientists, choice (A), are mentioned, but only as details. There is very little information about their influence as scientists, choice (B), and only Burbank is mentioned as being influenced by Darwin, choice (D).

13. **The correct answer is (A).** The word *drastically* is closest in meaning to *dramatically*.

14. **The correct answer is (D).** According to line 2, they "were close friends."

15. **The correct answer is (B).** This potato still "bears his name" (line 5), so it must be called the Burbank potato.

16. **The correct answer is (C).** The reference is to Burbank's work.

17. **The correct answer is (D).** The word *thwarted* means *defeated* or *obstructed*.

18. **The correct answer is (A).** The word *thorough* means *complete*.

19. **The correct answer is (A).** Line 12 states that Burbank "kept records only for his own use." Line 14 states that "Carver, on the other hand, was a careful researcher who took thorough notes."

20. **The correct answer is (B).** Lines 15-16 indicate that Carver earned his master's degree at Iowa State College.

21. **The correct answer is (A).** There is no mention that Carter developed new uses for cotton. In fact, according to lines 19-20, these other products were developed to "free Southern agriculture from the tyranny of cotton."

22. **The correct answer is (B).** The word *tyranny* is closest in meaning to the word *control*.

23. **The correct answer is (C).** The reference to his weaknesses as a researcher starts on line 11, beginning "However, the value of his contributions was diminished . . ."

24. **The correct answer is (C).** The focus of the passage is on Prince Edward Island's two main remaining natural habitats, sand dunes, and salt marshes.

25. **The correct answer is (C).** The quotation marks are used because the scenery looks unspoiled to visitors but has actually been tampered with since the eighteenth century.

26. **The correct answer is (A).** The word *hamlets* is closest in meaning to *villages*.

27. **The correct answer is (B).** The phrase *tampering with* is closest in meaning to *interfering with*.

28. **The correct answer is (B).** The second paragraph states that 80 percent of the trees had been cut down by 1900 to clear the land for farming and that more had been killed off by disease. However, the paragraph goes on to say that some of the farmland has been abandoned and returned to forest, so there must be more forest now than there was in 1900.

29. **The correct answer is (C).** Maple, birch, and oak are given as examples of the original climax forest. "Opportunist species," especially spruce (line 8) replaced these trees and would be more likely to be seen today.

30. **The correct answer is (B).** According to lines 15-16, beach pea and bayberry take root after marram grass stabilizes the dunes.

31. **The correct answer is (A).** According to lines 16-17, when marram grass is broken down, "the dunes may spread inland and inundate agricultural lands . . ."

32. **The correct answer is (C).** The word *trampled* is closest in meaning to *stepped on*.

33. **The correct answer is (C).** The word *bogs* is given as a synonym of the word *marshes* in line 22.

34. **The correct answer is (C).** According to line 19, "in the south are red dunes."

35. **The correct answer is (B).** Lines 20-21 state that "the dunes were once used as cattle pasture . . . but were abandoned." Line 25 states that marsh hay grown in the salt marshes was "used by the early settlers" but that "like the dunes, though, the marshes were soon dismissed as wasteland and escaped development" (lines 25-26).

36. **The correct answer is (B).** The author describes the destruction of one ecosystem—the original forest cover—in Paragraph 2.

37. **The correct answer is (D).** The first paragraph discusses the many environments in which lichens can live. Choice (A) is incorrect because lichens can live in the "driest desserts" (line 2). Choice (B) is incorrect because they can live in "steaming tropical rain forests" (line 1) and in hot springs. Choice (C) is incorrect because lichens can live "on the bricks of big-city buildings" (lines 1-2).

38. **The correct answer is (C).** The author refers to lichens as pioneers because they start "the formation of soil in which mosses, then ferns, and then other plants can take root."

39. **The correct answer is (A).** The word *barren* means *lifeless*.

40. **The correct answer is (D).** *Symbiosis* is defined in the passage as a relationship in which two organisms "live together to the benefit of both" (lines 7-8). In choice (A) the tiger and the grass do not actually live together, and while the tiger may benefit, the grass is unaffected. The same is true in choice (B), in which there is no mention that the shark benefits. In choice (C) the mistletoe benefits, but the trees are harmed. (This relationship is known as *parasitism*.) In choice (D), both the protozoa and the termites benefit by obtaining nutrition.

41. **The correct answer is (A).** Line 9 states that fungi "shelter the tender algae from direct sunlight," indicating that direct sunlight could damage the algae.

42. **The correct answer is (C).** The fungi are considered strange because they are "unlike any species that live independently" (line 12).

43. **The correct answer is (A).** The paragraph explains why lichens' characteristics as double organisms make them difficult to classify. Choice (B) is only a detail of the paragraph; there is no reason to believe that the author thinks choice (C) is true; choice (D) is too general to be the main idea of the paragraph, and there is no information in the passage to support this idea.

44. **The correct answer is (C).** The word *splendid* means *excellent* or *fine*.

45. **The correct answer is (B).** The passage primarily deals with the conflict between the states supporting the Large State Plan and those supporting the Small State Plan, and the Great Compromise that worked out the differences between the two groups.

46. **The correct answer is (A).** According to line 1, there were representatives from all thirteen states except Rhode Island—a total of twelve.

47. **The correct answer is (D).** The first paragraph indicates that the delegates to the Constitutional Convention had been told to revise the Articles of Confederation but that most delegates "believed that a strong central government was needed" (lines 3-4). This implies that the Articles provided for only a weak form of government.

48. **The correct answer is (B).** According to lines 6-7, in 1787 Virginia was the largest state in population; its population was twice that of New York, four times that of New Jersey, and ten times that of Delaware. Delaware, therefore, had the smallest population of the four states listed.

49. **The correct answer is (C).** The phrase refers to the Large State Plan.

50. **The correct answer is (A).** Angry debate was "heightened by a stifling heat wave" (line 13), while "a cooling of tempers seemed to come with lower temperatures" (line 14).

51. **The correct answer is (D).** The word *shrewd* means *clever* or *cunning*.

52. **The correct answer is (B).** There is no mention in the passage of how the president would be chosen under the compromise plan.

53. **The correct answer is (B).** The phrase *broke the logjam* means that problems were cleared up and progress became possible.

54. **The correct answer is (D).** The primary purpose of the passage is to discuss the development of balloon-frame houses, a "revolution in building" (line 11).

55. **The correct answer is (A).** Lines 7-8 indicate that the balloon-frame house was "invented . . . by a carpenter from Hartford, Connecticut."

56. **The correct answer is (B).** Choice (A) is answered: it was invented in Chicago (line 8). Choice (C) is answered: it was 2 × 4 and 2 × 6 inches (line 9). Choice (D) is answered: it was invented in 1833 (line 7). However, the inventor is not named in the passage.

57. **The correct answer is (C).** Choices (A) and (B) are colonial wooden homes, and, according to the passage, most of these "could be built with simple tools and minimal skills" (lines 3-4). Choice (D) "could be assembled by any careful worker who could saw in a straight line and drive a nail" (lines 9-10). Choice (C), however, "required highly-skilled workers with special tools" (line 7).

58. **The correct answer is (A).** Choices (B), (C), and (D) are listed in the third paragraph. Choice (A) is not given. In fact, the author implies that sophisticated tools were not needed to build this type of house.

59. **The correct answer is (D).** Because of the lightweight materials used to build balloon-frame houses, "skeptics predicted that a strong wind would send such houses flying through the air like balloons" (lines 13-14).

60. **The correct answer is (C).** The word *derision* means *ridicule* or *mockery*.

61. **The correct answer is (D).** The passage concentrates on the books written by Rachel Carson and on her career as a writer.

62. **The correct answer is (D).** Lines 1-2 state that Carson studied zoology at Johns Hopkins University.

63. **The correct answer is (C).** Carson was born in 1907 (line 1) and published *Under the Sea Wind* in 1941 (line 4), so she must have been about 34 years of age at the time of publication.

64. **The correct answer is (D).** According to lines 4-5, when *Under the Sea Wind* was first published, "it received excellent reviews, but sales were poor until it was reissued in 1952."

65. **The correct answer is (C).** There is no mention that Rachel Carson took part in a research expedition. The other sources are given in lines 7-9.

66. **The correct answer is (A).** Carson "realized the limitations of her nontechnical readers" (line 9), implying that the book was not highly technical. It did have a poetic quality (line 7), and it was fascinating (interesting), according to line 6, and well researched (lines 7-9).

67. **The correct answer is (D).** The word *reckless* is closest in meaning to *irresponsible*.

68. **The correct answer is (C).** Line 11 states that the book *Silent Spring* "proved how much harm was done by the reckless use of insecticides."

69. **The correct answer is (A).** The word *faulty* is closest in meaning to the word *flawed*.

70. **The correct answer is (B).** Carson's work "was vindicated" by the report (lines 14-15), implying that the report contradicted the chemical industry's claims and supported her ideas.

Practice Test 4

Answer Key

1. B	11. A	21. C	31. D	41. B
2. D	12. A	22. C	32. B	42. A
3. C	13. B	23. B	33. B	43. A
4. D	14. A	24. C	34. D	44. B
5. D	15. C	25. A	35. C	45. C
6. A	16. B	26. C	36. D	46. C
7. C	17. A	27. D	37. A	47. C
8. C	18. D	28. A	38. C	48. A
9. A	19. B	29. B	39. D	49. D
10. D	20. B	30. D	40. D	50. B

PART A

TRANSCRIPT*

1. F1: We need someone to put together a slide show for our class presentation.
    M1: How about Donna?
    F2: What does the man mean?

2. F1: Could you hand me a teaspoon, please?
    M2: Hang on, let me wash one.
    F2: What is the man going to do?

3. M1: Steve hasn't been himself lately, has he?
    F1: Well, no, he hasn't. He's had a lot on his mind.
    F2: What do the speakers say about Steve?

4. F1: What's Nancy doing this afternoon?
    M1: Playing golf, probably. She never wants to do anything else.
    F2: What does the man say about Nancy?

5. F1: How's that soup you ordered, Max?
    M2: Not as warm as I'd like it to be.
    F2: What does Max say about the soup?

6. M1: So, where are the books being stored?
    M2: In a warehouse somewhere.
    F2: What is learned from this conversation?

7. F1: Have you heard the good news about Marilyn?
    M1: You mean that she won a prize for her poetry?
    F2: What has the man heard about Marilyn?

8. F1: You sure checked a lot of books out of the library.
    M2: Oh, these aren't library books. I went to a used book sale. They were practically giving them away!
    F2: What does the man imply about the books?

---
* Note: M1 = first male voice   M2 = second male voice   F1 = first female voice   F2 = second female voice

9. M1: I heard your guitar was damaged.
    F1: Yes, but thanks to Mr. Benson, now it's as good as new.
    F2: What can be inferred about Mr. Benson from the conversation?

10. F1: All my papers almost blew away.
    M1: Windy out there today, isn't it?
    F2: What does the man mean?

11. F1: You know, whenever I read a book, I always wonder what the author looks like. For example, I'd like to see a picture of Robert Kurtz.
    M1: Well, if you're that interested, there's a photograph of him on the back of his new book.
    F2: What does the man say about Robert Kurtz?

12. F1: You don't know how to set up the printer? Try reading the manual, why don't you?
    M1: I did, and I'm still in the dark.
    F2: What is the man's problem?

13. Listen to a telephone conversation.
    (RING . . . RING . . . SOUND OF PHONE BEING PICKED UP.)
    M2: Hello?
    F1: Hello, is Rita there?
    M2: Hang on a minute. I'll see.
    F2: What does the man imply about Rita?

14. F1: I should have spent more time practicing the piano to get ready for the concert. I don't think I played well at all.
    M2: If I were you, I wouldn't dwell on it another minute.
    F2: What does the man suggest the woman do?

15. F1: I can't understand why Harold changed majors. He would have made a great mathematician.
    M1: I don't know either. He loved the subject, and his grades were good.
    F2: What can be concluded about Harold from this conversation?

16. M1: Robin, do you realize you had a dental appointment an hour ago?
    F1: I *did?*
    F2: What is Robin's reaction to the man's remark?

17. M1: Oh, so Charlene *was* able to get reservations for dinner here tonight.
    F1: Yes, just at the last minute.
    F2: What had the man initially assumed?

18. M1: I don't suppose you're free to go bowling Saturday evening, are you?
    F1: As a matter of fact, I *am.* I was planning to go to a lecture with my sister, but it was called off.
    F2: What will the woman probably do on Saturday evening?

19. M1: I just bought a camcorder. It's used, but it's in pretty good condition.
    F1: What's a good used camcorder going for these days?
    F2: What does the woman ask the man?

20. F1: These new glasses are giving me headaches.
    M1: Mine did, too, as first. That should wear off soon.
    F2: What does the man tell the woman?

21. F1: Today's the first of the month. Isn't your rent due today?
    M1: Yes, but I always pay it the day before it's due.
    F2: What does the man say about his rent?

22. M2: Is Roberta at home yet?
    F1: No, she had to work late again today.
    F2: What does the woman say about Roberta?

23. M1: I've never taken a class as hard as the first half of the accounting course.
F1: You think *that* was hard—wait till you take the second half!
F2: What does the woman imply about the accounting course?

24. M2: Have you ever read the book *The Great Gatsby*?
F1: Only a couple of dozen times!
F2: What does the woman imply about the book?

25. M2: I understand you intend to become a research biologist.
F1: My dream is that someday, I'll discover something as important as penicillin.
F2: What does the woman want to do?

26. F1: A lot of people were planning to attend the debate.
M1: Not many were there, though.
F2: What does the man mean?

27. F1: I need to pay my check and leave.
M1: I'll try to catch the waiter's eye.
F2: What does the man intend to do?

28. F1: I heard someone say that Sally needs a lot of improvement if she hopes to win the tennis match on Saturday.
M2: Whoever said that obviously hasn't seen her out on the court recently!
F2: What does the man imply about Sally?

29. M1: Wow, your apartment looks great! I've never seen it so clean.
F1: Well, my roommates pitched in and helped me, and the work was done in no time.
F2: What does the woman say about her roommates?

30. M1: Professor Atkinson, can I see you after this class?
M2: I'm due at a faculty meeting then—how about the same time on Friday?
F2: When does Professor Atkinson suggest that they meet?

PART B

Questions 31–33: Listen to a conversation between two students.

M1: Want to go out and get something to eat?
F1: I can't. I have a chemistry midterm on Monday and a German exam on Tuesday.
M1: I have a geology exam Monday myself, but I think I'm ready for it.
F1: What kind of exam is it going to be—multiple choice or essay?
M1: Neither. The professor is going to give us a mineral sample and we have to identify it.
F1: How do you do that? I mean, a rock's a rock, isn't it?
M1: Actually, there are a lot of tests you can perform on minerals to help you figure out what they are. Probably the first tests I'll do are scratch tests. When you do a scratch test, you rub the sample on a known mineral to see if the unknown mineral scratches the known mineral or vice versa. That tells you the relative hardness of the sample.
F1: What other tests will you do?
M1: I'll probably do a streak test next. In that test, you rub an unknown mineral against a piece of unglazed porcelain to see what color the streak is.
F1: Why can't you just *look* at the mineral to see what color it is?
M1: Well, you can, but sometimes a mineral has a lot of impurities, and they can change its color, but a streak test shows the mineral's true color. Then there's always the specific gravity test, the blowpipe test . . . oh, and the ultraviolet test, and . . .
F1: And after you've done all these tests, you can positively identify any mineral?
M1: Well, usually . . . but not always. I just hope I can on Monday!

31. F2: What type of exam is the man taking on Monday?

32. F2: According to the man, what does a streak test show about a mineral?

33. F2: What does the man imply about the tests used to identify minerals?

Questions 34–37: Listen to a telephone conversation.

(RING . . . RING . . . SOUND OF PHONE BEING PICKED UP.)

    M2: Hello?

    F1: Hi, Mike, this is Polly at Via Tours. Hope I didn't catch you at a bad time. I just wanted to give you an update on your travel plans for next week.

    M2: No, no. I'm glad you called. What have you found out?

    F1: Well, I've made hotel reservations for you in Key West at the Beachcomber Hotel.

    M2: Oh, great! That's my favorite hotel there.

    F1: And I've got you a rental car so that you can get from the Miami airport down to Key West.

    M2: Perfect. And what about the airline reservations?

    F1: That's the problem. There aren't any direct flights from here to Miami, you know. You'll have to fly through either Minneapolis or Chicago. I went ahead and put you on a flight from here to Chicago for next Monday, and I've got you on stand-by from Chicago to Miami.

    M2: Stand-by? You mean I don't have confirmed reservations to Miami?

    F1: I'm afraid not, but I'm pretty confident that something will open up and we'll be able to get you on a flight.

    M2: I hope so. Well, let me know as soon as you hear something. And next year, I've got to be sure to book my flights earlier.

34. F2: What is Polly's probable occupation?

35. F2: According to the conversation, where does Mike hope to spend his vacation?

36. F2: For which of the following does Mike not have confirmed reservations?

37. F2: What does Mike tell Polly he will do next year?

PART C

Questions 38–42: Listen to a talk given at an art exhibit.

    M2: I'd like to take this opportunity to welcome all of you to the opening of the American Folk Art Exhibit here at the Hotchkiss Museum. Some of the pieces in this exhibit have been displayed in other museums, but this is the first time they've all been shown together. Of course, most folk artists would be surprised to find their work in a museum. That's because folk artists created their art for practical purposes, or sometimes simply for the pleasure of creating art, but *not* because they expected their work to wind up in an exhibit in a museum, in a private gallery, or in the home of a collector.

    As you look around, you'll see that the work of these early American artists is delightful if simple and it still feels fresh. Our exhibit includes many types of folk art, but I suggest we begin with a look at the work of sign painters from the eighteenth and nineteenth centuries. Although the paint on these signs has faded, they were surely painted in bright colors to catch the eye of prospective customers. Keep in mind that before around 1870, the majority of Americans couldn't read. Shopkeepers wanted practical signs to advertise their wares. This sign, for example, with its picture of a steaming soup kettle, once hung in front of a restaurant in colonial Boston. This one, in the shape of a horseshoe, hung in front of a blacksmith's shop. You can probably guess where that sign with a picture of a boot on it once hung.

    You may have noticed that there are no plaques to tell you the names of these sign painters. Sometimes we do know the names of folk artists because they signed their work or had a particularly distinctive style, but there were no signatures on any of these signs, and the artists' names have long since been forgotten.

38. F2: Where is this talk being given?

39. F2: What does the speaker say about the art that appears in this exhibit?

40. F2: What can be inferred about the sign with the picture of a boot on it?

41. F2: Which of the following words would the speaker probably use to describe American folk art?

42. F2: Why does the speaker not mention the names of the sign painters?

Questions 43–46: Listen to a talk given at an academic awards ceremony.

M1: Good evening. I'd like to welcome the president of Colton College, the chancellors, the administrators, my fellow faculty members, and the students to the Academic Excellence Awards Night. Our first award, for Faculty Member of the Year, goes to Professor Patricia Callaghan. I'm particularly pleased that this year's winner is from my own department. Professor Callaghan has been at Colton College for a total of eight years now—two as a graduate student and six as a faculty member. She has consistently received top evaluations from the students as well as from her department head. Her papers on historical economics are well respected by all of her colleagues—including myself, if I may say so—and this year she received a government grant to continue her work on generating computer models of the economy. Please join me, ladies and gentlemen, in giving a round of applause to Professor Callaghan.

43. F2: What is the purpose of this talk?

44. F2: Who is the speaker?

45. F2: What subject does Professor Callaghan probably teach?

46. F2: For how many years has Professor Callaghan been a teacher at Colton College?

Questions 47–50: Listen to part of a lecture given in a class in American Literature.

F1: Good morning, class. In our last class, we talked about Walt Whitman, and said he was one of the two greatest voices of American poetry in the nineteenth century. The other was Emily Dickinson. Now, their poetry could not have been more different. Dickinson claimed that she never even read Whitman's poems. Their lifestyles could not have been more different. But they were both important innovators.

Now, I said before that Whitman became well known around the world. Dickinson was famous only in her own village—Amherst, Massachusetts—and that was not for her poetry but for her mysterious ways. You see, she almost never left the house of her father, who was a wealthy lawyer. When she did appear, she always wore white dresses. Although this may not seem too strange to us today, it was pretty unusual for Amherst in the 1800s!

For a woman who lived such an uneventful life, though, she wrote amazingly perceptive poems about nature, love, and death. Her poems are all short and untitled. What I particularly admire about these poems is their economy—she was able to say so much in so few words!

She never intended her poems to be published. At least ten of them were published during her lifetime, but that was against her will. After her death in 1886, her family discovered that she had written over 1,700 poems. They published a collection of about thirty of her poems a few years later, and eventually, all of them appeared in print.

Now, we'll take a look at some of her poems, but first . . . questions, anyone?

47. F2: What point does the speaker make about Walt Whitman?

48. F2: Why was Emily Dickinson famous in her hometown?

49. F2: What does the speaker say she particularly admires about the poems of Emily Dickinson?

50. F2: About how many of Emily Dickinson's poems were published when she was alive?

SECTION 2: STRUCTURE

Answer Key

1. D	11. B	21. C	31. A
2. A	12. C	22. B	32. B
3. B	13. A	23. D	33. D
4. D	14. C	24. B	34. B
5. C	15. B	25. A	35. A
6. A	16. B	26. D	36. C
7. A	17. D	27. D	37. C
8. D	18. C	28. A	38. D
9. B	19. C	29. D	39. D
10. A	20. D	30. C	40. A

EXPLANATION: ERROR IDENTIFICATION

16. **The correct answer is (B).** The possessive adjective *its* should replace *one's*.

17. **The correct answer is (D).** A noun (*sanitation*) is needed in place of the adjective *sanitary*.

18. **The correct answer is (C).** When used before a noun, a number + measurement is not pluralized; the correct phrase is *60-mile*.

19. **The correct answer is (C).** The correct word order is *long before*.

20. **The correct answer is (D).** The noun *humor* is needed in place of the adjective *humorous*.

21. **The correct answer is (C).** Before a clause (*bacteria are the chief decomposers of grassland soil*) the word *as* must be used instead of *like*. (*Like* is only used before noun phrases.)

22. **The correct answer is (B).** The correct superlative form of the one-syllable adjective *safe* is *safest*.

23. **The correct answer is (D).** The plural possessive form *their* must be used to refer to the plural noun phrase *ballpoint pens*.

24. **The correct answer is (B).** The definite article *the* should not be used before the names of fields of study, such as *archaeology*.

25. **The correct answer is (A).** The word *such* should replace the word *so*.

26. **The correct answer is (D).** The noun *life* should be used in place of *live*.

27. **The correct answer is (D).** For parallelism, an *-ing* form (*hiking*) is needed in place of the plural noun *hikes*.

28. **The correct answer is (A).** The noun *ability* should be used in place of the adjective *able*.

29. **The correct answer is (D).** The correct pattern is *not only . . . but also*.

30. **The correct answer is (C).** The plural verb *do* should be used in place of the singular *does* in order to agree with the plural subject *gases*.

31. **The correct answer is (A).** The word *Most* should be used in place of *Almost*. (This sentence could also be corrected by using the phrase *Almost all*.)

32. The correct answer is (B). The expression *both . . . and* is used to join two words or phrases, but this sentence contains a series of three words: *nails, claws,* and *hooves.* Therefore, the word *both* should be eliminated.

33. The correct answer is (D). The correct word order is *did they.* Sentences beginning with negative adverbials (such as *not until*) follow the question pattern: auxiliary + subject + main verb.

34. The correct answer is (B). The expression *percent* must be used in place of *percentage.*

35. The correct answer is (A). The plural noun *Mathematicians* (people who study mathematics) must be used in place of the singular noun *Mathematics* (the field); this is clear because the verb *have* is plural.

36. The correct answer is (C). An adjective (*wild*) is needed in place of the adverb *wildly.* (The word *lovely* is an adjective that ends with *-ly*, not an adverb.)

37. The correct answer is (C). The definite article *the* is needed in place of the indefinite article *a.*

38. The correct answer is (D). After the adjective *essential* the preposition *to* or *for* should be used.

39. The correct answer is (D). The correct word choice in this sentence is *earliest.*

40. The correct answer is (A). A noun (*marriage*) is needed in place of the participle *married.*

Answer Key

1.	C	11.	B	21.	B	31.	B	41.	C
2.	A	12.	D	22.	A	32.	D	42.	A
3.	B	13.	C	23.	B	33.	D	43.	C
4.	D	14.	A	24.	A	34.	A	44.	A
5.	B	15.	D	25.	D	35.	D	45.	D
6.	C	16.	A	26.	C	36.	A	46.	B
7.	C	17.	B	27.	B	37.	C	47.	A
8.	B	18.	C	28.	A	38.	C	48.	C
9.	B	19.	D	29.	C	39.	A	49.	D
10.	A	20.	C	30.	D	40.	D	50.	B

EXPLANATION: READING

1. **The correct answer is (C).** The first paragraph presents an overall definition of cooperation. Choice (A) is incorrect because the first paragraph explains what cooperation has in common with competition and conflict, but not how it differs from them. Choice (B) is incorrect because examples of specific forms of cooperation are given in the second, third, and fourth paragraphs, not the first. Choice (D) is incorrect; at no point in the passage does the author urge readers to cooperate.

2. **The correct answer is (A).** The word *cherished* means *prized, loved*.

3. **The correct answer is (B).** The word *fuse* means *unite, join together*.

4. **The correct answer is (D).** According to line 8, primary cooperation "is most often characteristic of preliterate societies"—in other words, societies in which people have generally not developed the ability to read and write.

5. **The correct answer is (B).** Lines 11-12 state that "members perform tasks so that they can *separately* enjoy the fruits of their cooperation in terms of salary, prestige, or power."

6. **The correct answer is (C).** The passage states that in tertiary cooperation, "latent conflict underlies the shared work" and that it "involves common means to achieve antagonistic goals." The situation described in choice (C) best fits this definition. Choice (A) is an example of secondary cooperation; choice (B) is an example of competition; choice (D) is an example of primary (or perhaps secondary) competition.

7. **The correct answer is (C).** In the fourth paragraph, the author calls the third type *tertiary cooperation*, or *accommodation* (line 14). At the end of that paragraph, the author states that "the term *antagonistic cooperation* is sometimes used for this relationship" as well. Latent conflict is NOT another term for this relationship; it is a characteristic of it.

8. **The correct answer is (B).** The word *fragile* means *weak* or *easily broken*.

9. **The correct answer is (B).** In this passage, *common* means *shared* or *jointly held*.

10. **The correct answer is (A).** The author defines a concept (*cooperation*) by discussing each of its three forms in the second, third, and fourth paragraphs of the passage.

11. **The correct answer is (B).** Only one of Schaefer's contributions to science is noted and that only briefly in the first paragraph. There is no description in the passage of the process by which snow crystals are formed. The effects of cloud seeding are not directly discussed. The passage is mainly an introduction to the basics of cloud seeding or weather modification.

12. **The correct answer is (D).** In this passage, the word *spawned* means *created or generated.* (It literally means to give birth to.)

13. **The correct answer is (C).** According to the first paragraph, farmers and ranchers first felt optimism (lines 3–4). However, because it was not clear whether "the cloud-seeding operations of the late 1940s and 1950s . . . had any effect" it is reasonable to believe that the farmers' and ranchers' optimism must have turned to disappointment.

14. **The correct answer is (A).** Line 7 states that cloud seeding came to be called "weather modification," indicating that cloud seeding is the older term.

15. **The correct answer is (D).** According to lines 10–11, winter orographic clouds are "formed when air currents encounter a mountain slope and rise."

16. **The correct answer is (A).** The reference is to water droplets (line 17).

17. **The correct answer is (B).** The passage states that in ground-based seeding, silver iodide is burned in ground generators and that the "smoke rises into the clouds where the tiny silver iodide particles act as nuclei for the formation of ice crystals" (lines 13–15).

18. **The correct answer is (C).** Choice (A) is not correct because seeding from planes is "more expensive" (line 18). Choice (B) is not correct; when clouds are seeded from airplanes, the process of spontaneous nucleation is employed (lines 17–18). Choice (D) cannot be correct; there is no information about the effect of temperature on cloud-seeding operations. Choice (B) is best because the passage says that seeding from airplanes is "more efficient" (line 18).

19. **The correct answer is (D).** Line 21 states, "About 85 percent of the waters in the rivers of the West comes from melted snow."

20. **The correct answer is (C).** The author quotes an expert in lines 22–23 who says that "the water problems of the future may make the energy problem of the 1970s seem like child's play to solve." (*Child's play* means a simple problem.)

21. **The correct answer is (B).** In line 24, the author mentions "private interests such as ski areas and agricultural cooperatives."

22. **The correct answer is (A).** In line 28, the author calls the effort to produce precipitation in 1976–77 a "crash program" (meaning an urgent or emergency program) and later classes it with "hurry-up programs" (line 29).

23. **The correct answer is (B).** The passage begins "The biological community changes once again as one moves from the city to the suburbs," indicating that the probable subject of the previous paragraph was the biological community in the city.

24. **The correct answer is (A).** Most of the trees "have been deliberately planted" (lines 2–3), while mammals "have moved in from the surrounding countryside" (lines 3–4).

25. **The correct answer is (D).** The word *thoroughfares* means *streets* or *roads.*

26. **The correct answer is (C).** Line 6 states that "usually only one species" of squirrel is found "in any given suburb."

27. **The correct answer is (B).** The word *thrive* means *flourish* or *prosper.*

28. **The correct answer is (A).** The word *odd* means *strange* or *unusual.*

29. **The correct answer is (C).** The topic of the second paragraph is "the odd biological sameness in these suburban communities" (line 10).

30. **The correct answer is (D).** The author states in lines 13-14 that "unlike the natural biomes, the urban and suburban communities exist in spite of, not because of, the climate." This means that the climate actually creates the conditions in the natural biomes, so the effect there is much more noticeable.

31. **The correct answer is (B).** The passage mainly discusses the potential use of Hot Dry Rock. There is no mention in the passage of the drawbacks (disadvantages) of using Hot Dry Rock nor does the passage explain how Hot Dry Rock was discovered; choice (D) is merely a detail of the third paragraph.

32. **The correct answer is (D).** The term *pressurized reservoir* refers to a supply of water that has been superheated by Hot Dry Rock. The other terms refer to Hot Dry Rock itself.

33. **The correct answer is (D).** The word *adjacent* means *side-by-side* or *next to.*

34. **The correct answer is (A).** Lines 4-5 state that "the concept . . . is quite simple, at least in theory," indicating that putting the concept into practice might be difficult.

35. **The correct answer is (D).** The reference is to the surface of the earth.

36. **The correct answer is (A).** According to the second paragraph, the heat energy of the water "is transferred to a volatile liquid that in turn drives an electric power-producing turbine."

37. **The correct answer is (C).** According to lines 10-12, Duchane thinks that a 1-megawatt plant will be built "in around two decades" (twenty years) and that "a small prototype station will be built in half that time" (ten years).

38. **The correct answer is (C).** The "grander dream" refers to the possibility of pumping seawater into the Hot Dry Rock, turning some of it to vapor, and thus obtaining pure water while producing electricity at the same time (lines 12-15).

39. **The correct answer is (A).** The reference is to seawater (line 13).

40. **The correct answer is (D).** The passage mainly focuses on historic houses in Taos that have been restored and are now open to the public.

41. **The correct answer is (C).** The word *meticulously* means *carefully* or *painstakingly.*

42. **The correct answer is (A).** The word *imposing* means *striking* or *impressive.*

43. **The correct answer is (C).** According to line 7, "Its twenty-one rooms and two courtyards now house a living museum."

44. **The correct answer is (A).** Bent was "a trader who later became governor of the New Mexico territory" (lines 9-10) and was thus a merchant and a politician.

45. **The correct answer is (D).** According to lines 10-11, "Carson's house was built in 1843, Bent's three years later"—in other words, 1846.

46. **The correct answer is (B).** The term *bigger sister* indicates that Sante Fe is similar to Taos but has a larger population.

47. **The correct answer is (A).** The author mentions "the works of Jack London and other bestselling authors," (lines 14–15) so in this context, *works* means *books.*

48. **The correct answer is (C).** Line 15 states that Blumenschein was on a "Denver-to-Mexico City sketching tour."

49. **The correct answer is (D).** The artist Nicolai Fechin was "Russian-born" (line 18) and he carved and decorated the furniture and so on to look like that "of a traditional country house in his homeland" (line 20). The style must have been traditional Russian.

50. **The correct answer is (B).** Jack London is not given in the passage as a resident of Taos. He is mentioned because Ernest Blumenschein illustrated his books.

Practice Test 5

Answer Key

1. **D**	11. **B**	21. **C**	31. **D**	41. **D**
2. **D**	12. **A**	22. **A**	32. **C**	42. **C**
3. **C**	13. **B**	23. **D**	33. **C**	43. **B**
4. **A**	14. **B**	24. **A**	34. **A**	44. **D**
5. **B**	15. **C**	25. **A**	35. **A**	45. **C**
6. **B**	16. **A**	26. **D**	36. **B**	46. **D**
7. **D**	17. **A**	27. **D**	37. **C**	47. **B**
8. **D**	18. **D**	28. **D**	38. **B**	48. **D**
9. **C**	19. **B**	29. **C**	39. **D**	49. **C**
10. **A**	20. **D**	30. **A**	40. **A**	50. **B**

PART A

TRANSCRIPT*

1. F1: I thought you were going to pick up some strawberries to have after dinner.
   M1: I went by Bailey's Market to get some, but they were fresh out.
   M2: What does the man mean?

2. M1: That has to be one of the worst lectures Professor Fowles has ever given.
   F2: It certainly wasn't up to his usual standards.
   M2: What do the speakers say about Professor Fowles?

3. M1: I *hate* missing breakfast!
   F1: Me too, but if we'd stopped for breakfast, we would have missed the appointment.
   M2: What did the speakers do this morning?

4. M1: I bought a new bicycle this week.
   F2: Glad to hear it. What kind?
   M2: What does the woman ask the man about the bicycle?

5. M1: Have you ever watched that program *Family Tree* on television?
   F2: Well, I *tried* to a couple of times.
   M2: What does the woman imply about the program?

6. F2: Let's make some sandwiches before we go. Then we won't have to eat lunch at the ski lodge.
   M1: That's not a bad idea. The restaurant there is *so* expensive!
   M2: What will the speakers probably do?

7. M1: I had to miss Dr. Hudson's first class. What was the lecture about?
   F2: For one thing, she talked about the differences between planets and stars.
   M2: What course does Professor Hudson probably teach?

---
* Note: M1 = first male voice   M2 = second male voice   F1 = first female voice   F2 = second female voice

8. M1: If you'd like to sing along, here are the lyrics for that song.
    F1: Oh, I already know them by heart!
    M2: What does the woman mean?

9. F1: Excuse me, do you know where the Admiral Hotel is?
    M1: I can't say that I do. Why don't you walk over and ask that taxi driver? He should know.
    M2: What does the man suggest the woman do?

10. F1: Tim sure got these clean!
    F2: I'll say! You can hardly tell that there are panes of glass in them.
    M2: What are the two speakers probably discussing?

11. F2: What time is Dean Metzger's reception tonight? Seven?
    M1: That's *tonight*?
    M2: What had the man NOT been aware of?

12. F2: Weren't you in my advanced math class last semester?
    M1: Me? You must be joking. I can barely add 2 and 2 together.
    M2: What does the man imply?

13. M1: You let Vince plan this event?
    F1: This time, but never again!
    M2: What does the woman imply about Vince?

14. F2: What was the matter with Jack last night?
    F1: I don't know. He was a nervous wreck, though, wasn't he?
    M2: What do the speakers say about Jack?

15. F1: I just walked by Professor Dixon's classroom, and there was no one in there.
    M1: That's because he always takes his class outside when the weather is nice.
    M2: What can be inferred from this conversation?

16. M1: On second thought, I'm going to take statistics instead of computer science.
    F2: Are you *sure* this time?
    M2: What does the *man* tell the woman?

17. F1: What did you think of the opera you saw Saturday night?
    M1: Frankly, I don't have much to compare it with.
    M2: What does the man imply?

18. F1: Here's the tape, some scissors, and some brown paper.
    M1: Thanks. Now I just need to find Richard's address.
    M2: What is the man probably going to do?

19. M1: Bob was late for the dinner because he was helping his roommate.
    F2: Isn't that just like Bob?
    M2: What does the woman imply about Bob?

20. F2: What did you think of Brenda's story?
    M1: To tell you the truth, I found it hard to keep a straight face while she was telling it.
    M2: How did the man feel about the story?

21. M1: Is this Dr. Goldsmith's office?
    F2: No, this is room 301. Dr. Goldsmith's office is right downstairs from here.
    M2: Where is Dr. Goldsmith's office?

22. F1: I saw Suzanne at the meeting this afternoon.
    M1: Yeah, she was the *last* person I expected to see there.
    M2: What does the man imply about Suzanne?

23. M1: Marie's picture was in the newspaper.
F2: Oh? What for?
M2: What does the woman ask?

24. M1: Traffic was so bad on the way to the airport that I almost missed my flight to Boston.
F2: I could have told you that it would be.
M2: What does the woman mean?

25. F1: That seafood restaurant on College Avenue is going to close down after just two months.
M1: So I heard. Too bad.
M2: What does the man mean?

26. F2: Here you are, sir—a hamburger and a large drink.
M1: Wait a second—that's what you call *large*?
M2: What does the man imply?

27. F1: Peter, want to play softball?
M1: No, I have to go down to the lumber yard now. I'm building some bookshelves.
M2: What will Peter probably do next?

28. F2: No, Emma's not here. She went to choir practice.
M1: Oh, she must be feeling much better then.
M2: What had the man assumed about Emma?

29. M1: How did you find out about this lecture series?
F1: Just through word of mouth.
M2: What does the woman say about the lecture series?

30. F1: Have you decided whether you're staying at the Buckley House or the Sherman Hotel during the conference?
M1: I didn't have to decide—the Buckley was already completely booked.
M2: What can be inferred from this conversation?

PART B

Questions 31-33: Listen to a conversation between two students.

M1: Hey, Amy, where are you off to?
F2: To the Recreation Center. I've got a physical education class.
M1: What course are you taking?
F2: Fencing.
M1: Oh, really? Is it hard?
F2: I was in the fencing club in high school, so for me it's mostly review.
M1: I once heard someone call fencing "the thinking person's sport." Would you agree with that?
F2: It *does* require lots of concentration, and if you want to win matches, tactics are important— just like in a game of chess.
M1: And I suppose you have to be fast and strong to win.
F2: Speed is important, and agility, but you don't have to be particularly strong to be a good fencer. The main reason I like fencing, though, is that it's great exercise. I find an hour of fencing is as good a workout as, say, an hour of tennis.

31. M2: What is the woman going to do?

32. M2: Which of the following does the woman say is *not* particularly important in fencing?

33. M2: Why does the woman compare fencing to tennis?

Questions 34–37: Listen to a conversation in a university bookstore.

F1: That comes to $160.

M1: One hundred and sixty dollars! I just can't believe how expensive textbooks are. And that's just for required texts. Why, if I had to buy all the books on my suggested reading lists, I'd have to take out a bank loan!

F1: You could save some money if you bought used texts, you know.

M1: I suppose, but it's hard for me to study from a text that's been marked up. Tell me, if I don't need some of these books, can I get a full refund?

F1: Sure, if the professor changes his mind about a book or if you drop a course, just return it and we'll give you your money back, but only for the first three weeks of class. So don't write your name in the text or mark it up until you're sure you're going to keep it all semester.

M1: And what about at the end of the semester? What's your buy-back policy?

F1: As long as the books are in reasonably good condition, and they're going to be used in class the next semester, we'll give you 50 percent of their original value, even if you didn't buy them at this store. Of course, if a professor changes texts or if a new edition comes out, we won't buy them back at all.

M1: Fifty percent—that's all?

F1: Well, I suppose that doesn't sound like much, but that's the store policy.

34. M2: What is the man buying?

35. M2: At what point in the semester does this conversation take place?

36. M2: If the man sells all the books that he buys today back to the store at the end of the semester, how much money will he receive?

37. M2: Why would the bookstore NOT buy back the man's books at any price?

PART C

Questions 38–42: Listen to a presentatoin given in an architecture class.

F1: Good afternoon, everyone. As you all know, our class project was to investigate some unconventional styles of housing and report on one. The one I chose is called the Earthship. It was developed by an architect named Michael Reynolds about twenty-five years ago, and there are about a thousand of them in existence today. One remarkable thing about the Earthship is that it is built almost entirely of recycled materials. The exterior walls are made of used tires packed with soil. Aluminum cans are tucked between the tires and the exterior walls are coated with straw and mud. Interior walls are made of cement and glass bottles. This may not sound very attractive, but, to learn more about these houses, I visited one not too far from here and, I can tell you, the finished building is very beautiful. And these houses use no outside electricity. They generate electricity from rooftop solar panels. They produce no sewage and don't pump water from the ground. So, what about costs? You can buy a book describing the building process for around $25 and architectural drawings for $2,000. A small, basic house—called a "nest"—can be built for about $35,000. Larger Earthships can cost hundreds of thousands of dollars. Now, I've brought a small model of an Earthship that I built myself. I hope that when I graduate and am designing houses myself, I can incorporate some of these ideas into my own designs. So come on up and take a close look at it.

38. F2: Who is the speaker?

39. F2: Which of these would NOT be needed to build an Earthship?

40. F2: What did the speaker do to research her project?

41. F2: According to the speaker, what is a "nest"?

42. F2: What did the speaker bring with her?

Questions 43–46: Listen to an announcement made on a university radio station.

M1: The Central State University School of Engineering invites you to go fly a kite—that is, once you've designed it. This weekend, the Third Annual Kite Competition will take place. Building a kite poses a number of engineering problems, and we want to see how you solve them. As in the two previous years, there are lots of prizes. There will be prizes for the kite with the largest surface area and for the kite with the smallest; for the kite that can lift the heaviest load and for the kite made from the most unusual material; there's even one for the funniest kite. Of course, all winning kites must be working models; you must be able to fly them at least 100 feet in the air. You don't have to be an engineering student to compete; all interested students at Central State are invited to enter. Preliminary events take place Saturday in the commons south of the Engineering Tower. Final events will be held at the stadium on Sunday afternoon.

43. M2: According to the speaker, how many times has the kite competition been held before this year?

44. M2: Which of the following would win a prize in the kite competition?

45. M2: According to the speaker, who is eligible to enter the kite competition?

46. M2: According to the speaker, when and where will the final portion of the kite competition be held?

Questions 47–50: Listen to part of a lecture given in an anthropology class.

F2: Students, have you ever been to a potluck dinner, where all the guests bring a different dish? The English word *potluck* is believed to come from an American Indian word *potlatch*. Today we're going to continue our discussion of Native American ceremonies by taking a look at this fascinating ceremonial activity—the potlatch. The potlatch was practiced among all the tribes of Native Americans who lived in the Pacific Northwest region of North America. Among members of these cultures, the concepts of prestige and rank were very important, and potlatches were the primary way to advance their social position. The potlatch reached its most elaborate form among a tribe called the Kwakiutl, who lived in British Columbia, Canada.

Potlatches were held to commemorate important events in the families of the hosts, such as births, naming ceremonies, or marriages. After feasting and dancing, the host would give away valuable gifts, such as blankets, jewelry, or food.

So, potlatches were a little like our birthday parties in reverse! At potlatches, the host might also throw copper money into the sea and destroy some of his most valuable possessions, such as canoes. As for the guests at potlatches, well, it was their turn next. They were required to hold potlatches of their own and to give away even more valuable gifts than they had received. As you can see, potlatches were a form of investment.

47. M2: What is the speaker primarily describing in this talk?

48. M2: According to the speaker, which of the following groups held potlatches?

49. M2: According to the speaker, what was a host's primary purpose for having a potlatch?

50. M2: Why does the speaker refer to a potlatch as a form of investment?

SECTION 2: STRUCTURE

Answer Key

1. **B**	11. **A**	21. **D**	31. **D**
2. **D**	12. **A**	22. **A**	32. **D**
3. **B**	13. **B**	23. **C**	33. **B**
4. **C**	14. **D**	24. **C**	34. **A**
5. **B**	15. **B**	25. **A**	35. **A**
6. **A**	16. **C**	26. **C**	36. **D**
7. **C**	17. **C**	27. **A**	37. **B**
8. **D**	18. **D**	28. **C**	38. **B**
9. **A**	19. **B**	29. **D**	39. **D**
10. **C**	20. **B**	30. **C**	40. **D**

EXPLANATION: ERROR IDENTIFICATION

16. **The correct answer is (C).** The correct pattern is *either . . . or.*

17. **The correct answer is (C).** The word *other* should not be pluralized when used before a plural noun.

18. **The correct answer is (D).** For parallelism, a superlative form (*heaviest*) is needed.

19. **The correct answer is (B).** The noun *replica* should be pluralized. (After the word *many*, a plural noun is used.)

20. **The correct answer is (B).** The preposition *during* should be used in place of *when* before a noun phrase *(construction of . . .)*; the word *when* is used before clauses.

21. **The correct answer is (D).** The noun *development* should be used in place of the verb *develop.*

22. **The correct answer is (A).** After a modal auxiliary verb (*must*), the simple form of the verb (*learn*) should be used in place of the *-ing* form.

23. **The correct answer is (C).** The pronoun *it* is an unnecessary repetition of the subject and should be omitted.

24. **The correct answer is (C).** With the verb *derived*, the preposition *from* should be used in place of the preposition *of.*

25. **The correct answer is (A).** The verb *differ* is needed in place of the adjective *different.*

26. **The correct answer is (C).** The adverb *primarily* should be used in place of the adjective *primary.*

27. **The correct answer is (A).** The word *runners* should be used in place of *running* to be parallel with *walkers.*

28. **The correct answer is (C).** The adjective *simple* should be used in place of the adverb *simply* to modify the noun *existence.*

29. **The correct answer is (D).** The correct word order is *future time.* (The phrase *at some time in the future* would also be correctly used here.)

30. **The correct answer is (C).** The gerund form (*understanding*) is needed in place of the simple form *understand*.

31. **The correct answer is (D).** The correct word choice is *twice*.

32. **The correct answer is (D).** The possessive form *his* should replace the definite article *the*.

33. **The correct answer is (B).** The noun *part* is needed in place of the adverb *partly* after the preposition *in*.

34. **The correct answer is (A).** The correct word order is *Of all mammals*.

35. **The correct answer is (A).** To be parallel with the other items in the series (*rhythm* and *melody*), a noun (*harmony*) is needed in place of the verb *harmonize*.

36. **The correct answer is (D).** The correct word is *them* because the pronoun refers to *objects* not to *babies*.

37. **The correct answer is (B).** The plural verb *have* should be used in place of the singular form *has* in order to agree with the plural subject *loblolly pines*.

38. **The correct answer is (B).** Because the information in the second clause is in contrast with the information in the first clause, the two clauses should be joined with the word *but* instead of the word *and*.

39. **The correct answer is (D).** The plural form *humans* should be singular (*human*) because in a compound noun such as *human beings*, only the second noun is pluralized.

40. **The correct answer is (D).** In a passive verb phrase, the past participle *polished* must be used in place of the simple form.

SECTION 3: READING

Answer Key

1.	A	11.	D	21.	B	31.	C	41.	A
2.	A	12.	B	22.	D	32.	A	42.	A
3.	D	13.	B	23.	D	33.	A	43.	C
4.	B	14.	A	24.	C	34.	C	44.	C
5.	C	15.	C	25.	A	35.	A	45.	A
6.	D	16.	B	26.	C	36.	B	46.	D
7.	D	17.	A	27.	B	37.	D	47.	B
8.	C	18.	A	28.	D	38.	A	48.	A
9.	C	19.	C	29.	C	39.	B	49.	D
10.	B	20.	A	30.	D	40.	C	50.	D

EXPLANATION: READING

1. **The correct answer is (A).** The passage mainly describes clusters and superclusters of galaxies. There is no information about the other three choices.

2. **The correct answer is (A).** The word *evenly* means *uniformly*.

3. **The correct answer is (D).** Lines 1-2 state that "a few are found alone, but almost all are grouped in formations termed *galactic clusters.*" Therefore, solo galaxies must be outnumbered by galaxies in clusters.

4. **The correct answer is (B).** The word *globular* means shaped like a globe—in other words, *spherical*.

5. **The correct answer is (C).** Line 6 states that "It is surmised that even clusters of superclusters are possible." Since their existence is possible but not proven, the author would probably describe them as theoretical.

6. **The correct answer is (D).** Line 8 says that the Local Group "is typical in terms of the types of galaxies it contains."

7. **The correct answer is (D).** This question involves some simple arithmetic: the Local Group contains twenty galaxies (line 8); there are three large spirals, four medium-size spiral galaxies, and four regular elliptical galaxies. The total of these three types is eleven. Since "the remainder are dwarf ellipticals," (line 12) there must be nine of those, making dwarf ellipticals," the most numerous.

8. **The correct answer is (C).** According to lines 8-14, in addition to our own galaxy (the Milky Way), only Andromeda and the Clouds of Magellan can be seen from somewhere on the earth with the naked eye (i.e., without a telescope). Therefore, the Triangulum Spiral must be invisible to the unaided eye.

9. **The correct answer is (C).** Lines 17-18 state that "the Local Group . . . and the Virgo Cluster form part of a much larger cluster of clusters—the Local Supercluster."

10. **The correct answer is (B).** The word *riddle* means *puzzle, mystery*.

11. **The correct answer is (D).** Lines 22-23 state that "galaxies contain great amounts of 'dark matter,'" indicating that dark matter does NOT lie between galaxies but inside them. The fourth paragraph provides information to show that choices (A), (B), and (C) are true.

12. The correct answer is (B). The word *members* is used throughout the passage to refer to members of galactic clusters—in other words, to galaxies.

13. The correct answer is (B). The passage deals mainly with Sequoyah's accomplishment—especially the creation of the Cherokee alphabet. The passage supplies only a little information about choices (A), (C), and (D)

14. The correct answer is (A). Lines 2–3 indicate that the invention of the Cherokee alphabet was accomplished in just a dozen (twelve) years.

15. The correct answer is (C). The first paragraph indicates that Sequoyah was a hunter, a silversmith, and an intrpreter as a young man. He did not serve as a representative in Washington until "his later life" (lines 18–19).

16. The correct answer is (B). According to lines 6–7, Sequoyah used the term "talking leaves" to refer to the books of white people.

17. The correct answer is (A). Lines 7–8 state that "his chief aim was to record their ancient tribal customs."

18. The correct answer is (A). The word *cumbersome* means *awkward* or *clumsy*.

19. The correct answer is (C). Lines 10–11 state that "he made symbols for the sounds of the Cherokee language."

20. The correct answer is (A). There is no mention that Sequoyah borrowed symbols from the Egyptian alphabet. The other choices are given in line 12.

21. The correct answer is (B). The word *wholeheartedly* means *enthusiastically* or *eagerly*.

22. The correct answer is (D). Lines 21–22 state that "a statue of Sequoyah represents Oklahoma in the Statuary Hall in the Capitol building in Washington, D.C."

23. The correct answer is (D). Lines 23–24 indicate that Sequoyah is rembered today chiefly because the sequoia trees of California are named in his honor.

24. The correct answer is (C). The reaction to the alphabet is given in lines 13–14 in the sentence "The response was phenomenal."

25. The correct answer is (A). The passage offers a basic definition and description of the amphibian class of animals.

26. The correct answer is (C). Line 3 states that "unlike reptiles, amphibians never have claws on their toes." The other characteristics are listed in the first paragraph.

27. The correct answer is (B). In the context of the passage, the term *scales* refers to the plates that cover certain animals, such as fish.

28. The correct answer is (D). According to lines 10–11, amphibians that undergo a double metamorphosis change "not only from gill breathers to lung breathers but also from vegetarians to insectivores."

29. The correct answer is (C). Amphibians' ability to breathe through their skin is most useful when they are in hibernation "during the coldest months," lines 8–9 (i.e., in the winter).

30. The correct answer is (D). The first paragraph deals with the similarities and differences between amphibians and reptiles. Line 2 says that "some amphibians, such as salamanders, are even shaped like lizards," indicating that lizards must not be amphibians. The other three choices are mentioned as amphibians in the third paragraph.

31. The correct answer is (C). The word *stubby* means *short and thick*.

32. The correct answer is (A). The reference is to toads.

33. **The correct answer is (A).** The passage is basically a history of animated film from its beginnings in 1906 to the 1990s. Choice (B) is briefly described in the passage, but is not the main idea. Choice (C) is incorrect because the passage discusses the development of animation in general, not of one specific film. Choice (D) is mentioned in the last paragraph but is not the main idea of the whole passage.

34. **The correct answer is (C).** According to line 4, McCay's films "featured . . . characters with individual personalities."

35. **The correct answer is (A).** The word *streamlined* means *simplified* or *made easier and faster.*

36. **The correct answer is (B).** The reference is to the cartoon character Felix the Cat.

37. **The correct answer is (D).** Since the first cartoon with sound (*Steamboat Willie*) was made in 1928, earlier cartoons must have been silent films.

38. **The correct answer is (A).** Lines 13–14 state, "The results of this are apparent in *Snow White and the Seven Dwarfs.*" (The word *this* refers to the training in anatomy, acting, drawing, and motion studies.)

39. **The correct answer is (B).** The phrase *splintered off from* means *broke away from.* (A splinter is a small piece that breaks off a larger piece.)

40. **The correct answer is (C).** The author DOES mention characters used by Disney (Mickey Mouse, Snow White), by Hanna and Barbera (Yogi Bear, the Flintstones), and Warner Brothers (Bugs Bunny, Daffy Duck). There is NO mention of any of the characters used by United Productions of America.

41. **The correct answer is (A).** The phrase *blurred the lines* means *eliminated the distinctions.*

42. **The correct answer is (A).** Lines 27–28 state that animators first experimented with computer animation in the 1950s, but the first full-length computer-animated film was not made until the 1990s.

43. **The correct answer is (C).** The word *heyday* means *prime* or *peak.*

44. **The correct answer is (C).** The first mention of animation on television is in lines 20–21, in the sentence beginning "In the 1950s children's cartoons began to be broadcast . . ."

45. **The correct answer is (A).** The first paragraph deals mostly with the dangers created by fog.

46. **The correct answer is (D).** The word *catastrophic* means *disastrous* or *calamitous.*

47. **The correct answer is (B).** According to line 10, "This type of fog (advection fog) often occurs along the California coast . . ."

48. **The correct answer is (A).** Advection fog occurs when "a warm ocean current blows across the surface of a cold current" (lines 11–12). This type of fog occurs off Newfoundland, where the Labrador Current meets the Gulf Stream. Since the Gulf Stream is identified as warm (line 13) the Labrador Current must be cold.

49. **The correct answer is (D).** The author first discusses "the most common type of fog," radiation fog. He then describes advection fog—"another common type." Finally, he mentions two kinds of fog that "are somewhat more unusual"—frontal fog and steam fog.

50. **The correct answer is (D).** Since fog is a weather phenomenon, it is likely that the passage was written by an expert in meteorology (the study of weather).

Practice Tests 1-5
Answer Sheets

Answer Sheet

Practice Test 1

Section 1: Listening

Part A

1. Ⓐ Ⓑ Ⓒ Ⓓ
2. Ⓐ Ⓑ Ⓒ Ⓓ
3. Ⓐ Ⓑ Ⓒ Ⓓ
4. Ⓐ Ⓑ Ⓒ Ⓓ
5. Ⓐ Ⓑ Ⓒ Ⓓ
6. Ⓐ Ⓑ Ⓒ Ⓓ
7. Ⓐ Ⓑ Ⓒ Ⓓ
8. Ⓐ Ⓑ Ⓒ Ⓓ
9. Ⓐ Ⓑ Ⓒ Ⓓ
10. Ⓐ Ⓑ Ⓒ Ⓓ
11. Ⓐ Ⓑ Ⓒ Ⓓ
12. Ⓐ Ⓑ Ⓒ Ⓓ
13. Ⓐ Ⓑ Ⓒ Ⓓ
14. Ⓐ Ⓑ Ⓒ Ⓓ
15. Ⓐ Ⓑ Ⓒ Ⓓ
16. Ⓐ Ⓑ Ⓒ Ⓓ
17. Ⓐ Ⓑ Ⓒ Ⓓ
18. Ⓐ Ⓑ Ⓒ Ⓓ
19. Ⓐ Ⓑ Ⓒ Ⓓ
20. Ⓐ Ⓑ Ⓒ Ⓓ

21. Ⓐ Ⓑ Ⓒ Ⓓ
22. Ⓐ Ⓑ Ⓒ Ⓓ
23. Ⓐ Ⓑ Ⓒ Ⓓ
24. Ⓐ Ⓑ Ⓒ Ⓓ
25. Ⓐ Ⓑ Ⓒ Ⓓ
26. Ⓐ Ⓑ Ⓒ Ⓓ
27. Ⓐ Ⓑ Ⓒ Ⓓ
28. Ⓐ Ⓑ Ⓒ Ⓓ
29. Ⓐ Ⓑ Ⓒ Ⓓ
30. Ⓐ Ⓑ Ⓒ Ⓓ

Part B

31. Ⓐ Ⓑ Ⓒ Ⓓ
32. Ⓐ Ⓑ Ⓒ Ⓓ
33. Ⓐ Ⓑ Ⓒ Ⓓ
34. Ⓐ Ⓑ Ⓒ Ⓓ
35. Ⓐ Ⓑ Ⓒ Ⓓ
36. Ⓐ Ⓑ Ⓒ Ⓓ
37. Ⓐ Ⓑ Ⓒ Ⓓ
38. Ⓐ Ⓑ Ⓒ Ⓓ

Part C

39. Ⓐ Ⓑ Ⓒ Ⓓ
40. Ⓐ Ⓑ Ⓒ Ⓓ
41. Ⓐ Ⓑ Ⓒ Ⓓ
42. Ⓐ Ⓑ Ⓒ Ⓓ
43. Ⓐ Ⓑ Ⓒ Ⓓ
44. Ⓐ Ⓑ Ⓒ Ⓓ
45. Ⓐ Ⓑ Ⓒ Ⓓ
46. Ⓐ Ⓑ Ⓒ Ⓓ
47. Ⓐ Ⓑ Ⓒ Ⓓ
48. Ⓐ Ⓑ Ⓒ Ⓓ
49. Ⓐ Ⓑ Ⓒ Ⓓ
50. Ⓐ Ⓑ Ⓒ Ⓓ

Practice Test 1

Section 2: Structure

1. Ⓐ Ⓑ Ⓒ Ⓓ	21. Ⓐ Ⓑ Ⓒ Ⓓ
2. Ⓐ Ⓑ Ⓒ Ⓓ	22. Ⓐ Ⓑ Ⓒ Ⓓ
3. Ⓐ Ⓑ Ⓒ Ⓓ	23. Ⓐ Ⓑ Ⓒ Ⓓ
4. Ⓐ Ⓑ Ⓒ Ⓓ	24. Ⓐ Ⓑ Ⓒ Ⓓ
5. Ⓐ Ⓑ Ⓒ Ⓓ	25. Ⓐ Ⓑ Ⓒ Ⓓ
6. Ⓐ Ⓑ Ⓒ Ⓓ	26. Ⓐ Ⓑ Ⓒ Ⓓ
7. Ⓐ Ⓑ Ⓒ Ⓓ	27. Ⓐ Ⓑ Ⓒ Ⓓ
8. Ⓐ Ⓑ Ⓒ Ⓓ	28. Ⓐ Ⓑ Ⓒ Ⓓ
9. Ⓐ Ⓑ Ⓒ Ⓓ	29. Ⓐ Ⓑ Ⓒ Ⓓ
10. Ⓐ Ⓑ Ⓒ Ⓓ	30. Ⓐ Ⓑ Ⓒ Ⓓ
11. Ⓐ Ⓑ Ⓒ Ⓓ	31. Ⓐ Ⓑ Ⓒ Ⓓ
12. Ⓐ Ⓑ Ⓒ Ⓓ	32. Ⓐ Ⓑ Ⓒ Ⓓ
13. Ⓐ Ⓑ Ⓒ Ⓓ	33. Ⓐ Ⓑ Ⓒ Ⓓ
14. Ⓐ Ⓑ Ⓒ Ⓓ	34. Ⓐ Ⓑ Ⓒ Ⓓ
15. Ⓐ Ⓑ Ⓒ Ⓓ	35. Ⓐ Ⓑ Ⓒ Ⓓ
	36. Ⓐ Ⓑ Ⓒ Ⓓ
16. Ⓐ Ⓑ Ⓒ Ⓓ	37. Ⓐ Ⓑ Ⓒ Ⓓ
17. Ⓐ Ⓑ Ⓒ Ⓓ	38. Ⓐ Ⓑ Ⓒ Ⓓ
18. Ⓐ Ⓑ Ⓒ Ⓓ	39. Ⓐ Ⓑ Ⓒ Ⓓ
19. Ⓐ Ⓑ Ⓒ Ⓓ	40. Ⓐ Ⓑ Ⓒ Ⓓ
20. Ⓐ Ⓑ Ⓒ Ⓓ	

Practice Test 1

Section 3: Reading

1. (A) (B) (C) (D)
2. (A) (B) (C) (D)
3. (A) (B) (C) (D)
4. (A) (B) (C) (D)
5. (A) (B) (C) (D)
6. (A) (B) (C) (D)
7. (A) (B) (C) (D)
8. (A) (B) (C) (D)
9. (A) (B) (C) (D)
10. (A) (B) (C) (D)

11. (A) (B) (C) (D)
12. (A) (B) (C) (D)
13. (A) (B) (C) (D)
14. (A) (B) (C) (D)
15. (A) (B) (C) (D)
16. (A) (B) (C) (D)
17. (A) (B) (C) (D)
18. (A) (B) (C) (D)

19. (A) (B) (C) (D)
20. (A) (B) (C) (D)
21. (A) (B) (C) (D)
22. (A) (B) (C) (D)
23. (A) (B) (C) (D)
24. (A) (B) (C) (D)
25. (A) (B) (C) (D)
26. (A) (B) (C) (D)
27. (A) (B) (C) (D)
28. (A) (B) (C) (D)
29. (A) (B) (C) (D)
30. (A) (B) (C) (D)

31. (A) (B) (C) (D)
32. (A) (B) (C) (D)
33. (A) (B) (C) (D)
34. (A) (B) (C) (D)
35. (A) (B) (C) (D)
36. (A) (B) (C) (D)
37. (A) (B) (C) (D)
38. (A) (B) (C) (D)
39. (A) (B) (C) (D)

40. (A) (B) (C) (D)
41. (A) (B) (C) (D)
42. (A) (B) (C) (D)
43. (A) (B) (C) (D)
44. (A) (B) (C) (D)
45. (A) (B) (C) (D)
46. (A) (B) (C) (D)
47. (A) (B) (C) (D)
48. (A) (B) (C) (D)
49. (A) (B) (C) (D)
50. (A) (B) (C) (D)

Answer Sheet

Practice Test 2

Section 1: Listening

Part A

1. Ⓐ Ⓑ Ⓒ Ⓓ
2. Ⓐ Ⓑ Ⓒ Ⓓ
3. Ⓐ Ⓑ Ⓒ Ⓓ
4. Ⓐ Ⓑ Ⓒ Ⓓ
5. Ⓐ Ⓑ Ⓒ Ⓓ
6. Ⓐ Ⓑ Ⓒ Ⓓ
7. Ⓐ Ⓑ Ⓒ Ⓓ
8. Ⓐ Ⓑ Ⓒ Ⓓ
9. Ⓐ Ⓑ Ⓒ Ⓓ
10. Ⓐ Ⓑ Ⓒ Ⓓ
11. Ⓐ Ⓑ Ⓒ Ⓓ
12. Ⓐ Ⓑ Ⓒ Ⓓ
13. Ⓐ Ⓑ Ⓒ Ⓓ
14. Ⓐ Ⓑ Ⓒ Ⓓ
15. Ⓐ Ⓑ Ⓒ Ⓓ
16. Ⓐ Ⓑ Ⓒ Ⓓ
17. Ⓐ Ⓑ Ⓒ Ⓓ
18. Ⓐ Ⓑ Ⓒ Ⓓ
19. Ⓐ Ⓑ Ⓒ Ⓓ
20. Ⓐ Ⓑ Ⓒ Ⓓ

21. Ⓐ Ⓑ Ⓒ Ⓓ
22. Ⓐ Ⓑ Ⓒ Ⓓ
23. Ⓐ Ⓑ Ⓒ Ⓓ
24. Ⓐ Ⓑ Ⓒ Ⓓ
25. Ⓐ Ⓑ Ⓒ Ⓓ
26. Ⓐ Ⓑ Ⓒ Ⓓ
27. Ⓐ Ⓑ Ⓒ Ⓓ
28. Ⓐ Ⓑ Ⓒ Ⓓ
29. Ⓐ Ⓑ Ⓒ Ⓓ
30. Ⓐ Ⓑ Ⓒ Ⓓ

Part B

31. Ⓐ Ⓑ Ⓒ Ⓓ
32. Ⓐ Ⓑ Ⓒ Ⓓ
33. Ⓐ Ⓑ Ⓒ Ⓓ
34. Ⓐ Ⓑ Ⓒ Ⓓ
35. Ⓐ Ⓑ Ⓒ Ⓓ
36. Ⓐ Ⓑ Ⓒ Ⓓ
37. Ⓐ Ⓑ Ⓒ Ⓓ
38. Ⓐ Ⓑ Ⓒ Ⓓ

Part C

39. Ⓐ Ⓑ Ⓒ Ⓓ
40. Ⓐ Ⓑ Ⓒ Ⓓ
41. Ⓐ Ⓑ Ⓒ Ⓓ
42. Ⓐ Ⓑ Ⓒ Ⓓ
43. Ⓐ Ⓑ Ⓒ Ⓓ
44. Ⓐ Ⓑ Ⓒ Ⓓ
45. Ⓐ Ⓑ Ⓒ Ⓓ
46. Ⓐ Ⓑ Ⓒ Ⓓ
47. Ⓐ Ⓑ Ⓒ Ⓓ
48. Ⓐ Ⓑ Ⓒ Ⓓ
49. Ⓐ Ⓑ Ⓒ Ⓓ
50. Ⓐ Ⓑ Ⓒ Ⓓ

Practice Test 2

Section 2: Structure

1. Ⓐ Ⓑ Ⓒ Ⓓ
2. Ⓐ Ⓑ Ⓒ Ⓓ
3. Ⓐ Ⓑ Ⓒ Ⓓ
4. Ⓐ Ⓑ Ⓒ Ⓓ
5. Ⓐ Ⓑ Ⓒ Ⓓ
6. Ⓐ Ⓑ Ⓒ Ⓓ
7. Ⓐ Ⓑ Ⓒ Ⓓ
8. Ⓐ Ⓑ Ⓒ Ⓓ
9. Ⓐ Ⓑ Ⓒ Ⓓ
10. Ⓐ Ⓑ Ⓒ Ⓓ
11. Ⓐ Ⓑ Ⓒ Ⓓ
12. Ⓐ Ⓑ Ⓒ Ⓓ
13. Ⓐ Ⓑ Ⓒ Ⓓ
14. Ⓐ Ⓑ Ⓒ Ⓓ
15. Ⓐ Ⓑ Ⓒ Ⓓ

16. Ⓐ Ⓑ Ⓒ Ⓓ
17. Ⓐ Ⓑ Ⓒ Ⓓ
18. Ⓐ Ⓑ Ⓒ Ⓓ
19. Ⓐ Ⓑ Ⓒ Ⓓ
20. Ⓐ Ⓑ Ⓒ Ⓓ

21. Ⓐ Ⓑ Ⓒ Ⓓ
22. Ⓐ Ⓑ Ⓒ Ⓓ
23. Ⓐ Ⓑ Ⓒ Ⓓ
24. Ⓐ Ⓑ Ⓒ Ⓓ
25. Ⓐ Ⓑ Ⓒ Ⓓ
26. Ⓐ Ⓑ Ⓒ Ⓓ
27. Ⓐ Ⓑ Ⓒ Ⓓ
28. Ⓐ Ⓑ Ⓒ Ⓓ
29. Ⓐ Ⓑ Ⓒ Ⓓ
30. Ⓐ Ⓑ Ⓒ Ⓓ
31. Ⓐ Ⓑ Ⓒ Ⓓ
32. Ⓐ Ⓑ Ⓒ Ⓓ
33. Ⓐ Ⓑ Ⓒ Ⓓ
34. Ⓐ Ⓑ Ⓒ Ⓓ
35. Ⓐ Ⓑ Ⓒ Ⓓ
36. Ⓐ Ⓑ Ⓒ Ⓓ
37. Ⓐ Ⓑ Ⓒ Ⓓ
38. Ⓐ Ⓑ Ⓒ Ⓓ
39. Ⓐ Ⓑ Ⓒ Ⓓ
40. Ⓐ Ⓑ Ⓒ Ⓓ

Practice Test 2

Section 3: Reading

1. Ⓐ Ⓑ Ⓒ Ⓓ	23. Ⓐ Ⓑ Ⓒ Ⓓ	42. Ⓐ Ⓑ Ⓒ Ⓓ
2. Ⓐ Ⓑ Ⓒ Ⓓ	24. Ⓐ Ⓑ Ⓒ Ⓓ	43. Ⓐ Ⓑ Ⓒ Ⓓ
3. Ⓐ Ⓑ Ⓒ Ⓓ	25. Ⓐ Ⓑ Ⓒ Ⓓ	44. Ⓐ Ⓑ Ⓒ Ⓓ
4. Ⓐ Ⓑ Ⓒ Ⓓ	26. Ⓐ Ⓑ Ⓒ Ⓓ	45. Ⓐ Ⓑ Ⓒ Ⓓ
5. Ⓐ Ⓑ Ⓒ Ⓓ	27. Ⓐ Ⓑ Ⓒ Ⓓ	46. Ⓐ Ⓑ Ⓒ Ⓓ
6. Ⓐ Ⓑ Ⓒ Ⓓ	28. Ⓐ Ⓑ Ⓒ Ⓓ	47. Ⓐ Ⓑ Ⓒ Ⓓ
7. Ⓐ Ⓑ Ⓒ Ⓓ	29. Ⓐ Ⓑ Ⓒ Ⓓ	48. Ⓐ Ⓑ Ⓒ Ⓓ
8. Ⓐ Ⓑ Ⓒ Ⓓ	30. Ⓐ Ⓑ Ⓒ Ⓓ	49. Ⓐ Ⓑ Ⓒ Ⓓ
9. Ⓐ Ⓑ Ⓒ Ⓓ		50. Ⓐ Ⓑ Ⓒ Ⓓ
10. Ⓐ Ⓑ Ⓒ Ⓓ	31. Ⓐ Ⓑ Ⓒ Ⓓ	
11. Ⓐ Ⓑ Ⓒ Ⓓ	32. Ⓐ Ⓑ Ⓒ Ⓓ	
12. Ⓐ Ⓑ Ⓒ Ⓓ	33. Ⓐ Ⓑ Ⓒ Ⓓ	
	34. Ⓐ Ⓑ Ⓒ Ⓓ	
13. Ⓐ Ⓑ Ⓒ Ⓓ	35. Ⓐ Ⓑ Ⓒ Ⓓ	
14. Ⓐ Ⓑ Ⓒ Ⓓ	36. Ⓐ Ⓑ Ⓒ Ⓓ	
15. Ⓐ Ⓑ Ⓒ Ⓓ	37. Ⓐ Ⓑ Ⓒ Ⓓ	
16. Ⓐ Ⓑ Ⓒ Ⓓ	38. Ⓐ Ⓑ Ⓒ Ⓓ	
17. Ⓐ Ⓑ Ⓒ Ⓓ	39. Ⓐ Ⓑ Ⓒ Ⓓ	
18. Ⓐ Ⓑ Ⓒ Ⓓ	40. Ⓐ Ⓑ Ⓒ Ⓓ	
19. Ⓐ Ⓑ Ⓒ Ⓓ	41. Ⓐ Ⓑ Ⓒ Ⓓ	
20. Ⓐ Ⓑ Ⓒ Ⓓ		
21. Ⓐ Ⓑ Ⓒ Ⓓ		
22. Ⓐ Ⓑ Ⓒ Ⓓ		

Answer Sheet

Practice Test 3 (Long Form)

Section 1: Listening

Part A

1. (A) (B) (C) (D)
2. (A) (B) (C) (D)
3. (A) (B) (C) (D)
4. (A) (B) (C) (D)
5. (A) (B) (C) (D)
6. (A) (B) (C) (D)
7. (A) (B) (C) (D)
8. (A) (B) (C) (D)
9. (A) (B) (C) (D)
10. (A) (B) (C) (D)
11. (A) (B) (C) (D)
12. (A) (B) (C) (D)
13. (A) (B) (C) (D)
14. (A) (B) (C) (D)
15. (A) (B) (C) (D)
16. (A) (B) (C) (D)
17. (A) (B) (C) (D)
18. (A) (B) (C) (D)
19. (A) (B) (C) (D)
20. (A) (B) (C) (D)
21. (A) (B) (C) (D)
22. (A) (B) (C) (D)
23. (A) (B) (C) (D)
24. (A) (B) (C) (D)
25. (A) (B) (C) (D)

26. (A) (B) (C) (D)
27. (A) (B) (C) (D)
28. (A) (B) (C) (D)
29. (A) (B) (C) (D)
30. (A) (B) (C) (D)
31. (A) (B) (C) (D)
32. (A) (B) (C) (D)
33. (A) (B) (C) (D)
34. (A) (B) (C) (D)
35. (A) (B) (C) (D)
36. (A) (B) (C) (D)
37. (A) (B) (C) (D)
38. (A) (B) (C) (D)
39. (A) (B) (C) (D)
40. (A) (B) (C) (D)
41. (A) (B) (C) (D)
42. (A) (B) (C) (D)
43. (A) (B) (C) (D)
44. (A) (B) (C) (D)
45. (A) (B) (C) (D)
46. (A) (B) (C) (D)
47. (A) (B) (C) (D)
48. (A) (B) (C) (D)
49. (A) (B) (C) (D)
50. (A) (B) (C) (D)

Part B

51. (A) (B) (C) (D)
52. (A) (B) (C) (D)
53. (A) (B) (C) (D)
54. (A) (B) (C) (D)
55. (A) (B) (C) (D)
56. (A) (B) (C) (D)
57. (A) (B) (C) (D)
58. (A) (B) (C) (D)
59. (A) (B) (C) (D)
60. (A) (B) (C) (D)
61. (A) (B) (C) (D)
62. (A) (B) (C) (D)
63. (A) (B) (C) (D)

Part C

64. (A) (B) (C) (D)
65. (A) (B) (C) (D)
66. (A) (B) (C) (D)
67. (A) (B) (C) (D)
68. (A) (B) (C) (D)
69. (A) (B) (C) (D)
70. (A) (B) (C) (D)
71. (A) (B) (C) (D)
72. (A) (B) (C) (D)
73. (A) (B) (C) (D)
74. (A) (B) (C) (D)
75. (A) (B) (C) (D)
76. (A) (B) (C) (D)
77. (A) (B) (C) (D)
78. (A) (B) (C) (D)
79. (A) (B) (C) (D)
80. (A) (B) (C) (D)

Practice Test 3

Section 2: Structure

1. Ⓐ Ⓑ Ⓒ Ⓓ	21. Ⓐ Ⓑ Ⓒ Ⓓ	41. Ⓐ Ⓑ Ⓒ Ⓓ
2. Ⓐ Ⓑ Ⓒ Ⓓ	22. Ⓐ Ⓑ Ⓒ Ⓓ	42. Ⓐ Ⓑ Ⓒ Ⓓ
3. Ⓐ Ⓑ Ⓒ Ⓓ	23. Ⓐ Ⓑ Ⓒ Ⓓ	43. Ⓐ Ⓑ Ⓒ Ⓓ
4. Ⓐ Ⓑ Ⓒ Ⓓ		44. Ⓐ Ⓑ Ⓒ Ⓓ
5. Ⓐ Ⓑ Ⓒ Ⓓ	24. Ⓐ Ⓑ Ⓒ Ⓓ	45. Ⓐ Ⓑ Ⓒ Ⓓ
6. Ⓐ Ⓑ Ⓒ Ⓓ	25. Ⓐ Ⓑ Ⓒ Ⓓ	46. Ⓐ Ⓑ Ⓒ Ⓓ
7. Ⓐ Ⓑ Ⓒ Ⓓ	26. Ⓐ Ⓑ Ⓒ Ⓓ	47. Ⓐ Ⓑ Ⓒ Ⓓ
8. Ⓐ Ⓑ Ⓒ Ⓓ	27. Ⓐ Ⓑ Ⓒ Ⓓ	48. Ⓐ Ⓑ Ⓒ Ⓓ
9. Ⓐ Ⓑ Ⓒ Ⓓ	28. Ⓐ Ⓑ Ⓒ Ⓓ	49. Ⓐ Ⓑ Ⓒ Ⓓ
10. Ⓐ Ⓑ Ⓒ Ⓓ	29. Ⓐ Ⓑ Ⓒ Ⓓ	50. Ⓐ Ⓑ Ⓒ Ⓓ
11. Ⓐ Ⓑ Ⓒ Ⓓ	30. Ⓐ Ⓑ Ⓒ Ⓓ	51. Ⓐ Ⓑ Ⓒ Ⓓ
12. Ⓐ Ⓑ Ⓒ Ⓓ	31. Ⓐ Ⓑ Ⓒ Ⓓ	52. Ⓐ Ⓑ Ⓒ Ⓓ
13. Ⓐ Ⓑ Ⓒ Ⓓ	32. Ⓐ Ⓑ Ⓒ Ⓓ	53. Ⓐ Ⓑ Ⓒ Ⓓ
14. Ⓐ Ⓑ Ⓒ Ⓓ	33. Ⓐ Ⓑ Ⓒ Ⓓ	54. Ⓐ Ⓑ Ⓒ Ⓓ
15. Ⓐ Ⓑ Ⓒ Ⓓ	34. Ⓐ Ⓑ Ⓒ Ⓓ	55. Ⓐ Ⓑ Ⓒ Ⓓ
16. Ⓐ Ⓑ Ⓒ Ⓓ	35. Ⓐ Ⓑ Ⓒ Ⓓ	56. Ⓐ Ⓑ Ⓒ Ⓓ
17. Ⓐ Ⓑ Ⓒ Ⓓ	36. Ⓐ Ⓑ Ⓒ Ⓓ	57. Ⓐ Ⓑ Ⓒ Ⓓ
18. Ⓐ Ⓑ Ⓒ Ⓓ	37. Ⓐ Ⓑ Ⓒ Ⓓ	58. Ⓐ Ⓑ Ⓒ Ⓓ
19. Ⓐ Ⓑ Ⓒ Ⓓ	38. Ⓐ Ⓑ Ⓒ Ⓓ	59. Ⓐ Ⓑ Ⓒ Ⓓ
20. Ⓐ Ⓑ Ⓒ Ⓓ	39. Ⓐ Ⓑ Ⓒ Ⓓ	60. Ⓐ Ⓑ Ⓒ Ⓓ
	40. Ⓐ Ⓑ Ⓒ Ⓓ	

Practice Test 3

Section 3: Reading

1. Ⓐ Ⓑ Ⓒ Ⓓ	24. Ⓐ Ⓑ Ⓒ Ⓓ	45. Ⓐ Ⓑ Ⓒ Ⓓ
2. Ⓐ Ⓑ Ⓒ Ⓓ	25. Ⓐ Ⓑ Ⓒ Ⓓ	46. Ⓐ Ⓑ Ⓒ Ⓓ
3. Ⓐ Ⓑ Ⓒ Ⓓ	26. Ⓐ Ⓑ Ⓒ Ⓓ	47. Ⓐ Ⓑ Ⓒ Ⓓ
4. Ⓐ Ⓑ Ⓒ Ⓓ	27. Ⓐ Ⓑ Ⓒ Ⓓ	48. Ⓐ Ⓑ Ⓒ Ⓓ
5. Ⓐ Ⓑ Ⓒ Ⓓ	28. Ⓐ Ⓑ Ⓒ Ⓓ	49. Ⓐ Ⓑ Ⓒ Ⓓ
6. Ⓐ Ⓑ Ⓒ Ⓓ	29. Ⓐ Ⓑ Ⓒ Ⓓ	50. Ⓐ Ⓑ Ⓒ Ⓓ
7. Ⓐ Ⓑ Ⓒ Ⓓ	30. Ⓐ Ⓑ Ⓒ Ⓓ	51. Ⓐ Ⓑ Ⓒ Ⓓ
8. Ⓐ Ⓑ Ⓒ Ⓓ	31. Ⓐ Ⓑ Ⓒ Ⓓ	52. Ⓐ Ⓑ Ⓒ Ⓓ
9. Ⓐ Ⓑ Ⓒ Ⓓ	32. Ⓐ Ⓑ Ⓒ Ⓓ	53. Ⓐ Ⓑ Ⓒ Ⓓ
10. Ⓐ Ⓑ Ⓒ Ⓓ	33. Ⓐ Ⓑ Ⓒ Ⓓ	
11. Ⓐ Ⓑ Ⓒ Ⓓ	34. Ⓐ Ⓑ Ⓒ Ⓓ	54. Ⓐ Ⓑ Ⓒ Ⓓ
	35. Ⓐ Ⓑ Ⓒ Ⓓ	55. Ⓐ Ⓑ Ⓒ Ⓓ
12. Ⓐ Ⓑ Ⓒ Ⓓ	36. Ⓐ Ⓑ Ⓒ Ⓓ	56. Ⓐ Ⓑ Ⓒ Ⓓ
13. Ⓐ Ⓑ Ⓒ Ⓓ		57. Ⓐ Ⓑ Ⓒ Ⓓ
14. Ⓐ Ⓑ Ⓒ Ⓓ	37. Ⓐ Ⓑ Ⓒ Ⓓ	58. Ⓐ Ⓑ Ⓒ Ⓓ
15. Ⓐ Ⓑ Ⓒ Ⓓ	38. Ⓐ Ⓑ Ⓒ Ⓓ	59. Ⓐ Ⓑ Ⓒ Ⓓ
16. Ⓐ Ⓑ Ⓒ Ⓓ	39. Ⓐ Ⓑ Ⓒ Ⓓ	60. Ⓐ Ⓑ Ⓒ Ⓓ
17. Ⓐ Ⓑ Ⓒ Ⓓ	40. Ⓐ Ⓑ Ⓒ Ⓓ	
18. Ⓐ Ⓑ Ⓒ Ⓓ	41. Ⓐ Ⓑ Ⓒ Ⓓ	61. Ⓐ Ⓑ Ⓒ Ⓓ
19. Ⓐ Ⓑ Ⓒ Ⓓ	42. Ⓐ Ⓑ Ⓒ Ⓓ	62. Ⓐ Ⓑ Ⓒ Ⓓ
20. Ⓐ Ⓑ Ⓒ Ⓓ	43. Ⓐ Ⓑ Ⓒ Ⓓ	63. Ⓐ Ⓑ Ⓒ Ⓓ
21. Ⓐ Ⓑ Ⓒ Ⓓ	44. Ⓐ Ⓑ Ⓒ Ⓓ	64. Ⓐ Ⓑ Ⓒ Ⓓ
22. Ⓐ Ⓑ Ⓒ Ⓓ		65. Ⓐ Ⓑ Ⓒ Ⓓ
23. Ⓐ Ⓑ Ⓒ Ⓓ		66. Ⓐ Ⓑ Ⓒ Ⓓ
		67. Ⓐ Ⓑ Ⓒ Ⓓ
		68. Ⓐ Ⓑ Ⓒ Ⓓ
		69. Ⓐ Ⓑ Ⓒ Ⓓ
		70. Ⓐ Ⓑ Ⓒ Ⓓ

Answer Sheet

Practice Test 4

Section 1: Listening

Part A

1. Ⓐ Ⓑ Ⓒ Ⓓ
2. Ⓐ Ⓑ Ⓒ Ⓓ
3. Ⓐ Ⓑ Ⓒ Ⓓ
4. Ⓐ Ⓑ Ⓒ Ⓓ
5. Ⓐ Ⓑ Ⓒ Ⓓ
6. Ⓐ Ⓑ Ⓒ Ⓓ
7. Ⓐ Ⓑ Ⓒ Ⓓ
8. Ⓐ Ⓑ Ⓒ Ⓓ
9. Ⓐ Ⓑ Ⓒ Ⓓ
10. Ⓐ Ⓑ Ⓒ Ⓓ
11. Ⓐ Ⓑ Ⓒ Ⓓ
12. Ⓐ Ⓑ Ⓒ Ⓓ
13. Ⓐ Ⓑ Ⓒ Ⓓ
14. Ⓐ Ⓑ Ⓒ Ⓓ
15. Ⓐ Ⓑ Ⓒ Ⓓ
16. Ⓐ Ⓑ Ⓒ Ⓓ
17. Ⓐ Ⓑ Ⓒ Ⓓ
18. Ⓐ Ⓑ Ⓒ Ⓓ
19. Ⓐ Ⓑ Ⓒ Ⓓ
20. Ⓐ Ⓑ Ⓒ Ⓓ

21. Ⓐ Ⓑ Ⓒ Ⓓ
22. Ⓐ Ⓑ Ⓒ Ⓓ
23. Ⓐ Ⓑ Ⓒ Ⓓ
24. Ⓐ Ⓑ Ⓒ Ⓓ
25. Ⓐ Ⓑ Ⓒ Ⓓ
26. Ⓐ Ⓑ Ⓒ Ⓓ
27. Ⓐ Ⓑ Ⓒ Ⓓ
28. Ⓐ Ⓑ Ⓒ Ⓓ
29. Ⓐ Ⓑ Ⓒ Ⓓ
30. Ⓐ Ⓑ Ⓒ Ⓓ

Part B

31. Ⓐ Ⓑ Ⓒ Ⓓ
32. Ⓐ Ⓑ Ⓒ Ⓓ
33. Ⓐ Ⓑ Ⓒ Ⓓ
34. Ⓐ Ⓑ Ⓒ Ⓓ
35. Ⓐ Ⓑ Ⓒ Ⓓ
36. Ⓐ Ⓑ Ⓒ Ⓓ
37. Ⓐ Ⓑ Ⓒ Ⓓ

Part C

38. Ⓐ Ⓑ Ⓒ Ⓓ
39. Ⓐ Ⓑ Ⓒ Ⓓ
40. Ⓐ Ⓑ Ⓒ Ⓓ
41. Ⓐ Ⓑ Ⓒ Ⓓ
42. Ⓐ Ⓑ Ⓒ Ⓓ
43. Ⓐ Ⓑ Ⓒ Ⓓ
44. Ⓐ Ⓑ Ⓒ Ⓓ
45. Ⓐ Ⓑ Ⓒ Ⓓ
46. Ⓐ Ⓑ Ⓒ Ⓓ
47. Ⓐ Ⓑ Ⓒ Ⓓ
48. Ⓐ Ⓑ Ⓒ Ⓓ
49. Ⓐ Ⓑ Ⓒ Ⓓ
50. Ⓐ Ⓑ Ⓒ Ⓓ

Practice Test 4

Section 2: Structure

1.	Ⓐ	Ⓑ	Ⓒ	Ⓓ		21.	Ⓐ	Ⓑ	Ⓒ	Ⓓ
2.	Ⓐ	Ⓑ	Ⓒ	Ⓓ		22.	Ⓐ	Ⓑ	Ⓒ	Ⓓ
3.	Ⓐ	Ⓑ	Ⓒ	Ⓓ		23.	Ⓐ	Ⓑ	Ⓒ	Ⓓ
4.	Ⓐ	Ⓑ	Ⓒ	Ⓓ		24.	Ⓐ	Ⓑ	Ⓒ	Ⓓ
5.	Ⓐ	Ⓑ	Ⓒ	Ⓓ		25.	Ⓐ	Ⓑ	Ⓒ	Ⓓ
6.	Ⓐ	Ⓑ	Ⓒ	Ⓓ		26.	Ⓐ	Ⓑ	Ⓒ	Ⓓ
7.	Ⓐ	Ⓑ	Ⓒ	Ⓓ		27.	Ⓐ	Ⓑ	Ⓒ	Ⓓ
8.	Ⓐ	Ⓑ	Ⓒ	Ⓓ		28.	Ⓐ	Ⓑ	Ⓒ	Ⓓ
9.	Ⓐ	Ⓑ	Ⓒ	Ⓓ		29.	Ⓐ	Ⓑ	Ⓒ	Ⓓ
10.	Ⓐ	Ⓑ	Ⓒ	Ⓓ		30.	Ⓐ	Ⓑ	Ⓒ	Ⓓ
11.	Ⓐ	Ⓑ	Ⓒ	Ⓓ		31.	Ⓐ	Ⓑ	Ⓒ	Ⓓ
12.	Ⓐ	Ⓑ	Ⓒ	Ⓓ		32.	Ⓐ	Ⓑ	Ⓒ	Ⓓ
13.	Ⓐ	Ⓑ	Ⓒ	Ⓓ		33.	Ⓐ	Ⓑ	Ⓒ	Ⓓ
14.	Ⓐ	Ⓑ	Ⓒ	Ⓓ		34.	Ⓐ	Ⓑ	Ⓒ	Ⓓ
15.	Ⓐ	Ⓑ	Ⓒ	Ⓓ		35.	Ⓐ	Ⓑ	Ⓒ	Ⓓ
						36.	Ⓐ	Ⓑ	Ⓒ	Ⓓ
16.	Ⓐ	Ⓑ	Ⓒ	Ⓓ		37.	Ⓐ	Ⓑ	Ⓒ	Ⓓ
17.	Ⓐ	Ⓑ	Ⓒ	Ⓓ		38.	Ⓐ	Ⓑ	Ⓒ	Ⓓ
18.	Ⓐ	Ⓑ	Ⓒ	Ⓓ		39.	Ⓐ	Ⓑ	Ⓒ	Ⓓ
19.	Ⓐ	Ⓑ	Ⓒ	Ⓓ		40.	Ⓐ	Ⓑ	Ⓒ	Ⓓ
20.	Ⓐ	Ⓑ	Ⓒ	Ⓓ						

Practice Test 4

Section 3: Reading

1.	Ⓐ Ⓑ Ⓒ Ⓓ	21. Ⓐ Ⓑ Ⓒ Ⓓ	40. Ⓐ Ⓑ Ⓒ Ⓓ
2.	Ⓐ Ⓑ Ⓒ Ⓓ	22. Ⓐ Ⓑ Ⓒ Ⓓ	41. Ⓐ Ⓑ Ⓒ Ⓓ
3.	Ⓐ Ⓑ Ⓒ Ⓓ	23. Ⓐ Ⓑ Ⓒ Ⓓ	42. Ⓐ Ⓑ Ⓒ Ⓓ
4.	Ⓐ Ⓑ Ⓒ Ⓓ	24. Ⓐ Ⓑ Ⓒ Ⓓ	43. Ⓐ Ⓑ Ⓒ Ⓓ
5.	Ⓐ Ⓑ Ⓒ Ⓓ	25. Ⓐ Ⓑ Ⓒ Ⓓ	44. Ⓐ Ⓑ Ⓒ Ⓓ
6.	Ⓐ Ⓑ Ⓒ Ⓓ	26. Ⓐ Ⓑ Ⓒ Ⓓ	45. Ⓐ Ⓑ Ⓒ Ⓓ
7.	Ⓐ Ⓑ Ⓒ Ⓓ	27. Ⓐ Ⓑ Ⓒ Ⓓ	46. Ⓐ Ⓑ Ⓒ Ⓓ
8.	Ⓐ Ⓑ Ⓒ Ⓓ	28. Ⓐ Ⓑ Ⓒ Ⓓ	47. Ⓐ Ⓑ Ⓒ Ⓓ
9.	Ⓐ Ⓑ Ⓒ Ⓓ	29. Ⓐ Ⓑ Ⓒ Ⓓ	48. Ⓐ Ⓑ Ⓒ Ⓓ
10.	Ⓐ Ⓑ Ⓒ Ⓓ	30. Ⓐ Ⓑ Ⓒ Ⓓ	49. Ⓐ Ⓑ Ⓒ Ⓓ
			50. Ⓐ Ⓑ Ⓒ Ⓓ
11.	Ⓐ Ⓑ Ⓒ Ⓓ	31. Ⓐ Ⓑ Ⓒ Ⓓ	
12.	Ⓐ Ⓑ Ⓒ Ⓓ	32. Ⓐ Ⓑ Ⓒ Ⓓ	
13.	Ⓐ Ⓑ Ⓒ Ⓓ	33. Ⓐ Ⓑ Ⓒ Ⓓ	
14.	Ⓐ Ⓑ Ⓒ Ⓓ	34. Ⓐ Ⓑ Ⓒ Ⓓ	
15.	Ⓐ Ⓑ Ⓒ Ⓓ	35. Ⓐ Ⓑ Ⓒ Ⓓ	
16.	Ⓐ Ⓑ Ⓒ Ⓓ	36. Ⓐ Ⓑ Ⓒ Ⓓ	
17.	Ⓐ Ⓑ Ⓒ Ⓓ	37. Ⓐ Ⓑ Ⓒ Ⓓ	
18.	Ⓐ Ⓑ Ⓒ Ⓓ	38. Ⓐ Ⓑ Ⓒ Ⓓ	
19.	Ⓐ Ⓑ Ⓒ Ⓓ	39. Ⓐ Ⓑ Ⓒ Ⓓ	
20.	Ⓐ Ⓑ Ⓒ Ⓓ		

Answer Sheet

Practice Test 5

Section 1: Listening

1.	Ⓐ Ⓑ Ⓒ Ⓓ	21.	Ⓐ Ⓑ Ⓒ Ⓓ	38. Ⓐ Ⓑ Ⓒ Ⓓ
2.	Ⓐ Ⓑ Ⓒ Ⓓ	22.	Ⓐ Ⓑ Ⓒ Ⓓ	39. Ⓐ Ⓑ Ⓒ Ⓓ
3.	Ⓐ Ⓑ Ⓒ Ⓓ	23.	Ⓐ Ⓑ Ⓒ Ⓓ	40. Ⓐ Ⓑ Ⓒ Ⓓ
4.	Ⓐ Ⓑ Ⓒ Ⓓ	24.	Ⓐ Ⓑ Ⓒ Ⓓ	41. Ⓐ Ⓑ Ⓒ Ⓓ
5.	Ⓐ Ⓑ Ⓒ Ⓓ	25.	Ⓐ Ⓑ Ⓒ Ⓓ	42. Ⓐ Ⓑ Ⓒ Ⓓ
6.	Ⓐ Ⓑ Ⓒ Ⓓ	26.	Ⓐ Ⓑ Ⓒ Ⓓ	43. Ⓐ Ⓑ Ⓒ Ⓓ
7.	Ⓐ Ⓑ Ⓒ Ⓓ	27.	Ⓐ Ⓑ Ⓒ Ⓓ	44. Ⓐ Ⓑ Ⓒ Ⓓ
8.	Ⓐ Ⓑ Ⓒ Ⓓ	28.	Ⓐ Ⓑ Ⓒ Ⓓ	45. Ⓐ Ⓑ Ⓒ Ⓓ
9.	Ⓐ Ⓑ Ⓒ Ⓓ	29.	Ⓐ Ⓑ Ⓒ Ⓓ	46. Ⓐ Ⓑ Ⓒ Ⓓ
10.	Ⓐ Ⓑ Ⓒ Ⓓ	30.	Ⓐ Ⓑ Ⓒ Ⓓ	47. Ⓐ Ⓑ Ⓒ Ⓓ
11.	Ⓐ Ⓑ Ⓒ Ⓓ			48. Ⓐ Ⓑ Ⓒ Ⓓ
12.	Ⓐ Ⓑ Ⓒ Ⓓ	31.	Ⓐ Ⓑ Ⓒ Ⓓ	49. Ⓐ Ⓑ Ⓒ Ⓓ
13.	Ⓐ Ⓑ Ⓒ Ⓓ	32.	Ⓐ Ⓑ Ⓒ Ⓓ	50. Ⓐ Ⓑ Ⓒ Ⓓ
14.	Ⓐ Ⓑ Ⓒ Ⓓ	33.	Ⓐ Ⓑ Ⓒ Ⓓ	
15.	Ⓐ Ⓑ Ⓒ Ⓓ	34.	Ⓐ Ⓑ Ⓒ Ⓓ	
16.	Ⓐ Ⓑ Ⓒ Ⓓ	35.	Ⓐ Ⓑ Ⓒ Ⓓ	
17.	Ⓐ Ⓑ Ⓒ Ⓓ	36.	Ⓐ Ⓑ Ⓒ Ⓓ	
18.	Ⓐ Ⓑ Ⓒ Ⓓ	37.	Ⓐ Ⓑ Ⓒ Ⓓ	
19.	Ⓐ Ⓑ Ⓒ Ⓓ			
20.	Ⓐ Ⓑ Ⓒ Ⓓ			

Practice Test 5

Section 2: Structure

1. Ⓐ Ⓑ Ⓒ Ⓓ   21. Ⓐ Ⓑ Ⓒ Ⓓ
2. Ⓐ Ⓑ Ⓒ Ⓓ   22. Ⓐ Ⓑ Ⓒ Ⓓ
3. Ⓐ Ⓑ Ⓒ Ⓓ   23. Ⓐ Ⓑ Ⓒ Ⓓ
4. Ⓐ Ⓑ Ⓒ Ⓓ   24. Ⓐ Ⓑ Ⓒ Ⓓ
5. Ⓐ Ⓑ Ⓒ Ⓓ   25. Ⓐ Ⓑ Ⓒ Ⓓ
6. Ⓐ Ⓑ Ⓒ Ⓓ   26. Ⓐ Ⓑ Ⓒ Ⓓ
7. Ⓐ Ⓑ Ⓒ Ⓓ   27. Ⓐ Ⓑ Ⓒ Ⓓ
8. Ⓐ Ⓑ Ⓒ Ⓓ   28. Ⓐ Ⓑ Ⓒ Ⓓ
9. Ⓐ Ⓑ Ⓒ Ⓓ   29. Ⓐ Ⓑ Ⓒ Ⓓ
10. Ⓐ Ⓑ Ⓒ Ⓓ   30. Ⓐ Ⓑ Ⓒ Ⓓ
11. Ⓐ Ⓑ Ⓒ Ⓓ   31. Ⓐ Ⓑ Ⓒ Ⓓ
12. Ⓐ Ⓑ Ⓒ Ⓓ   32. Ⓐ Ⓑ Ⓒ Ⓓ
13. Ⓐ Ⓑ Ⓒ Ⓓ   33. Ⓐ Ⓑ Ⓒ Ⓓ
14. Ⓐ Ⓑ Ⓒ Ⓓ   34. Ⓐ Ⓑ Ⓒ Ⓓ
15. Ⓐ Ⓑ Ⓒ Ⓓ   35. Ⓐ Ⓑ Ⓒ Ⓓ
                 36. Ⓐ Ⓑ Ⓒ Ⓓ
16. Ⓐ Ⓑ Ⓒ Ⓓ   37. Ⓐ Ⓑ Ⓒ Ⓓ
17. Ⓐ Ⓑ Ⓒ Ⓓ   38. Ⓐ Ⓑ Ⓒ Ⓓ
18. Ⓐ Ⓑ Ⓒ Ⓓ   39. Ⓐ Ⓑ Ⓒ Ⓓ
19. Ⓐ Ⓑ Ⓒ Ⓓ   40. Ⓐ Ⓑ Ⓒ Ⓓ
20. Ⓐ Ⓑ Ⓒ Ⓓ

Practice Test 5

Section 3: Reading

1. Ⓐ Ⓑ Ⓒ Ⓓ
2. Ⓐ Ⓑ Ⓒ Ⓓ
3. Ⓐ Ⓑ Ⓒ Ⓓ
4. Ⓐ Ⓑ Ⓒ Ⓓ
5. Ⓐ Ⓑ Ⓒ Ⓓ
6. Ⓐ Ⓑ Ⓒ Ⓓ
7. Ⓐ Ⓑ Ⓒ Ⓓ
8. Ⓐ Ⓑ Ⓒ Ⓓ
9. Ⓐ Ⓑ Ⓒ Ⓓ
10. Ⓐ Ⓑ Ⓒ Ⓓ
11. Ⓐ Ⓑ Ⓒ Ⓓ
12. Ⓐ Ⓑ Ⓒ Ⓓ

13. Ⓐ Ⓑ Ⓒ Ⓓ
14. Ⓐ Ⓑ Ⓒ Ⓓ
15. Ⓐ Ⓑ Ⓒ Ⓓ
16. Ⓐ Ⓑ Ⓒ Ⓓ
17. Ⓐ Ⓑ Ⓒ Ⓓ
18. Ⓐ Ⓑ Ⓒ Ⓓ
19. Ⓐ Ⓑ Ⓒ Ⓓ
20. Ⓐ Ⓑ Ⓒ Ⓓ
21. Ⓐ Ⓑ Ⓒ Ⓓ
22. Ⓐ Ⓑ Ⓒ Ⓓ
23. Ⓐ Ⓑ Ⓒ Ⓓ
24. Ⓐ Ⓑ Ⓒ Ⓓ

25. Ⓐ Ⓑ Ⓒ Ⓓ
26. Ⓐ Ⓑ Ⓒ Ⓓ
27. Ⓐ Ⓑ Ⓒ Ⓓ
28. Ⓐ Ⓑ Ⓒ Ⓓ
29. Ⓐ Ⓑ Ⓒ Ⓓ
30. Ⓐ Ⓑ Ⓒ Ⓓ
31. Ⓐ Ⓑ Ⓒ Ⓓ
32. Ⓐ Ⓑ Ⓒ Ⓓ

33. Ⓐ Ⓑ Ⓒ Ⓓ
34. Ⓐ Ⓑ Ⓒ Ⓓ
35. Ⓐ Ⓑ Ⓒ Ⓓ
36. Ⓐ Ⓑ Ⓒ Ⓓ
37. Ⓐ Ⓑ Ⓒ Ⓓ
38. Ⓐ Ⓑ Ⓒ Ⓓ
39. Ⓐ Ⓑ Ⓒ Ⓓ

40. Ⓐ Ⓑ Ⓒ Ⓓ
41. Ⓐ Ⓑ Ⓒ Ⓓ
42. Ⓐ Ⓑ Ⓒ Ⓓ
43. Ⓐ Ⓑ Ⓒ Ⓓ
44. Ⓐ Ⓑ Ⓒ Ⓓ

45. Ⓐ Ⓑ Ⓒ Ⓓ
46. Ⓐ Ⓑ Ⓒ Ⓓ
47. Ⓐ Ⓑ Ⓒ Ⓓ
48. Ⓐ Ⓑ Ⓒ Ⓓ
49. Ⓐ Ⓑ Ⓒ Ⓓ
50. Ⓐ Ⓑ Ⓒ Ⓓ

ABOUT THE AUTHOR

Bruce Rogers has taught English as a Second language and test-preparation courses at the Economics Institute in Boulder, Colorado, since 1979. He also has taught in special programs in Indonesia, Vietnam, South Korea, and the Czech Republic. He is the author of *TOEFL Success* (Peterson's, Lawrenceville, NJ), *The Complete Guide to TOEFL* (Heinle & Heinle Publishers, Boston, MA), and *The Complete Guide to TOEIC* (International Thompson Publishing Asia, Singapore).

NOTES

Practice makes perfect!

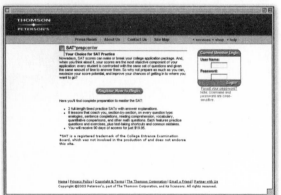

Improve your scores from the comfort of your own computer.

Online Practice Tests for the SAT*, ACT Assessment®, GRE® CAT, GMAT CAT®, TOEFL®, and ASVAB

No matter what test you're taking, the best ways to improve your scores are through repeated practice and a solid understanding of how the test works. Whether you're headed for college, graduate school, or a new career, if your test is computer-adaptive or paper-based, Peterson's online practice tests give you the convenience you crave. Each is completely self-directed. And you get 90 days access so you can log on and off whenever you like. Plus, automated essay question scoring for the GRE, GMAT, and TOEFL!

Visit the Test Preparation Channel of **www.petersons.com**, select your test, and get started.

*SAT is a registered trademark of the College Entrance Examination Board, which was not involved in the production of and does not endorse this product.

*ACT Assessment is a registered trademark of ACT™ Inc., which has no connection with this product.

*GRE and TOEFL are registered trademarks of Educational Testing Service (ETS). These products are not endorsed or approved by ETS.

*GMAT and GMAT CAT are registered trademarks of the Graduate Management Admission Council (GMAC). This product does not contain any actual GMAT test items, nor is it endorsed or approved by GMAC.